THE EUROPEAN ACADEMY OF LEGAL THEORY SERIES

ON LAW AND LEGAL REASONING

THE EUROPEAN ACADEMY OF LEGAL THEORY SERIES

General Editors

Professor Mark Van Hoecke
Professor François Ost
Professor Luc Wintgens

Other titles in this Series

Moral Conflict and Legal Reasoning
Scott Veitch

The Harmonisation of European Private Law
Mark van Hoecke and *François Ost* (eds)

Law as Communication
Mark van Hoecke

Legisprudence
A New Theoretical Approach to Legislation
Luc Wintgens (ed)

On Law and Legal Reasoning

FERNANDO ATRIA

HART PUBLISHING

OXFORD – PORTLAND OREGON

2001

Hart Publishing
Oxford and Portland, Oregon

Published in North America (US and Canada) by
Hart Publishing
c/o International Specialized Book Services
5804 NE Hassalo Street
Portland, Oregon
97213-3644
USA

Distributed in Netherlands, Belgium and Luxembourg by
Intersentia, Churchillaan 108
B2900 Schoten
Antwerpen
Belgium

Hart Publishing is a specialist legal publisher based in Oxford, England.
To order further copies of this book or to request a list of other
publications please write to:

Hart Publishing, Salters Boatyard, Folly Bridge, Abingdon Rd, Oxford,
OX1 4LB
Telephone: +44 (0)1865 245533 Fax: +44 (0) 1865 794882
email: mail@hartpub.co.uk
WEBSITE: http//:www.hartpub.co.uk

British Library Cataloguing in Publication Data
Data Available

ISBN 1-84113-275-6

Typeset by John Saunders Design & Production. Reading UK
Printed and bound in Great Britain by
Biddles Ltd www.biddles.co.uk

For Ximena

Acknowledgements

This book is a (hopefully) improved version of my *The powers of application*, a doctoral thesis submitted at the University of Edinburgh. Edinburgh is a beautiful city, and the *Centre for Law* and society must count among the most stimulating and engaging environments where such an enterprise could be undertaken. This has meant, unsurprisingly, that I have accumulated quite a number of debts over the years I spent there.

"It is an interesting fact," David Lodge has noticed, "that all modifications of a play that are made in rehearsal become the intellectual property of the author, whatever its source". In my experience of writing this book this is even more so. It is "interesting" that I hold exclusively the intellectual rights to this book, when so much of its content has been so heavily influenced by the constant criticism, encouragement and support Zenon Bankowski and Neil MacCormick offered me from the beginning. They made me feel at home from my first day at Edinburgh, and for this I have a great debt of gratitude.

Claudio Michelon and Kevin Walton read and discussed several parts of this book in different stages. They were always willing to engage with my arguments, put forward objections and evaluate my counter-objections. Every match of the 1998 World Cup could be used as a counter-example. With them I learned about legal theory, friendship and football.

Both Neil MacCormick and Kevin Walton read the whole manuscript with a view to improving its readability, and if it were not for their pains there would be even more mistakes and infelicities of English.

I have discussed different sections of the text with different audiences. In March 1997 I had the opportunity to discuss chapters 1, 2, 3, 4 and 7 with friends and colleagues at the University of Chile and the Diego Portales University at Santiago; sections of Chapter 3 were read at the seminar of the Philosophy Department of the Universidad de Puerto Rico (Recinto de Río Piedras) in May 1998; An early draft of chapter 1 was presented at the IV ERASMUS course in legal reasoning, held at Lund in 1995. The first sections of the same chapter were read at the Marvin Faber conference in Applied Legal Ontology held at Buffalo, NY in May 1998; the second half of Chapter 1 (where Roman law is discussed) was presented to the 15th Colloquium of the International Association for the Semiotics of Law, held at Arrabida (Portugal) in June 1999. Chapter 3 was presented to the 1999 IVR World Congress, held at New York in June 1999. In each of these opportunities I was shown ways in which the positions defended here had to be amended, abandoned or expanded, and though the result is not for me to judge, I believe that the book has significatively improved as a result.

I was invited to teach Philosophy of Law at the Universidad de Puerto Rico (Recinto de Río Piedras) in 1997–8. This provided me with an opportunity to test the whole of the argument contained in this book in front of an intelligent and critical audience, and I benefited greatly from it. I am particularly grateful to Dean Antonio García Padilla for offering me this opportunity.

Many people have read and commented upon different sections of this book. I am grateful to David Garland and Letizzia Gianformaggio for their comments on Chapter 1, and to Reinhard Zimmermann for his advice concerning my discussion of issues of Roman law; to Burkhard Schaeffer for his willingness to read and comment on Chapter 7; to John Searle for his comments on some sections on Chapter 1; to Emilios Christodoulidis and Stephen Guest who, as examiners of the thesis on which this book is based, offered very useful criticism and suggestions as how to improve it; to Jorge Streeter, relentlessly trying to bring down to (legal) earth my theoretical discussions; to Bert Roermund, who managed to find time to read the whole manuscript and made incredibly useful points at one crucial time; the final structure of the book closely reflects the advice I received from him. Lastly, to Ximena Fuentes, who thinks she has had no influence in the content of this book. This time, I'm afraid, she is wrong: she was working on the equitable utilisation of international watercourses during the years I was working on this book; her attempt to reason legally on the application of a rather abstract principle like "equitable utilisation", and the conversations we had about it, were highly instructive examples of the canon of (international) legal argument at work. When it has become rather fashionable for legal theorists not to discuss law (valid laws, judicial decisions, and the like) but theories about law, the need to offer an account that could do justice to endeavours like hers is all the greater.

Chapters 3 and 4 have suffered the most extensive interventions after I was awarded a doctorate. To complete them in their present version I was fortunate to be invited to spend some time at University College London's Faculty of Law in early 2001. I am particularly grateful to Dean Jeffrey Jowell and to Stephen Guest, who made that possible.

My stay at Edinburgh was made possible by a scholarship funded by the Chilean Government and by the generous support of the Universidad de Talca, for which I am indebted. Additional funding was provided by an ORS award granted by the Committee of Vice Chancellors and Principals of the Universities of the United Kingdom. My stay at UCL in early 2001 was made possible by a generous grant of the Dirección de programas de investigación y asistencia técnica (DIAT) of the Universidad de Talca, for which I am also grateful.

This book incorporates material previously published in 85 *Archiv für Rechts- und Sozialphilosophie* (1999) pp. 309–47 (Chapter 1); *Anuario de Filosofía Jurídica y Social*, (Valparaíso,1999) pp. 379–94 (part of Chapter 3), 34 *The Irish Jurist* (1999) pp. 276–99 (Chapter 6), and 18 *Law and Philosophy* (1999) pp. 537–77, © Kluwer Academic Publishers (Chapter 7).

Contents

Then came the churches then came the schools,
then came the lawyers and then came the rules

MARK KNOPFLER, *Telegraph Road* (1982)

1

Constitutive Rules, Institutions and the Weightier Matters of the Law

Football is not a matter of life and death:
it's much more important than that.
BILL SHANKLY

This book is intended as a contribution to the literature on legal theory and legal reasoning. In particular, it seeks to examine the relations that obtain between law and a theory of law and legal reasoning, and a theory of legal reasoning. Two features of law and legal reasoning will be particularly important in this regard: law is *institutional*, and legal reasoning is *formal*. These two features are so closely connected that it is reasonable to believe that in fact they are simply two ways of looking at the same issue. I hope this will become clearer as the focus of the book shifts from the institutional nature of law, with which this chapter is concerned, to the consequences of this for legal reasoning, which will entertain us in the following chapters.

The word "institution" encompasses a wide range of ideas that, at best, bear a tenuous family resemblance to one another. As a form of legal literature, it has a long and venerable tradition, going back to the *Institutes*, or brief expositions of the law, common since Roman times. In the literature of speech acts, the analysis of the so-called "institutional concepts" such as promises and the like plays a crucial role. A related legal usage is that in which a "trust" is an "institution" peculiar to the *common law*.

I believe that the idea of "institutional" facts, the existence, consequences and termination of which depend upon the existence and application of rules and the occurrence of some brute facts, can be highly successful in dealing with some of the insights offered by the literature on legal reasoning. To use this idea in understanding the law *and* legal reasoning, however, a distinction between "brute" and "institutional" facts is not enough. All institutional facts might be equal, but some of them are certainly more equal than others.

TWO CONCEPTS OF RULES

In his seminal article "Two concepts of rules", John Rawls drew a distinction between what he called the "summary" and the "practice" conception of rules. For Rawls, the "summary conception" regards rules as summaries of previous decisions. Each of these is made on the balance of all relevant considerations, and some kinds of cases will be recurrent: "thus it will happen that in cases of certain kinds the same decision will be made either by the same person at different times or by different persons at the same time" (Rawls, 1955: 34). In this context, a rule is formulated to encompass cases of that kind, so the next time the agent will have no need to ponder all the applicable moral considerations, and will instead be able "simply" to apply the rule. We see why in this conception rules are actually "summaries" of previous decisions: "rules are regarded as reports that cases of a certain sort have been found on *other* grounds to be properly decided in a certain way" (Rawls, 1955: 34).

The "summary conception" of rules is contrasted by Rawls to what he calls the "practice conception", in which rules are seen as

> defining a practice. Practices are set up for various reasons, but one of them is that in many areas of conduct each person's deciding what to do on utilitarian grounds case by case leads to confusion, and that the attempt to coordinate behavior by trying to foresee how others will act is bound to fail. As an alternative one realizes that what is required is the establishment of a practice, the specification of a new form of activity; and from this one sees that a practice necessarily involves the abdication of full liberty to act on utilitarian and prudential grounds. It is the mark of a practice that being taught how to engage in it involves being instructed in the rules which define it, and that appeal is made to those rules to correct the behavior of those engaged in it (Rawls, 1955: 36).

In this chapter the related concepts of "practice", "institution" and "rules" are to be discussed. In that discussion, I will look at games and the law as providing the standard instances of practices. Games, in fact, will constitute one paradigmatic case. This is not because games are the most important practices: indeed they are not. But they do present the features of institutional facts in a particularly pure and clear-cut way. They can be sliced off from their environment and studied in ways in which other institutional facts cannot. This is an important point in itself, and we shall see later on that an explanation for this feature of games is called for. For the time being I just want to emphasise that my choosing games as one paradigm of practices is intended in a purely analytical sense. Games are a kind of luxury we get on top of what is really important, rather than the real thing. But this need not bother us. To claim paradigmatic status for games in this respect is simply to make explicit what authors like John Searle, John Rawls and others did when they relied so heavily and interestingly upon the structure of games to clarify their ideas on institutional facts.

One need only read Rawl's article to see that he was indeed using games as a (at least one) paradigmatic instance of a practice. But on the other hand he believes the practice conception to be especially relevant in understanding "legal and legal-like arguments" (1955: 43 n. 27). Hence, we could start by trying to ascertain how naturally Rawl's conception of practice would fit the law on the one hand, and games on the other.

"Practices are set up for various reasons, but one of them is that in many areas of conduct each person's deciding what to do on utilitarian grounds case by case leads to confusion." *This* reason for setting up a practice seems clearly applicable to the law. Instead of having people autonomously deciding how much income tax to pay, it seems more convenient authoritatively to lay down the rate of income tax. Games are typically set up for other reasons. In the case of games, the practice is created *ex novo* for the sake of having one more activity to engage in.[1] Hence, here we have two reasons (there might be more: "various reasons" seems to suggest more than two) why practices are set up. So far so good.

Since "practices are set up for various reasons", those reasons mentioned by Rawls do not characterise the notion of practice. It is probably the fact that they are set up that is characteristic of institutions. For the time being I will bypass this issue, to which I will return shortly. One consequence of the creation of a practice is "the specification of a new form of activity; and from this one sees that a practice necessarily involves the abdication of full liberty to act on utilitarian and prudential grounds". This seems straightforwardly applicable to games and the law (though a complication will shortly appear). In both cases the agent is not supposed to act on the basis of an all-things-considered judgment, rather she is supposed to follow the rules. This must be understood as meaning that, from the point of view of the practice, it defines what is to be done in particular cases. Both citizens and players might find themselves in situations in which reasons external to the practice might require them to break the rules of practices. Normally, however, and unless the practice itself recognises an exception for those cases, the presence of those reasons will not constitute an excuse from the point of view of the practice. This is obviously true of games: think of a football player asking the referee to validate a hand-goal of his because he promised his dying son to score a goal (*see* Detmold, 1984: 49). In order to explain the idea of the agent's "abdication of full liberty to act on utilitarian and prudential grounds" in practices, Rawls uses the following example:

> In a game of baseball if a batter were to ask, "Can I have four strikes?" it would be assumed that he was asking what the rule was; and if, when told what the rule was, he were to say that he meant that on this occasion he thought it would be best on the whole for him to have four strikes rather than three, this would be most kindly taken as a joke. One might contend that baseball would be a better game if four strikes were allowed instead of three; but one cannot picture the rules as guides to what is best on the whole in particular cases, and question their applicability to particular cases as particular cases" (1955: 38).

[1] Bert Roermund showed me that I had to be more careful here: of course, we do have further reasons to invent this new activities. For example, games are usually contests, they typically involve some kind of competition between players. However, they are not reasons for a particular game, but reasons for a game of such-and-such features. There is a subtle distinction to be drawn here: "the value or point of chess [i.e. winning] is certainly artificial; chess constructs by its rules its unique method of winning. But the value of winning in general is an inseparable part of play [contest] and no more artificial than play itself is" (Detmold, 1984: 160–1).

Is this feature of games shared by the law? I believe it is not. "It would be better if I were allowed four strikes, hence I am allowed four strikes" shows without doubt that the speaker has not mastered baseball, or else that he is joking. In the context of a baseball game, that utterance is simply nonsense. Here it is indeed the case that "if one wants to do an action which a certain practice specifies then there is no way to do it except to follow the rules which define it" (Rawls, 1955: 38). But "it would be better if a legatee were not entitled to the legacy if he's been convicted for the murder of the testator, hence he is not so entitled" is radically different. Whether or not this is a good argument will depend, of course, on the peculiarities of the legal practice in question, but one cannot say that, in general, the mere fact of putting it forward shows ignorance or lack of seriousness about the law.

Here we should remember the context of Rawls's article. In it, the distinction between two concepts of rules was designed to defend utilitarianism "against those objections which have traditionally been made against it in connection with punishment and the obligation to keep promises" (Rawls, 1955: 21). Rawls's strategy was to claim that there were some spheres of social life that were, so to speak, insulated from the *direct* application of moral considerations. But by focusing upon those paradigmatic instances (games), he overemphasised that feature of practices, and tended to regard complete insulation as defining the notion of practice. When rules are practice-rules, "a player in a game cannot properly appeal to [moral] considerations as reasons for his making one move rather than another" (Rawls, 1955: 31). Indeed, "it is *essential to the notion of a practice* that the rules are publicly known and understood as definitive", because "those engaged in a practice recognize the rules as defining it" (*ibid.* 36, emphasis added).

So the picture we get is as follows: first, the notion of a practice is defined in such a way that it obviously includes, if anything at all, developed legal systems: "I use the word "practice" throughout as a sort of technical term meaning any form of activity specified by a system of rules which defines offices, roles, moves, penalties, defences, and so on, and which gives the activity its structure" (Rawls, 1955: 20 n.1). Secondly, the notion of practice is developed as showing that it *essentially* implies the insulation of some sphere of activity from the application of moral considerations (in this case, since the article is a defence of utilitarianism, the utilitarian principle); thirdly, and precisely because of the perfect isolation that characterises them, games are placed at the centre of the analysis, as "paradigmatic" instances; and fourthly, the conclusions thus obtained are said to belong to the *notion* of a practice, with the consequence that they clearly apply to the law, since the law obviously constitutes an instance of a practice in the sense defined at the beginning. But the problem is that the perfect insulation that characterises games is due to the *particular sort of practice* they are, and thus *that* aspect of games is not essential to the notion of a practice. It is certainly not shared by the law.

Let me explain this last point, to make it clear that I am not begging any question (I will come back to this point, hence all I need do here is to make this claim plausible enough for the reader to suspend disbelief and go on). A game-like insularity would imply a highly formalistic approach to law. I do not want to claim, of course, that such an approach is necessarily wrong (indeed we shall see that we can find instances of that formalist approach, and that that backs my general argument). But in the case of games such a formalistic approach is something *about* the practice that any would-be participant has to understand *before* actually engaging in it, while in law the correctness of such an approach is a substantive claim to be argued and defended inside the practice, as one more ordinary, first-order legal claim. To dispute the complete insulation that characterises games is to show lack of understanding about the practice of them; but to dispute that very same approach to the interpretation and application of rules of law is not to display ignorance regarding the fundamentals of legal practice, but to defend a substantive legal claim and in a particular case to advance moral arguments to ground an interpretation of the law is not to display ignorance or lack of seriousness about that practice.

In other words, one could say that a category is missing in Rawls's distinction. Rawls does say that his distinction is "not intended to be exhaustive" (1955: 40). Notice, if correct, what the argument so far implies and what it does not imply. Rawls's attempt to develop a distinction between a "summary" and a "practice" conception of rules is defective insofar as the notion of practice is supposed to be especially "relevant to understanding legal and legal-like arguments" (Rawls, 1955: 43 n. 27). But as a defence of utilitarianism, it might (or might not) well be the case that both kinds of practices (i.e. games and the law) are sufficiently insulated from moral considerations to allow for the distinction between "justifying a practice and justifying a particular action falling under it" (*ibid.* 20), which is Rawls's main purpose. If we are to follow Rawls's advice, however, and apply the distinction to the understanding of law and quasi-legal argument, we shall need a more sophisticated distinction, one that (ideally) is able to explain the difference in the insularity displayed by different practices. This is what I shall try to develop in this chapter.

Before that, however, it will be useful to refer to another aspect of Rawls's argument. What is the correct understanding of rules, the summary or the practice view? According to Rawls, that is the wrong question to ask. The point is not that either the practice or the summary conception has to be true of all rules: "Some rules will fit one conception, some rules the other; and so there are rules of practices (rules in the strict sense) and maxims and "rules of thumb"" (Rawls, 1955: 40).

But the problem is, how are we to know whether a particular rule is to be interpreted according to the "summary" or the "practice" view? Rawls believes that there might be cases in which "it will be difficult, if not impossible, to decide which conception of rules is applicable. One expects borderline cases with any concept, and they are specially likely in connections with such involved concepts as those of a practice, institution, game, rule and so on" (Rawls, 1955: 40). But can we make sense of the idea that it is sometimes *impossible* to decide which conception is applicable? "Summary" and "practice" rules are applied in radically different ways; what participants must know and master before being able to engage in each kind of practice is significantly different. In the "summary" conception, a rule is a rule of thumb: it has no normative force of its own (here a rule is *quae rem quae est breuiter enarrat* (*Digest* 51.17.1), something which briefly *describes* how a thing is: *see* below, at 151ff). In this conception an agent can reasonably apply a rule only if she has reason to believe that the proper application of the standards of which the rule is a summary leads to the same solution offered by the rule.[2] In the practice conception the agent is not supposed to act on her assessment of the situation beyond the assessment needed to establish that the rule applies. It follows that no agent can really participate in a practice unless she is able to decide whether the rule is a summary or a practice rule. An observer trying to understand what the agent is doing, on the other hand, might find it impossible to determine whether the agent treats the rule as a summary rule or as a practice rule. Indeed, we are in such a position concerning at least significant aspects of Roman law (for the full argument and examples, *see* below, at 141ff). The importance of this point for a theory of legal reasoning can hardly be overemphasised.

THE GAME-ANALOGY

An idea underlying Rawls's general notion of "practice" is, as we have seen, that both games and the law are correctly regarded as practices in his sense. Now, for Rawls this might not be a problematic point, since he was not concerned with providing an analysis of law, but that idea is also recurrent in contemporary legal theory. Among many other authors, as we shall see, H L A Hart seems to have shared this view and, in *The Concept of Law*, relied heavily on the similarities between them. In fact, he relied upon that analogy *so* heavily that it is not too big an exaggeration to say, with Judith Shklar, that games were "Hart's obsession" (Shklar, 1986: 105), or that "H L A Hart described law as a complex game" (Morawetz, 1992: 16).[3]

[2] Notice that this is not necessarily because the agent has actually applied those standards to the case and decided that the solution is the rule's solution. It might very well be that, e.g., the agent does not have time to consider how those standards apply, and so she relies on the previous decisions summarised by the rule. Still, the rule acquires its force from its being a good summary ("the law may not derive from a rule, but a rule must arise from the law as it is" says the *Digest* 51.17.1), and a conscientious agent would always try to check the accuracy of that summary, circumstances permitting (of course, in many cases circumstances will not).

[3] On Hart's "obsession", in addition to Hart, 1994: 310 (index entry for "Games"), see Hart (1953: *passim*).

One of the most important functions of the game-analogy in *The Concept of Law* was to help Hart in ascertaining the rights and wrongs of formalism and rule-scepticism. One of the rule-sceptic's arguments, Hart tells us, is based upon the fact that

> [a] supreme tribunal has the last word in saying what the law is and, when it has said it, the statement that the court was "wrong" has no consequences within the system: no one's rights or duties are thereby altered . . . . Consideration of these facts makes it seem pedantic to distinguish, in the case of a supreme tribunal's decisions, between their finality and their infallibility. This leads to another form of the denial that courts in deciding are ever bound by rules: "The law (or the constitution) is what the court says it is" (1994: 141).

To answer this argument, Hart considered what a game would be like if one were to see games as the sceptics see the law. According to him, such a game would not be like any ordinary game, but a rather odd one he called "scorer's discretion". In it, "rules" are mere predictions of what the referee will do, since they are what the scorer says they are. To see the law as "scorer's discretion", however, is a mistake, Hart claimed, for the same reason a normal game like football or cricket is *not* "scorer's discretion". Though it is strictly possible that any game may be transformed into "scorer's discretion", this possibility does not imply that all games are, actually, "scorer's discretion": "[t]he fact that isolated or exceptional official aberrations are tolerated does not mean that the game of cricket or baseball is no longer being played" (Hart, 1994: 144–5).

I do not want to discuss the whole of Hart's argument against the rule-sceptic (which might be right regardless of the flaws in the "scorer's discretion" argument), but only to note that this particular argument is not very convincing. The sceptic could answer by saying that in games people do not disagree about what the rules are, nor about how should they be applied. They might discuss whether or not Maradona used his hand to score his famous goal against England (though nobody would still like to deny that), rather than whether a particular player's touching the ball with his hands "counts" as a hand ball: is it not an amazing fact that however passionate participants and spectators can be (as is all too well-known nowadays, in Europe, particularly in England) no serious disagreement exists as to what the rules mean and what they demand?

It seems, though, that Hart would not agree with this. He believed that rules of games were as open-textured as any other rule. In games the scoring rule, "though it has, *like other rules*, its area of open texture where the scorer has to exercise a choice, yet has a core of settled meaning" (1994: 144; emphasis added).

It is at least arguable that this assimilation of rules of games to legal rules, on which Hart relied so heavily in his discussion of formalism and rule-scepticism in chapter VII of *The Concept of Law*, distorts the way in which rules of games are applied: they are not controversial (except in special cases, like the "dangerous play" rule, as we shall see). If this is correct, then there is no reason why the rule-sceptic must be committed to a denial of the difference between football and "scorer's discretion", and Hart's argument (at least his analogy with games) would become harmless. If, as Paul Valery has said, "no scepticism is possible where the rules of a game are concerned" (quoted in Huizinga, 1970: 30), then the analogy cannot be used against *legal* rule-scepticism, where scepticism is (to say the least) possible.

In other words, Hart thought that whatever was true concerning rules of games was also true concerning legal rules by virtue of the fact that in both games and the law "rules" are an important element. There is no obvious reason why the sceptic has to go along with this unstated premiss and Hart did not offer a non-obvious one.

As was said at the beginning of this section, however, Hart was not alone in thinking the game-analogy to be useful for the analysis of legal concepts. Ronald Dworkin's case is interesting for two reasons: on the one hand, he uses the game-analogy at two crucial moments: first, when introducing his (now famous) distinction between rules and principles, and then, to present his (also famous) thesis of what he called "the interpretive attitude". On the other hand, while in the first case he was interested in the *similarities* between games and the law, in the second his point was to *distinguish* one from the other. And in both cases the feature of games he relied upon was the same, i.e. the certainty of their rules.

In *Taking Rights Seriously*, he argued that there was a logical distinction between rules and principles, because only the former were applicable in an all-or-nothing fashion. Though this all-or-nothing aspect of *legal* rules might not be obvious, it "is seen most plainly if we look at the way rules operate, not in law, but in some enterprises they dominate—a game, for example" (Dworkin, 1977: 24).

The interesting point, in my view, is that the reason "this all-or-nothing feature is seen most plainly" in the case of games *is the very same reason* why "scorer's discretion" is so different from cricket or football: because of the certainty of the application of the rules of games. The game-analogy was meant to throw light on something important *about the law*, but it was (in both cases) based upon a feature of games that the law *does not share* (namely, its complete insulation from moral considerations). Here again, the unstated assumption is that "legal rules" are, so to speak, the same kind of entity as rules of games. But Dworkin himself later *distinguished* the law from games when he wanted to explain what is to have an "interpretive attitude". He argued that the two components[4] of the interpretive attitude were independent from each other, so that participants could accept one without necessarily having to accept the other: "We do that in the case of games and

[4] The two components are "the assumption that the practice . . . has some point", and that "the requirements of [the practice] are sensitive to its point" (Dworkin, 1986: 47).

contests. We appeal to the point of these practices in arguing about how their rules should be changed, but not (except in very limited cases) about what their rules now are; that is fixed by history and convention" (1986: 48).[5]

According to this passage, Dworkin would probably say that precisely because no interpretive attitude is adopted either by players or spectators of, say, football, the interpretation and application of the rules of football can have the very high level of certainty they do have. This, however, creates the problem of establishing in which way what we call "rules" in games are the same sort of thing that we call "rules" in law. Dworkin claimed that "legal rules" were all-or-nothing standards, and that this "is seen most plainly" if we look not to legal but to game-rules. There was, for Dworkin in 1967, a common feature between rules in games and rules in the law: they were both *rules*, i.e. standards that were "applicable in an all-or-nothing fashion".

Twenty years later, however, we were told that there was, after all, a fundamental difference between law and games: only the former is an "interpretive concept". So we can legitimately wonder, does this fundamental difference affect the "all-or-nothingness" of legal rules? Maybe the rules of games are all-or-nothing standards not because of a feature they have in virtue of their being rules, but because players and spectators have developed no interpretive attitude towards football. If this is true, then the conclusion would be that in Dworkin's definition there is no such a thing as a legal rule (more on this later, at 98).

The fact is, we are told both by Hart and Dworkin, that some (quite important) features of rules are easier to see if we look at games, but harder if we are looking at the law. This, however, does not necessarily mean that those features are to be equally found in the latter with only an extra effort of observation; maybe they can be easily seen in the former only because they cannot be seen at all in the latter.

INSULATION

Consider the case of the (now not-so-) recent modification of the offside rule in football. As is known, "a player is in an offside position if he is nearer to his opponents' goal line than both the ball and the second last opponent": "a player is not in an offside position if he is levelled with the second last opponent or with the last two opponents". A player in any of these last two situations would have been in an offside position under the old offside rule. We are told that after the 1990 World Cup played in Italy, in which most teams adopted highly conservative and defensive strategies (therefore diminishing the

[5] The "very limited cases" Dworkin had in mind in this passage are probably cases like the one he discussed in *Taking Rights Seriously*. These cases are not counter-examples to my argument, as I will try to show below (for the argument, *see* below, at 31ff; for Dworkin's very special case, *see* below, at Ch. 2, n. 19.

quality of a football match as a spectacle), FIFA modified the rule in an effort to make the game more aggressive and more attractive to audiences and so forth.

The following I take to be rather obvious: in the period between (some moment before the end of) the 1990 World Cup and the issuing of the new offside rule, all of the reasons for having the new rule existed, but they were irrelevant at the moment of applying the old rule. They are equally irrelevant *after* FIFA's decision: an umpire could not, after the new rule had been introduced, decide that he should apply the rule in the light of its goal, and hence that he was going to be (say) "less strict" in the application of the rule in those cases in which the involved play was likely to be part of an aggressive strategy, even if we are prepared to imagine that in so doing the referee would be likely to increase the desired effect of the new regulations. After the decision was taken, the reasons for it were as irrelevant in the context of adjudication as they were before. The very suggestion that the referee could apply the rule in this way seems to be nonsensical[6] (in fact, it is not clear what "less strict" could mean in this context).[7] Thus the rule is completely insulated from the reasons for it.

But in legal adjudication things are different. This will be discussed in considerably more detail below, but for the time being suffice it to say that lawyers do speak of interpretations being more or less strict, and the idea that a law should be interpreted in the light of its purpose is all too common. Needless to say, this is not the *only* kind of argument that can be used to interpret a law (some will say that it is not even a good argument), but for the time being, I only need to claim that this *makes sense*, in a way that the offside argument does not. The idea that interpretation should be purposive is not necessarily controversial insofar as it is limited: nobody would deny that legal rules should *sometimes* be interpreted in the light of the goals they are supposed to advance. What is controversial is whether or not this is *always* the case. But we need not adopt this strong Fullerian position to see that a football referee is not, except when the rules explicitly grant him that power, supposed to consider the purpose of the rules at the moment of applying them. This general feature of adjudication in games is absent in the law: even according to a positivistic theory of law there will be cases in which "assumptions about the purposes the rule is meant to advance would take a prominent—perhaps even pre-eminent—role in solving the particular difficulties encountered" (Marmor, 1994: 154).

The point is that in games the application of a rule is always straightforward, while in law, at least sometimes, the application of an otherwise valid and clear

[6] In this context, to say of an argument that it is nonsensical is to say that the fact of a speaker seriously offering that argument would be taken by others either as a joke or as proof that the speaker is not really playing, or does not understand the game, etc. This was Rawls's point discussed above (at 3).

[7] I am ignoring some complexities of the offside rule, like the so-called "passive" offside. They are not an objection to the thesis presented here, any more than the existence of "discretion-granting" rules like the dangerous play or advantage rules are (*see* below, at 31f).

rule can be contested. Notice that this claim does not amount to saying (not *now*, anyway) that there are no cases in which the application of legal rules is not as clear as the application of rules of games. My claim here amounts to the rather obvious observation that, while it would not lift a lawyer's eyebrow to notice that the application of a clear general rule to a particular case can sometimes be problematic, to find that referees and players disagree about what a penalty, or a goal, or a hand ball are, would indeed surprise any football fan.

In other words in football (as in all games) the fact that a rule does not make some aspect *x* of a concrete case relevant means that *x* is irrelevant for the application of that rule.[8] Part of what you need to learn when studying football is, for example, that during the course of the game the ball can only be handled by the goalkeepers in their penalty boxes, and that under no circumstances can a different player or the goalkeepers outside that area intentionally use their hands to move the ball. There might be disagreement about whether or not a particular touching of the ball was intentional, but a player that was to offer moral reasons to justify his handling of the ball would show, as Rawls claimed, that he does not understand, or else is joking.

The latter example was consciously selected for the discretion that the rule allows the referee to determine whether a particular hand ball was "intentional" or not. A rule against "touching" or "handling" the ball might be vague in the sense that it does not clarify whether an unintentional handling of the ball would count as a hand ball (is it a case of a player touching the ball or of the ball touching the hand of a player?). Since whether or not the semantic meaning of rule requires intentionality is not clear, there will be cases in which people will disagree about whether a player's touching the ball counts as a hand ball.[9] Insofar as rules of a game rely on the normal use of words, there will always be space for this kind of vagueness. Thus, *this* kind of vagueness is common to games and the law.

[8] Consider the following case: on Saturday, 13 February, 1999, Arsenal played Sheffield United at Highbury. The score was 1-1 with just over 10 minutes of the game to play. A Sheffield United player, Lee Morris, went down after a challenge by an Arsenal attacker. Since the referee did not stop the game, a Sheffield United player kicked the ball out. Morris recovered, and the match restarted. Arsenal's Ray Parlour tried to throw the ball to United keeper Alan Kelly to give the visitors unchallenged possession, but his team-mate, Nwankwo Kanu, hunted the ball down and slid a low cross into the path of Arsenal's Marc Overmars who then scored. Sheffield United failed to equalise and the match finished 2–1 for Arsenal. What is important here is that the goal was valid, though it was scored in violation of one of the most clear and undisputed requirements of *fair play*. The fact that Arsenal's goal was grossly unfair was irrelevant for its validity, because the scoring rule in football does not make any reference to the fairness of the scoring. The match was later ordered to be replayed, which is another way of emphasising the same: the possibility of simply "invalidating" the goal because of Arsenal's unfairness was not discussed (I am grateful to Kevin Walton for bringing this case to my attention).

[9] Remember the penalty that led to Italy's equaliser against Chile in their 1998 World Cup match (probably only we Chileans remember it, so here it is: seven minutes before the end of the match a Chilean defender, Ronald Fuentes, touched the ball with his hand inside Chile's penalty box (or the ball hit Fuentes' hand) and the referee awarded Italy a penalty kick. The decision was controversial, since the intentionality of Fuentes' hand ball was in question. Italy scored and the match ended 2–2). For the record, the official FIFA rule *does* require intentionality (Law 12).

Am I not conceding Hart's point here? Not really. We only need to look at the way in which rules of games are applied in *real matches* to see how restricted the vagueness warranted by this argument really is. The claim that the rules of football and legal rules are *equally* vague is so descriptively inaccurate that one wonders if it should receive any serious consideration. The problems that arise when applying *legal* rules to concrete cases go well beyond problems of uncertainty at the (semantic) borderline, and this is almost as old as the law itself. I will offer only three cases taken from different periods in a two thousand-year span:

(1) Roman jurists knew that not to take Rawls's batter's attitude at least sometimes was legally mistaken. In other words, for them not to take into account considerations other than those needed to ascertain whether or not the rule's operative facts were fulfilled would have demonstrated lack of mastery of the law, i.e. exactly the opposite of Rawls's batter. Consider just one example, a piece written by Paul, who lived in the third century AD:

> D.1.3.29 (Paul, *libri singulari ad legem Cinciam*). *Contra legem facit, qui id facit quod lex prohibet, in fraudem uero, qui saluis uerbis legis sententiam eius circumuenit* (it is a contravention of the law if someone does what the law forbids, but fraudulently, in that he sticks to the words of the law but evades its sense).

In other words, it is not possible to know whether by following a rule we are following the law unless we can ascertain the *ratio* (sensus) *legis*. Ascertaining the *ratio legis* supposes the ability to consider how some moral considerations bear on the issue. Marc Overmars did not infringe the rules of football when he scored his goal against Sheffield United, since the scoring rule in football was silent concerning *fair play* (see above at n. 8); but it is at least arguable that the court would be misapplying the law if it grants the legacy to the murderous legatee on the basis that the statute of wills is silent on the legatee's killing of the testator (see below, at 34ff).

(2) The second example dates back to 1688. Discussing the interpretation of laws, Samuel Pufendorf comments upon a Bolognese case:

> there was a law of Bologna, that whoever drew blood from another person in a public place should suffer the most severe penalties. On the basis of this law a barber was once informed upon, who had opened a man's vein in the square. And the fellow was in no little peril because it was added in the statute that the words should be taken exactly and without any interpretation.

This example is offered by Pufendorf as an illustration of his claim that

> When words, if taken in their plain and simple meaning, will produce an absurd or even no effect, some exception must be made from their generally accepted sense, that they may not lead to nothingness or absurdity (1688: Book V, Ch. 12, § 8, pp. 802–3 [547]).

Here we can find Pufendorf facing a legal problem and doing as a matter of course what for players and referees, when facing a similar problem in a football game, is always wrong: i.e. arguing that, since there is some value *beyond* the rule for which the rule is an instrument, (how could it be known that a given result is "absurd" if not by reference to such an external value?) the question of how the rule is to be applied to particular cases has to be answered taking that into account. And to take that into account (some) moral considerations have to be referred to. In this case Pufendorf is indeed behaving like Rawls's batter; he is claiming that since it would be better on the whole if the rule had an exception for barbers, the rule does have an exception. And one might think that Pufendorf is wrong, but if so, he is wrong as a matter of Bolognese law: we are not entitled to conclude that he did not understand the law or that he was joking.[10]

(3) Much the same can be said about many of the cases imagined by Lon Fuller in the second half of the twentieth century. I will only refer to one of them here. We are invited to consider the existence of a rule to the effect that 'It shall be a misdemeanour, punishable by fine of five dollars, to sleep in any railway station", and to imagine that

> two men are brought before me (i.e. the judge) for violating this statute. The first is a passenger who was waiting at 3 am for a delayed train. When he was arrested he was sitting upright in an orderly fashion, but was heard by the arresting officer to be gently snoring. The second is a man who had brought a blanket and pillow to the station and had obviously settled himself down for the night. He was arrested, however, before he had a chance to go to sleep (1958: 664).

Notice that in this and in Pufendorf's case there is no doubt as to the meaning of the words used by the rule. Anyone who was to say that the barber should not be punished or the businessman should not be fined because the former didn't "really" draw blood in a public space or the latter wasn't "really" sleeping in the station, would demonstrate lack of mastery of English. In fact, the problem is created rather than solved by the fact that the case is indeed uncontroversially covered by the semantic meaning of the rules.

This is important because there has been a strong tendency in contemporary legal theory to regard the issue of the defeasibility of legal rules as one that has to be tackled in terms of the general defeasibility of concepts.[11] But any sensible explanation of legal reasoning will find a form of defeasibility that is not reducible to semantic defeasibility. The cases discussed by Pufendorf and Fuller, and the danger we are warned against by Paul are not cases of what we

[10] This last sentence should not be interpreted as relying on Pufendorf as an authority concerning the law. The argument is not "look, Pufendorf was so clever, he could not have been joking or misunderstood the law". It is, rather, that Pufendorf is doing something that no lawyer would regard as off-limits.

[11] This is indeed what Hart himself, only sometimes I believe, thought: *see* Hart, 1994: 124ff; the issue is discussed below (at 89ff).

might call "semantic" defeasibility. In the case of Ronald Fuentes' hand ball we might disagree because we disagree about the case being covered by a rule against "intentionally" handling the ball, and we might not be sure about Fuentes' intentionality. But in the cases discussed by Pufendorf and Fuller this is not the reason why we might not be sure about the application of the rule. The truth is, we are unsure on the face of the fact that the cases can easily be shown to be covered by the semantic meaning of the relevant rules. This is a different sense in which a rule can be defeated. My claim is that *this* form of defeasibility, characteristic of legal reasoning, is not to be found in games. From now on, I will refer to this form of defeasibility every time I use that word without further explanations.

It is clear that the question of which legal cases will cause problems of this kind depends on the peculiarities of the legal practices involved (see Atiyah and Summers, 1987, as discussed below, at 207ff) . What in my view cannot be denied, however, is that the law as we understand it is a kind of practice in the context of which this is a (more or less) common problem. One could even say that mastery of the law (what law students are supposed to learn before becoming lawyers) *is* (or at least includes) the ability to recognise these cases, while mastery of football is (or at least includes) to understand that the application of a clear rule cannot be discussed during a match.

If this is correct so far, then it would naturally follow that an explanation of legal reasoning, or a criticism (like Hart's) of rule-scepticism cannot be based on an analogy between games and the law. A good starting point for an explanation of legal disagreement is, therefore, to give a closer to look at the similarities and differences between the two.

A GENERAL THEORY OF INSTITUTIONAL FACTS[12]

Both games and the law figure profusely in the literature on institutions. Both games and the law are (or allow for) paradigmatic instances of "institutional facts". I think that there is an important truth here, but that truth is obscured when some crucial differences (we have seen one; we shall see more shortly below) between the two are disregarded. The argument offered in the last section was designed to give this point initial plausibility: in some important sense rules seem to be much more well-behaved, so to speak, in games than in the law. If this feature of rules in games is not taken account of, the game-analogy can easily backfire: after all, it might be the case that *precisely* because rules of games are certain in their application when rules of law are not, that the rule-scepticism Hart was arguing against is right, or that *precisely* because

[12] This section benefited from Professor John Searle's detailed comments and criticism for which I am grateful (every now and then in the text I refer to what Searle said or did not say "at the Buffalo conference", meaning the Marvin Faber Conference in Applied Legal Ontology held at Buffalo, NY in May 1998).

of this certainty in the application of the rules of games, *legal* rules are not all-or-nothing, as Dworkin claimed.[13]

I want to claim that games and law are institutions of different *kinds*. A convenient way of developing the argument would be, therefore, to begin with what we could call a "unified" theory of institutional facts like goals, contracts, hand balls and the like. This is now possible since John Searle has recently offered what he called "a general theory of institutional facts" (1995). I will try to show that a theory that does not recognise the existence of two *kinds* of institutions cannot but fail to account for some peculiarities of the neglected kind.

Regulative and Constitutive Rules

In an often-quoted passage, Searle introduces his now famous distinction:

> I want to clarify a distinction between two different sorts of rules, which I shall call *regulative* and *constitutive* rules . . .. As a start, we might say that regulative rules regulate antecedently or independently existing forms of behaviour; for example, many rules of etiquette regulate inter-personal relationships which exist independently of the rules. But constitutive rules do not merely regulate, they create or define new forms of behaviour. The rules of football or chess, for example, do not merely regulate playing football or chess, but as it were they create the very possibility of playing such games (1969: 33).

Searle believes that this reflects an "intuitively obvious distinction" between two different kinds of rules. He himself acknowledged that he was "fairly confident about the distinction, but do[es] not find it easy to clarify" (*ibid.*). However obvious that distinction looked to Searle, it proved controversial. Among others, Anthony Giddens[14] has argued that "that there is something suspect in this distinction, as referring to two types of rule, is indicated by the etymological clumsiness of the term "regulative rule". After all, the word "regulative" already implies "rule": its dictionary definition is "controlled by rules'" (Giddens, 1984: 20). In other words, all rules can, in one way or another, be said to be regulative. This is, naturally, no objection to Searle's distinction, since he does not claim that constitutive rules *do not* regulate (notice, in the following displayed quotation, his qualification of "*purely* regulative" rules, and also his claim, in the previous quotation, that "constitutive rules do not

[13] I do not want to pursue these arguments here, since they are not important for the point discussed in the main text. It might be the case that, in the end, Hart is right against the rule-sceptic or Dworkin is right in his claim about the logical distinction between *legal* principles and rules. In both cases, however, once account is taken of the uncontroversial nature of the application of the rules of games, the game-analogy ceases to be a supporting reason (i.e. as it was used supporting Hart's or Dworkin's arguments) and provides the reader with a (not necessarily conclusive) reason to believe exactly the opposite.

[14] I begin with Giddens' criticism because he is the only critic to whom reference is made in *The Construction of Social Reality* (at 230 n. 10).

merely regulate"). "Constitutive rules"—this is Searle speaking at the Buffalo conference— "of course regulate behaviour, but they do something more, they create the possibility of forms of behaviour that would not exist without those rules."

This should be readily granted. But if all constitutive rules do regulate behaviour, then it cannot also be the case that *all* rules are also constitutive, since in that case there would be no distinction whatsoever. Are all rules, then constitutive? Searle answers:

> There is a trivial sense in which the creation of any rule creates the possibility of new forms of behaviour, namely, behaviour done in accordance with the rule. That is not the sense in which my remark is intended. What I mean can perhaps be best put in the formal mode. Where the rule is purely regulative, behaviour which is in accordance with the rule could be given the same description or specification . . . whether or not the rule existed, provided the description or specification makes no explicit reference to the rule. But where the rule (or system of rules) is constitutive, behaviour which is in accordance with the rule can receive specifications or descriptions which it could not receive if the rule or rules did not exist (1969: 35).

Some critics of Searle have not been convinced by this argument, and have pressed the point that all rules are, really, *both* constitutive *and* regulative. One of them is Joseph Raz, who invites us to compare the following two pairs of act-descriptions:

1 (a) "Giving £50 to Mr Jones" (b) "Paying income tax"
2 (a) "Saying 'I promise'" (b) "Promising".

In Raz's view,

> descriptions 1 (a) and 2 (a) specify acts which are in accordance with the rules in a way which could be given regardless of whether or not there is such a rule. Therefore, the rules are regulative. Descriptions 1 (b) and 2 (b) describe actions in accordance with the rule in a way that could not be given if there were no such rules. Therefore, the rules are constitutive, as well. Since for every rule one can formulate a similar pair of act descriptions, all rules are both constitutive and regulative (1992: 109).

But here there is a clear *non sequitur*. From the fact that in both 1 and in 2 "one can formulate a similar pair of descriptions" it does not follow that that is the case "for every rule". This is the more obvious when we notice that Searle would probably not object to Raz's claim that both taxes and promises are institutional facts. Searle would (rightly) claim that one can think of (other) rules for which the (b) item of the pair is missing. In other words, it is not the case that all actions in accordance with rules, because of that very fact, admit of this dual description. That *is* the case concerning tax law and promising, but not concerning rules of, say, the decalogue. The following is not a complete pair of act-descriptions:

3 (a) Honouring one's father and mother (b) (empty)

since, though in the relevant circumstances "giving £ 50 to Mr Jones" and "saying 'I promise'" counts as paying taxes and promising, 'honouring one's parents' does not count as anything. Hence not *all* rules are constitutive.

What about

4 (a) Being nice towards one's parents (b) Honouring one's parents?

In this case the description contained in 4 (b) is a form of *appraisal* rather than a specification (Searle, 1969: 36; *see* also Cherry, 1973: 302). If instead we had something like

5 (a) Not honouring one's parents (b) To be guilty of a sin

then the rule in question (the Fourth Commandment, Exod. 20:12) would indeed, I believe, be constitutive. But this would depend upon the (contingent, i.e. not necessarily implicated by the Fourth Commandment) existence of the institutional concept of *sin*.

Notice that the concept of sin is not conceptually (as opposed to theologically, as the case might or might not be) needed in order either to understand or to apply the Ten Commandments: they can be understood as simply stating what it is right and wrong to do. The institutional concept of sin is born, so to speak, when someone offers an interpretation of a (up-to-then-not-institutional) practice in terms of institutional facts (see below at 25ff). Notice further that, if we introduce the institutional concept of sin, not only the fourth, but *all* of the Ten Commandments suddenly become constitutive: each of the acts described by each commandment (taking the name of the Lord in vain, killing, committing adultery, stealing, etc.) becomes an X term to which the institutional Y term "sin" is attached.

Perhaps this is the gist of Raz's critique. Maybe he should be understood as saying that concerning legal rules in developed legal systems, there will be always a description available for the (b) item. This is, I believe, true, but it fails to follow that all rules are both regulative and constitutive. What follows is that a rule acquires its character (regulative or constitutive) from the normative system to which it belongs.

We can now go one step further. Since all rules are regulative, but some are also constitutive, it follows that some rules are purely regulative. But this, I believe, presents an interesting question: can "purely regulative" rules exist in the context of institutional systems ("institutions", following Searle for a while, being "systems of constitutive rules")? Are there purely regulative (say) legal rules, for example?

Tony Honoré, for instance, has claimed that a satisfactory theory of individuation of laws must allow for the following kinds of laws:

1. *Existence laws* create, destroy or provide for the existence or non-existence of entities.
2. *Rules of inference* provide how facts may or must or should preferably be proved and what inferences may or must or should preferably be drawn from evidence.
3. *Categorising laws* explain how to translate actions, events, and other facts into the appropriate categories.
4. *Rules of scope* fix the scope of other rules.
5. *Position-specifying rules* set out the legal position of persons or things in terms of rights, liabilities, status and the like.
6. *Directly normative rules* (which are few in number, but important) guide the conduct of the citizen as such (Honoré, 1977: 112; on the importance of a theory of individuation of the law, which gives the background of Honoré's claim, *see* Raz, 1980: Ch. 4).

I hope it is clear that items 1 to 5 cannot be purely regulative. Rules of the third type, for example, "A young person is any person who has attained the age of 14 years and is under the age of 17 years" (Honoré, 1977: 102) are plain instances of constitutive rules, i.e. rules of the form "*X* counts as *Y* in *C*" (Searle, 1995: 43ff). The same can be said of items 1, 4 and 5. Rules of inference, I believe, are also typically constitutive: they specify what counts as evidence for the existence of an institutional fact like a contract or a will.

This leaves only 6, "directly normative rules". Are they not purely regulative? They certainly do not *constitute* what they regulate: if they did, they would fall into another category. The problem is, these rules cannot be purely regulative since they are expressed in institutional terms. They are almost tautological (Searle seems to believe that they are, in fact, tautologies: 1969: 191).[15] As Honoré argued,

> the fact that criminal legislation by and large defined what constitutes an offence and does not directly forbid the obnoxious conduct . . . reveals . . . that the directly normative rules of a modern system are for the most part platitudinous generalities.

[15] Though I will not pursue this matter further, it is interesting to notice that it is dubious whether they can be tautologies. Barry Smith argues, following Adolf Reinach, that in (what Searle calls) "systems of constitutive rules" one must "eventually arrive at basic institutional concepts [BICs], which is to say: institutional concepts not capable of being further defined on the institutional level" (Smith, 1993: 318). They are not capable of being defined in non-circular ways in terms of non-institutional concepts, since then "all institutional concepts would turn out to be thus definable". This reinforces my conclusion that there is no space for purely regulative rules in "systems of constitutive rules". *See* Sergot *et al.* (1986), for an attempt to translate an actual piece of legislation, the British Nationality Act, into a set of definitions (i.e. rules of the form "X counts as Y in context C"). One could then take "citizenship" to be a basic institutional concept (or to be definable in BICs, or to be definable on the basis of concepts that are in turn definable on the basis of BICs, etc.). The nature of these BICs raises problems I need not pursue: Smith goes on to say that the only explanation available to Searle would be to accept that truths about BICs "express irreducible material necessities of the Reinachian sort, that is, express necessary relations between certain uninventable *sui generis* categories" (1993: 318–9; Smith's reference is to Reinach, 1913).

> "Do not commit an offence". "Abstain from torts". "Perform contract". "Pay debts". "Discharge liabilities", "Fulfil obligations" . . .. These basic norms are not tied to specific act-situations, and this confirms, if it needed confirmation, how unsatisfactory would be any general programme of individuating laws on the basis of act-situations. But of course the norms presuppose for their application in legal discourse that the system contains rules which do specify the act-situations falling within the general categories "offence", "tort", "contract", "debt", "liability", "obligation" (Honoré, 1977: 118).

Given that the act-situations these rules regulate are constituted by other rules, i.e. those defining "tort", "contract" and the like, these rules cannot be purely regulative. A rule like "perform contracts", for example, seems to be regulative, but it imposes on a party to a contract a "negative power" (which corresponds, naturally, to the other party's "positive power" of requiring compliance). This negative power (and its correlative positive) is necessarily part of any specification of the Y term in any rule of the form "X counts as Y in context C" when "Y" stands for "contract". Hence it is not only (part of) a constitutive rule, it is a rule without which nothing we would recognise as a contract could exist. This highlights an important feature of Searle's distinction: the distinction is not one between rules, but one between *systems of rules*.[16]

Searle does not agree. He believes that it is perfectly possible *both* for constitutive rules to exist without belonging to any system of rules (a kind of "stand-alone" constitutive rule) *and* that there can exist purely regulative rules in the context of institutions (we shall see how these two points are, really, the same). But I fail to see how he can allow for these possibilities without giving up the distinction altogether. At the Buffalo conference Searle offered the following examples:

(1) *Stand-alone constitutive rules*. "You might have a tribe that has a procedure for selecting a leader: he who can lift the biggest stone, like the Vikings. The one who can throw the rock the farthest, he is the boss. So there you got one constitutive rule. And there is no whole system. It's just that they recognise him as the boss".

The problem is, "being the boss" might receive a non-institutional interpretation. "Being the boss" can be a brute fact if it means that I recognise someone as the boss because she has shown that she is the strongest, and because of that it is better for me to do as she wants until I get as strong as she is (here "boss" works as a mere label for "strongest"). This involves no institutional fact (*see* Searle's remark on labels, quoted below), and hence "she's the boss" does not make reference to any constitutive rule.

Things are different, however, if by "she's the boss" I mean or imply that in

[16] To be sure, he recognises the fact that, usually, "constitutive rules come in systems" (1969: 36; *see* also 35). But constitutive rules are constitutive *because* they belong to institutions, not when they are floating in some kind of normative vacuum (*see* Cherry, 1973).

some sense I have the *duty* to do as she commands. *Now* we're talking institutional. By being chosen as the boss, she has acquired a new status that allows her to demand obedience from the rest of us: *X* counts as *Y* in context *C*. This normative language is made possible by constitutive rules. How can we distinguish the two situations? Well, we have to look at precisely what "being the boss" means. If "boss" is an institutional fact, we would expect to find not only a rule about how to choose the boss, but also rules that specify the consequences of being the boss: rules that confer powers to the boss and obligations to the subordinates, to say the least. If we have only a rule saying how we can find out who is he or she whose wants we better satisfy or else, then I do not see how we could say that "being he or she whose wants we better satisfy or else" can be an institutional fact. Indeed, it looks to be a good example of one of Rawls's "summary" rule. Contrariwise, if Searle wants to grant that "being he or she whose wants we better satisfy or else" is an institutional fact, then it seems likely that with some ingenuity we shall be able to make any regulative rule into a constitutive one, and the distinction would collapse.

Searle, I believe, saw this problem (the problem of all rules becoming trivially constitutive in this way) in *The Construction of Social Reality*, where he said that

> As I am using the formula (i.e. the formula "X counts as Y in context C") it would not be a statement of a constitutive rule to say "objects that are designed and used to be sat on by one person count as chairs", because satisfying the *X* term is already sufficient for satisfying the *Y* term, just from the definition of the word "chair". ***The "rule" does not add anything but a label*** so it is not a constitutive rule (Searle, 1995: 44, emphasis added).

In the situation imagined by Searle, in which we have only one rule specifying that he or she who can lift the biggest stone shall be the boss, there is no constitutive rule, but a mere label ("boss" a mere label for "strongest"), unless we find further rules specifying the status that goes with the *Y* term. It follows that precisely insofar as constitutive rules stand alone, they cease to be constitutive rules.

This is not just an amusing detail about institutional facts. The key difference between a label and a status is that only the latter is characterised by a set of powers or functions that are attached to it; hence *it is necessarily the case* that, insofar as there is only a rule saying "he or she who can throw the rock the farthest is the boss", without any function or status being attached to a person's being the boss, and *precisely because there is only one such rule*, "being the boss" would not count as an instance of an institutional fact. Indeed, Searle appears to grant this when he talks about money:

> But to describe these bits of paper with the *Y* term "money" does more than provide a shorthand for the features of the *X* term; it describes a new status, and that status, viz. Money, has a set of functions attached to it, e.g. medium of exchange, store of value, etc. (1995: 46).

(2) *Purely regulative, institutional rules.* At the Buffalo conference Searle offered rule 48 of Baseball as an example of this: "no player, coach or manager shall dispute a decision of an umpire". But this rule is not purely regulative, since it contributes to defining the positions of players, referees and coaches in the game of baseball. A person's having the status of referee in baseball is an institutional fact that is defined (among other things) by the fact that no player or coach can dispute his decisions as to how the rules are to be applied. If rule 48 is not constitutive of what a referee (a player, a coach) is, then it is difficult to see how powers can be ascribed to institutional statuses.

We see how points (1) and (2) are linked: a constitutive rule of the form "X counts as Y in context C" must indicate not only how something or someone gets to occupy the Y position (i.e. not only how you go about choosing the boss, hence the Viking rule either was not constitutive or did not stand alone), but it also "has to assign a new *status* that the object does not already have just in virtue of satisfying the X term" (Searle, 1995: 44). This status gets assigned by further rules specifying what the powers of the status-holder are. Among those rules, in the case of baseball, we shall find rule 48. Rule 48 cannot be a purely regulative rule.

Before pursuing this point any further, let us go back to the beginning and consider the criteria offered by Searle to distinguish regulative from constitutive rules. In *Speech Acts* Searle offered two different criteria: one at p. 33 and another at p. 35 (I will call them "33" and "35", respectively. Both of them were quoted above, at 15f). What is the relation between these two criteria? I think it can be shown that they do not necessarily coincide, because they answer different questions. As Geoffrey Warnock said:

> This supposed distinction between "two sorts" of rules is really, I think, a confused groping after two other distinctions. There is, first, a distinction between two ways of saying what people do—one way which, as for instance walking, or hitting balls about, or waving flags, involves no reference to any rules, and another which, as for instance playing tennis, or signalling, or bequeathing property, does essentially make reference to rules, or presupposes them. Then, second, there is a broad and rather woolly distinction between two different "objects" of rules, or reasons for having them. It is not the *object*, presumably, of the criminal law to "create the possibility" of committing criminal offences, though it incidentally does so; the object is to "regulate" in certain respects the conduct of members of society. By contrast, while the rules of, say, soccer do "regulate" the way in which balls are kicked about in fields, it is in this case the *object* of (some of) the rules to "constitute" a certain exercise in physical skill and ingenuity, to "create" a particular game for people to play (1971: 38).

Now having Warnock's idea in mind, let us consider the two criteria of Searle's distinction. As should be remembered, the first criterion (33) was that while regulative rules regulate "antecedently or independently existing forms of behaviour", constitutive rules create or define *new* forms of behaviour, like playing chess or football.

Strictly speaking, as Searle saw, what *creates* the possibility of playing chess or football is not *a* rule, but a *system* of rules ("the *rules* of chess..."). We have already seen that no single rule can allow for institutional facts. Hence this is not a criterion to distinguish constitutive from regulative *rules* but *systems of rules*. Some systems of rules exist, as Warnock said, in order to "regulate in certain respects the conduct of members of society", i.e. to regulate antecedently or independently existing behaviour. The point of some other systems of rules is, on the other hand, to "create" particular activities (both Warnock, as we have seen, and Searle (1995: 50) agree that while chess is an instance of the latter, criminal law is one of the former).

The second criterion (35) looked at the description of behaviour which is in accordance with the rule. When the rule is constitutive, the action in accordance with it can be given a description which would not be available if the rule did not exist; concerning regulative rules, this is not the case.

Now, this criterion tells a rather different story: criminal law, for example, is typically regulative in the first sense, a point that, as we saw, is uncontroversial. Criminal law does not exist *in order to* create the possibility of committing offences, but to regulate antecedently existing forms of behaviour. But in (not necessarily too) developed legal systems, the rules of criminal law are necessary to describe, for example, that Jones is "guilty" of "murder in the first degree" though he is "excused" by "mitigating circumstances" etc. Hence, according to the second criterion, the rules of criminal law are constitutive (*see* MacCormick, 1998: 335, where he argues that "the boundary between regulative and constitutive is unclear in Searle's schema"; *see* also MacCormick and Weinberger, 1986: 23, where they claim that "particularly unsatisfactory is the Searlean distinction between constitutive and regulative rules").

Searle's new general theory of institutional facts is still liable to this problem. This time the distinction makes its appearance in the book with the help of the following pair of examples: "drive on the right-hand side of the road" (regulative) and "the rules of chess" (constitutive). Here we can see Searle using the first criterion. The "drive on the right" rule is said to be regulative because it regulates driving and driving is an antecedently existing form of behaviour (Searle, 1995: 27), while rules of chess are constitutive because they "create the very possibility" of playing chess (notice again the singular of the former as opposed to the plural of the latter).

Now consider for a moment Searle's new paradigmatic regulative rule: "drive on the right-hand side of the road". If the rule's literal formulation is (something like) "drive on the right-hand side of the road, or you shall be forced to pay £5" the rule does not create "new possibilities of behaviour" and is, therefore, (purely) regulative. But if the rule's formulation were "failure to drive on the right-hand side of the road shall constitute an offence" (as it is, in fact, likely to be), it would indeed be creating such a new possibility (to wit, to commit an offence), and it would be constitutive.

I do not believe Searle would like to accept that the selfsame rule can be regulative or constitutive according to its literal formulation. But the only way in which this can be avoided is to focus not upon the rule, but upon the whole system of rules to which the rule belongs: if it is a legal rule in a developed legal system ("developed" here excludes "systems of primary rules" in the sense of Hart, 1994: 91), then it will be constitutive, since it will single out one form of behaviour as the X term to attach to an institutional Y term like "being guilty of an offence", with a particular set of negative and positive powers. If it is only a rule of etiquette (like the "stand on the right" rule that applies in the escalators of the London Tube), then it would be purely regulative (but it could even be a rule of a weird game: "driving on the right counts as scoring one point").

As mentioned before, Searle does not agree with my talk of two criteria. He claimed (at the Buffalo Conference) that 33 is a definition (rather than a criterion), and 35 simply a "pedagogical device", another way of looking at the issue, but this does not seem to be more than a verbal disagreement. Searle does agree that one consequence of the existence of institutional facts is that one can use something one might want to call "institutional language". I would also like to distinguish 35 from 33. I would like to say that 33 is the important idea, and that whether or not one would use institutional language to describe institutional facts (i.e. whether or not 35 obtains) depends, to an important extent, upon technical details about the canonical formulation of the rules involved. But whether or not a system of rules is institutional in 33's sense is not something that 33 makes dependent upon the canonical formulations of the involved rules. As we have seen 33 is not a definition that singles out a constitutive rule, but a *system of rules*. The distinction is, therefore, between systems of rules that have as their main point the creation of a new activity and those whose main point is to regulate a pre-existing practice. Systems of the first kind, however, do regulate pre-existing forms of behaviour (e.g. the rules of football regulate the ways in which players can get the ball moving), and systems of the second kind do constitute new forms of behaviour (e.g. to be guilty of an offence). The distinction contained in 33 is not based on the fact that some systems constitute and others regulate, but on the fact that some systems regulate pre-existing forms of behaviour in order to create a new activity, while others create the possibility of new forms of behaviour in order to regulate some pre-existing form of behaviour.

This is not a particularly strong objection to Searle's original claims: for some purposes it might be of use to focus upon particular rules only. Indeed, since both systems do constitute (though in different directions: one constitutes in order to regulate and the other regulates in order to constitute), if all we want to talk about is the fact that institutional language introduces a special ontology, it might be enough simply to talk about "systems that allow for institutional facts" and in this sense we might legitimately refer to both games and law, to institutions that regulate-to-constitute and those that constitute-to-regulate. The argument contained in this Chapter is not designed to show that Searle's original distinction was mistaken. It is, rather, that the possibilities that are opened up for the analysis of the "institutional ontology" are missed if one stops simply at the point where one can glance at institutional facts. My claim, to speak metaphorically, is that one can use more sophisticated glasses, glasses that allow one to see the differences between the inhabitants of this institutional world. Leaving the metaphor behind, the claim is that to put systems of rules, rather than rules, under the spotlight, provides far greater insight into the way rules work.

In the next section I will try to provide some examples of this last claim. I will try to show that, because he uses a distinction that is designed only to show whether institutional facts are possible, when it comes to explaining the features of that institutional ontology, Searle tends to ascribe to all institutional fact features that in truth belong to some of them not because they are institutional, but because they are the particular sort of institution they actually are. Thus, he is led to distort one kind of institution by forcing upon it the features of another.

A Critique of Searle's General Theory

The Evolution of Institutions

The first problem I want to discuss is related to the issue of the evolution of institutions. Can an institution evolve without the participants being aware that they are evolving one?

Searle's answer is, indeed they can. Consider the example of money. People can go around buying, selling and exchanging, without their thinking that the particular goods they use as a medium of exchange is "money":

> The evolution may be such that the participants think, e.g. "I can exchange this for gold', "this is valuable", or even simply "this is money". They need not think "we are collectively imposing a value on something that we do not regard as valuable because of its purely physical features", even though that is exactly what they are doing . . .. In the course of consciously buying, selling, exchanging, etc., they may simply evolve institutional facts (Searle, 1995: 47).

Now, why is it possible for people to evolve institutional facts without being aware of it? The answer is that they can keep doing what they were doing all along, and the institution will grow, so to speak, on the back of the practice. As Zenon Bankowski has argued, concerning promises:

> the institution comes about because gradually a practice grows up where, for example, we do something we say we will, not merely because of the substantive reasons we had in saying we would do it, but also because of the reason that we said we would do it. At first that is one among all the reasons but gradually it excludes the others and so we might say the convention of promising grows up. We do it

because we promised and the other reasons are excluded. Thus the institution grows up on the back of the substantive reasons since the reason that it is a promise can be seen as the universalisation of the substantive reasons (1993: 13; *see*, for a similar point, Atiyah, 1981: 120).

Before proceeding any further, notice that Bankowski is *not* trying to offer a reductionist analysis of promising in terms of whatever substantive reasons the parties might think they have for promising. There is no need to emphasise that any such reductionist account cannot be a complete analysis of promising. I think that Bankowski's point here should be understood as aiming at the same target as Searle's assertion (1995: 50f), that "in many cases the X term is chosen precisely because it is supposed to have the features necessary to perform the function specified by the Y term", though "even in these cases, something is added by the Y term". Bankowski's claim, from this point of view, is that the Y term "grows up on the back" of the substantive reasons *normally* behind the X term, and that it adds to it *some degree* of insulation from the actual presence or absence of those substantive reasons in a particular instance of the X term. Under normal circumstances, we have good substantive reasons to grant an agreement (the X term) the binding force of a promise (the Y term). Therefore, we treat agreements as binding promises without having to check, in every instance, whether those substantive reasons are actually present.

This growing of the Y term on the back of the X term, however, is something that can only happen regarding institutions that "constitute to regulate", that is, institutions that create the possibility of institutional facts because of the improved regulatory effects this *technique* allows. Because the institutions of criminal law are not necessary to sustain the practice of punishing people for failing to behave according to what Hart called "primary" rules (in much the same way in which we saw that the concept of sin was not conceptually necessary either to understand or to apply the Ten Commandments), those who administer the punishments need not think of the rules of criminal law in constitutive terms (in an "undeveloped" system, it could be enough to have a list of "do's" and "don'ts"; or, rather, a list of "don'ts—or else"). They can simply continue the practice of punishing people, and at some point in time a writer (what in Scotland, for example, is called an *institutional* writer)[17] can offer an interpretation of the practice of punishing

[17] See Cairns (1994: 90): "In France and Spain, institutional works were obviously linked to attempts to create and to promote a unified national law. This cannot be so for Scotland, since Scots law was unified. It is, however, worth considering that Scots law did require unification in a different sense, in that the separate constituent parts of the law—customary, Canon, Roman and statute—had to be worked into a convincing whole; and this unification of the law into a general Scots law is generally taken to have been carried out by the Scottish institutional writers, especially Stair. The disparate elements of Scots law are connected with the various different jurisdictions—royal, heritable and ecclesiastical—and it must be of importance in this respect that in the seventeenth and eighteenth centuries all the various jurisdictions tended to be united into one centrally organised system of justice."

people in terms of institutional facts (*see* MacCormick, 1974: 62f; 1998: 333; MacCormick and Weinberger, 1986: 12).[18] But when the institution is one that "regulates to constitute" (one that specifies how things are to be done in order to create a new activity e.g. how a ball is to be kicked about in fields in order to create the game of football) it cannot evolve on the back of the practice, since without the institution there is no practice at all. There cannot be a pre-institutional practice of football, in the sense in which it is possible for a pre-institutional legal practice to exist; a Hartian "regime of primary rules" of football is, I believe, a conceptual impossibility (*see* Amselek, 1988: 209: "it is impossible to imagine that one can play a game without implying that one is following the corresponding collections of rules") . The first group of people who thought of football, for example, must have been aware of the fact that they were imposing a particular meaning on three wooden posts that did not have that meaning by virtue of their physical characteristics.[19]

(When I was a boy we used to play football in a park. As there were, of course, no goal posts in the park, we had to use our jumpers and bags as goalposts. The first time my friends started to throw their bags and jumpers around I could not understand what were they up to, until one of them said: "this is your goal, and that is ours": everything was clear from then on. We could not have played football in the park had we not been aware of the fact that by placing those bags and jumpers where we placed them we were collectively assigning meaning to them, a meaning that was not exhausted by the physical properties of the bags and jumpers. But the POWs who, in German concentration camps, as the standard story goes, started to give and accept packages of cigarettes in exchange for other goods need not have been aware of the fact that by their giving and taking cigarettes in those circumstances they were assigning to cigarettes a meaning not exhausted by their physical characteristics).[20]

Systematic relationships between institutional facts

One feature of institutional facts, according to Searle, is that they "cannot exist in isolation but only in a set of systematic relationships to other facts" (1995: 35). For money to exist, a system of exchange has to exist beforehand, and for a system of exchange there has to be a system of property and

[18] I am not saying that the writer *creates* institutional facts where there were none; she makes explicit what was up to then implicit in the practice: this is Searle's point. What we have is a seamless process from pure brute facts to implicit institutional facts to explicit institutional facts (for an illustration of this process in legal history, *see* Cairns, 1994; Stein, 1983) .

[19] But they could, couldn't they, think that the posts had some magical feature, so that football was something that had to be played in those terms because of broader considerations (such as the aim of not insulting the Gods, etc.)? This answer is not available to Searle, who would not be willing to call this "game" a game (1995: 36n): "to the extent that professional sports have such [broader] consequences, they cease to be just games and become something else, e.g. big business".

[20] See Wonnacott and Wonnacott (1990: 38–41) for the text-book version of this story. Wonnacott and Wonnacott follow Radford (1945).

property ownership. "Similarly, in order that society should have marriages, they must have some form of contractual relationships. But in order that they can have contractual relationships, they must have such things as promises and obligations" (*ibid.*)

Generally speaking, the existence of systems that "constitute to regulate" presupposes the existence of the practice the system is created to regulate. This is, obviously, because the point of the development of the system is its regulatory impact on the practice. But this shows that this (i.e. the fact that some institutions presuppose other institutional and non-institutional facts) is not the case by virtue of some mysterious characteristic of institutional facts, but because of the particular kind of institutional facts under consideration. Concerning games, again, the point is less straightforward.

Searle, however, thinks that games are not counterexamples to his claim, though "it might seem" that they are, "because, of course, games are designed to be forms of activity that do not connect with the rest of our lives in a way that institutional facts characteristically do". When this point is looked at carefully, Searle claims,

> even in the case of games there are systematic dependencies on other forms of institutional facts. The position of the pitcher, the catcher, and the batter, for example, all involve rights and responsibilities; and their positions and actions or inactions are unintelligible without an understanding of these rights and responsibilities; but these notions are in turn unintelligible without the general notions of rights and responsibilities (1995: 36).

It is not clear whether Searle thinks that *baseball* is unintelligible without such notions as rights and responsibilities or, as he later claims, that this fact (the fact that baseball so depends) is a consequence of games generally "employ[ing] an apparatus—of rights, obligations, responsibilities, etc.—that is intelligible only given all sorts of other social facts" (*ibid.*, 56). In any case, this does not seem to be the case. We can understand, make sense of, and even *play* chess without knowing a thing about the "apparatus" used in India during or before the sixth century (or wherever and whenever it was invented: that we do not need to be sure of its origins to play is another way of making the point). Baseball and football are played all over the world, and that is not a proof that the notions of "rights, obligations and responsibilities" are common to the human race at large, unless one wants to hold on to Searle's point and claim that the fact that we can understand games is a proof of a shared "apparatus" between human beings of all times and places (a weird argument, would it not be, for a natural law doctrine?)

Granted, today we would use some idea of responsibility to understand the different functions of, say, a goalkeeper, a defender, etc. in a football team, but without such notions one is still able to play football. Those notions seem to me to be linked more to the idea of a successful strategy than to the very notion of what football is.

Finding in games this feature, which is obviously present in legal concepts (money, marriage and the like) forces Searle to weaken his requirement. At the Buffalo Conference, Searle's explanation for our ability to understand chess in the face of our ignorance about sixth century India was that "we do have to know that they spoke a language, and that they understood such things as, the queen has more power than the pawn . . .. The basic institutional form is language; the basic institutional move is the speech act, and that's universal".

This is, of course, something I do not want to deny. But notice how weak in content this requirement is when compared to the heavily loaded requirement that "in order to . . . have money, that society must have a system of exchanging goods and services for money. But in order that it can have a system of exchange, it must have a system of property and property ownership" (Searle, 1995: 35). We are not talking about language here, we are talking of social structures, production relations and the like: in order to have institutions, some social structures must be in place. When it comes to games, all we are told is that the society must have a language. This is common, says Searle, to all institutional facts, and I do not want to deny it. Using Barry Smith's language (Smith, 1993), we might say that all institutions stand in a relation of ontological necessity to language; but some of them (like those Searle referred to in the first paragraph of section 4 at page 35 of *The Construction of Social Reality*) also stand in such relations to much more concrete and contingent practices (like private property and the like). This is something that is relevant for the ontology of different kinds of institutional facts, something that is missed by Searle's too rough conceptual apparatus.

Institutions and their Consequences

So let us go back to Searle's statement in *The Construction of Social Reality*, where he claims that "It might seem that games are counterexamples to this general principle, because, of course, games are designated to be forms of activity that do not connect with the rest of our lives in a way that institutional facts characteristically do" (1995: 36). To the best of my knowledge he does not explicitly refer to this characteristic of institutional facts elsewhere in the book, and it is not clear what he has in mind. One characteristic way in which institutions (i.e. systems of constitutive rules) connect with our lives is that they allow us to do things that we could not otherwise do: we can promise, we can play football and so on. But in this sense games *do* connect with our lives in the same way, hence this is not the sense in which Searle intends his remark on page 36 (where he claimed that games *do not* connect in the way institutional facts characteristically do). The sentence that immediately follows the one discussed here seems to imply that the way in which institutional facts characteristically connect to our lives is that the former have *consequences* for the latter: "Today's philosophy department softball game need have no consequences for tomorrow, in a way that today's wars . . . are intended precisely to have consequences for tomorrow".

Hence, the fact that institutional facts have "consequences for tomorrow" is characteristic of them. This is why the caveat above concerning the paradigmatic *status* of games as institutional facts is important: we have seen that, concerning two important features of institutional facts, games are unlike the institutions that are really important. Indeed, I do not want to object to the thesis that *some* institutions stand in systematic relationships with other institutional and non-institutional facts. In fact, this is an extraordinarily important feature of institutions like the law. But this is not a characteristic of institutions *qua* institutions (since there are institutions that have no systematic relationships to other facts), but only of institutions that "constitute to regulate", *because* they do so. The reason for this is simple: since the institutional (i.e. constitutive) apparatus is used to regulate a practice that exists independently, that apparatus must, of necessity, have "systematic relationships" with the institutional and non-institutional facts that are part of the practice to be regulated.

I take Searle's point of institutions "having consequences for tomorrow" to be his way of singling out what I have been calling institutions that "constitute to regulate" from those that "regulate to constitute". My last claim can, therefore, be expressed in Searle's terms by saying that institutions have "systematic relationships to other facts" *because* they have "broader consequences": games do not have consequences, hence they need not have those relationships. Indeed, insofar as games do develop those relationships, Searle himself believes that they "cease to be just games" (*cf.* 1995: 36).

Constitutive and Regulative Institutions

I agree with Searle when he says that the important criterion to characterise institutions is the first one (i.e. 33). According to it, the law is a "regulative" institution, since its point is to regulate antecedently existing forms of behaviour (and to do that in a better and more efficient way it creates the possibility of new forms of behaviour). Games, on the other hand, are "constitutive" institutions, that is, systems of rules whose point is to create new possibilities of behaviour rather than to regulate antecedently existing forms of it (though they doubtless do regulate some pre-existing forms of behaviour in order to do this). A distinction of this kind is obviously behind Ronald Dworkin's claim that

> chess is, in this sense, an autonomous institution; I mean that it is understood, among its participants, that no one may claim an institutional right by direct appeal to general morality . . .. But legislation is only partly autonomous in this sense (1977: 101).

Thus, it transpires that the important distinction is not based on whether the *rules* are constitutive of institutional facts or regulative of pre-existing forms of behaviour, since we might find rules of both kinds in either system. Thus "thou shalt not drive on the left" would be regulative (because it is not needed to describe the action), but "it shall be an offence to drive on the left" counts as constitutive (since it *is* required to describe the action of committing an offence).

Because "regulative" (regulatory) institutions are justified by their regulatory effects (i.e. by their "broader consequences") those effects have an impact upon the application of the rules. In regulative (regulatory) institutions the rules set out only what is "presumptively" the case, and the fact that that presumption can be defeated in concrete cases allows for problems like those discussed by Paul, Fuller and Pufendorf. In "constitutive" (autonomous) institutions, since the institution is not justified by its regulatory effects, consideration of those effects need not affect the application of the rules, which can (but need not) be indefeasible: here we go back to the initial observation, i.e. the fact that disagreement about what is the law is a common phenomenon while it is most *un*common concerning games. The defeasibility of *legal* reasoning, then, is a consequence of the *kind* of institution the law is understood to be (we shall soon see that some forms of ancient law can be said to have been "autonomous": *see* below at 49ff). But to see this, to understand legal reasoning, we need a theory of institutional facts that can account for this distinction.[21]

A note about the word "institution". As should by now be evident, I am using this word in a loose sense. Or rather, I am using it as defined by Searle, as "systems of constitutive rules" (1969: 51). I understand "constitutive rules" in this definition as meaning "rules that provide for the existence of institutional facts". Therefore, both "constitutive" (autonomous) and "regulative" (regulatory) institutions are in this sense institutional: both of them allow for the existence of institutional facts (an example of a non-institutional system of rules is Hart's "régime of primary rules" in Hart, 1994: 91ff). My reason for using the word "institution" in this sense is to emphasise the fact that what I take to be the true distinction between the regulative and the constitutive is not the fact that only the former regulates and only the latter allows for institutional facts. Both kinds of institutions do both, but in different directions, so

[21] After the next paragraph I will cease to talk of "constitutive" and "regulative" institutions. I believe that the argument presented in this section is best viewed as a way of taking Searle beyond Searle, that is to say, of building upon Searle's "general theory of institutional facts". But even if my argument fails as a critique of Searle's views, I still think it has intrinsic value. For this reason, from now on I will label "autonomous" institutions those that "regulate to constitute", like games (i.e. those systems of rules that if my argument is correct correspond to Searle's "constitutive rules"). The other kind (i.e. those that "constitute to regulate") I will call "regulatory" institutions; they would correspond to Searle's regulative rules. In choosing these labels I have tried to give them a Searlean flavour, while at the same time suggesting that they represent a different (i.e. hopefully improved) version of Searle's two kinds of rules. Beyond that there is nothing to be read in the labels. They could be replaced by "A-" and "B-institutions" (in fact, labels of this latter kind were used in a previous draft of this chapter, and I am grateful to Professor David Garland who suggested to me the labels I am using now).

to speak: one regulates in order to constitute, the other constitutes in order to regulate.[22]

However, there still remain some objections that could be presented against the thesis that there is a difference in *kind* between two models of institution. These objections take the form of alternative explanations for the differences between legal and game-adjudication, explanations that would not be committed to the claim that they are qualitatively different. To them we should turn now.

THE GAME OF LAW

In this section I want to address some objections to the thesis presented above, objections that amount to the claim that the difference between institutions like games and institutions like the law is not one of kind, but one of (at most) degree. Needless to say, since the argument up to now has effectively claimed precisely the contrary, I have to show why all these objections fail.

To begin with, however, it could be said (i) that I have overvalued the certainty of norms of games. Is it not the case that some norms of games are, after all, indeterminate in a Hartian sense? Any football fan knows that some actions are *core* instances of, say, *dangerous play*, but also that the referee will have to exercise discretion to decide whether or not some actions—which can be said to be penumbra instances of "dangerous play"—are to be punished (my stipulation concerning the word "defeasibility" above at 14 goes some way towards answering this objection). Furthermore, (ii) the fact that these controversial applications do not generate the same controversy as hard cases in law might be due to the existence of a secondary rule of adjudication in football according to which decisions must be produced on the spot and without further consideration (indeed, it is very difficult to imagine a game like football without such a rule).

In my view, however, both of these facts are explained, not by the reason that natural languages are necessarily open-textured, but by the existence of rules to that effect. With regard to (i), the use of vague standards like "dangerous play"[23] is, himself tells us, a particular legislative "technique"

[22] Again, this is basically a stipulative definition, and for that reason it is important to see its implications. It follows Searle's stipulation, but it would not be agreed upon by, e.g. Neil MacCormick, who claims that a definition of institution in terms of constitutive rules "would simply involve an obvious confusion between the law of contract and the legal institution "contract" itself which is regulated by that branch of the law" (1974: 51). It would also commit one to say that a contract is a different institution in Germany than in France, while it could at least be claimed that the (same) institution of contract exists both in German and in French law, though subject to different rules. I believe that MacCormick is right in making the distinction between the system of rules and the institution that exists under it, but for ease of exposition I will use one word to refer to both, hoping that the context will make the precise meaning clear.

[23] "An indirect free kick is awarded to the opposing team if a player, in the opinion of the referee . . . plays in a dangerous manner" (Law 12).

(1994: 132) that it is reasonable to use when "it is impossible to identify a class of specific actions to be uniformly done or forborne and to make them the subject of a simple rule" (*ibid.*). This must be distinguished from the philosophical claim about language according to which "whichever device . . . is used to communicate standards of behaviour, these . . . *will* prove indeterminate" (*ibid.* 128, emphasis added), since, even if the latter claim were false, that "legislative technique" could still be useful in many cases (thus, we shall see that the Hartian open texture thesis can receive two wildly different interpretations). With regard to (ii), it clearly cannot be the case that we have no disagreement about what the rules of football are for concrete cases *because* the referee has the final say on the matter, since if that were the case we would not be playing (or watching or talking about) football but some form of "scorer's discretion".

But maybe a more sophisticated version of this argument could be advanced along lines suggested by Neil MacCormick. He first noticed and then tried to offer an explanation for what he called the "variable practical force" of rules (1998: 316–7). He argues that rules are of ***absolute application*** if the "O[perative] *F*[acts] must be attended unfailingly by *N*[ormative] C[onsequence], and *NC* may not be put into effect except when either *OF* obtains or some other rule independently providing for *NC* is satisfied by virtue of the ascertained presence of its operative facts"; of ***strict application*** if "the person charged with applying the rule and managing the activity within which the rule has application is given some degree of guided discretion to make exceptions, or to override the rule, in special, or very special cases"; and of ***discretionary application*** "if the decision-maker is expected to consider every case in the light of all factors that appear relevant".

Now, what, according to MacCormick, determines the kind of rule a rule belongs to? "The answer is obvious—it depends not on the content of the first-tier rules about a practice, but on second-tier norms laying down the terms of authorization or empowerment of the decision maker" (*ibid.* 317).

The variable practical force of rules is an important feature of them (and fatal to any account of rules as exclusionary reasons, as we will see), but if my argument is correct, MacCormick's explanation cannot be enough. The "second-tier" rules arise when a person is appointed to monitor the application of the rules of the practice (MacCormick, 1998: 312). But MacCormick's own example of rules of absolute application (rules of chess) shows that the practical force of rules is determined even in the absence of second-tier rules. Indeed, Hart (1994) noticed that "many competitive games are played without an official scorer: notwithstanding their competing interest, the players succeed tolerably well in applying the scoring rule to particular cases; they usually agree in their judgements, and unresolved disputes may be few" (at 142). It is the nature of the institution, what determines the practical force of the rules of it (needless to say, second-tier rules, when they exist) that can affect the practical force of rules. But even when they purport to do so, the nature of the institution sets them an important limit, since they also belong to it, *see* below at 118ff.[24]

So let us look elsewhere for an explanation. It could be argued, to support the thesis that the difference between games and the law is not one of *kind*, but rather one of *degree*, that this difference of degree is explained by the difference in the *complexity* of the regulations that games and the law involve: games restrict the reality they deal with, and so they create a world artificially simple (Huizinga, 1970: 28). The law, on the other hand, at least potentially regulates any situation. In a more restricted world, it is possible to predict and to anticipate any problem the application of a rule will present in the future, while this is impossible in law. The law has what, following Emilios Christodoulidis, we could call a "complexity deficit" (Christodoulidis, 1999).

This view appears promising at first sight, but it is wrong, and to see why, compare the two following cases:

Edson's Case. During a football match, each team is allowed to replace a given number of players only (three in the last World Cup). If one team has already made those replacements, it cannot make any further under any circumstance whatsoever. Now, suppose that this is the case, and that one of the players of team *A* (call him Edson) is an extraordinarily good player: the performance of *A* is largely improved when Edson is playing. Now, team *B*'s manager knows this, so he decides to instruct Harald, one of his players, to severely injure Edson. The manager knows that if Harald succeeds he is likely

[24] The distinction between first- and second-tier rules, however, can be of use in a different sense. Every time I have tried to explain the argument contained in this chapter to others, they have felt challenged to try their best to produce counter-examples (memorable discussions about football ensuing). It is an interesting point that the most convincing counter-examples are rules that have as their obvious point to secure the continuity of a match. Bert Roermund offered the best example: a referee has constantly to balance his whistling in accordance with the rules against his responsibility in keeping the match attractive. In deciding whether or not to award a free kick after a very minor fault, the referee might encounter an application problem. My answer to Roermund's example would be that one can distinguish first-tier rules *of* football (like the rule against handling the ball) from second-tier rules *about* football, rules that purport to facilitate the development of the game. The obvious way in which such a distinction could be made would be to say that the first-tier rules define what football is, while the second-tier rules are rules which take football as something already existing and tries to single out some ways of playing as to be preferred. This explanation would fit perfectly well the argument I am developing here, for it would take rules *of* football as constitutive of that new (i.e. non-existing before the rules) activity, football, and rules *about* football as regulating something already existing, i.e. something not created by them. The reason why I confined this discussion to a footnote, however, is that this explanation would commit me to say that what I used to play with my friends at the park was not "football" since we did not consider the offside rule (clearly a rule *of* football rather than one *about* football), and this conclusion seems to me to be rather pedantic. I will not go further into this problem: the distinction might be difficult to pinpoint with complete accuracy, but it seems to me a natural distinction to make. Strictly, a proper counter-example to my claim would be a rule *of* football (or *of* any other game) that were open to challenge by substantive considerations in the absence of a rule of the game granting discretion to the rule-applier (or, as Pufendorf's rule, in the presence of a rule instructing the rule-applier to apply the other rules in a strict manner). I suppose that if FIFA were to pass a rule instructing referees not to balance their whistling against their responsibility to keep the match attractive, then referees would not have any balancing to do. I have not yet heard such a counter-example.

to be sent off, but he also knows that if the injury Edson suffers is bad enough, Edson will not be able to continue playing and, since *A* cannot make further replacements, both teams will continue the game with ten players (with a significant advantage for *B*, since Edson will not be playing for *A*). So Harald breaks Edson's leg in a vicious tackle.

Elmer's Case. Now imagine that Elmer wants his grandfather's money. He knows that his grandfather has made a will in his favour, but he needs the money now (and his grandfather is, alas, very healthy), so he murders him. Imagine further that none of the provisions of the statute of wills said anything about a legatee killing the testator, and all the requirements it does contain for the validity of a will have been fulfilled by Elmer (and Elmer's grandfather). After he has been convicted for the killing, Elmer goes on to claim the inheritance (*Riggs* v. *Palmer*, 115 NY 506, 22 NE 188 [1889]).

Elmer's case is discussed by the jurisprudential literature as a standard example of a hard case. On the other hand, I submit that Edson's cannot but be a clear case, and that any football fan will agree with me if I say that, however reasonable from a moral point of view that might be, the referee *cannot* (without violating the rules of football) allow *A* to make a fourth replacement. I want to argue that *no difference in complexity* can account for this fact (i.e. the fact that the former is or at least can be a hard case while the latter is definitively a clear one). In Edson's case, the rule does not leave any margin to the referee to decide . . . what? to allow Edson's team a fourth replacement? to declare Edson's team the winner?[25] to grant it an extra goal? an extra yellow card for every player in *B*? to send off one additional player of Harald's team, chosen at random? In Elmer's case, however, though the rule does not appear to leave the judge any scope, it does: the possibility of discussing the application of the rule contained in the statute of wills is present, any sensible counsel would see the possible arguments each side could use in court (it does not matter for the time being whether or not these arguments are good enough to carry the day, but only that they are not to be taken as evidence that the speaker does not really understand what lawyers are supposed to do).

To be useful in this context, the recourse to the different level of complexity between a game like football and the law must be related to the (supposed) inability of the law-maker to predict future cases in such a complex normative system as the law is said to be. This was the idea behind Hart's view on the convenience of uncertainty given by our "relative ignorance of fact" and

[25] Bert Roermund advised me to think about this possibility more seriously than I had. The referee could stop the game, in his opinion, and declare Edson's team the winner. But this is because the rules of the game allow the referee to "stop, suspend or terminate the match, at his discretion, for any infringements of the Laws" (Law 5), if he thinks the infringement is sufficiently serious. But it is, of course, not part of my argument that the referee cannot be *granted* discretion explicitly, as in this case. Incidentally, Harald may, of course, be sued by Edson (or sanctioned by FIFA) after the match, that is something for the law, but it is something that, of course, I need not deny.

"relative indeterminacy of aim" (1994: 128). The solution would then be: in a "simple" normative system (e.g. football) the legislator (i.e. FIFA) can predict all possible combinations of relevant facts in the future, so that any participant can safely assume that the solution provided by the rule is the solution actually sought by the authority. Hence, as all participants acknowledge the authority of FIFA, the rule can be applied to any conceivable case without controversy. In a "complex" normative system (e.g. law), on the other hand, participants cannot assume this knowledge on the part of the authority, because, as the reality the law is dealing with is so complex, it is empirically impossible for any legislator actually to predict all of the possible combinations of relevant factual features in the future. So the complexity of the system (strictly, the enormous number of possible combinations of relevant factual features the system purports to take into account) allows space for the following argument: "this rule should not be applied to this case because it was not *meant* to". That would be the reason, on this interpretation, why purposive interpretation is so useful in legal hard cases.

The problem with this approach is simply that there is *no* reason *at all* to assume that a case like Edson's was actually predicted by FIFA (in fact, I would think that Elmer's case is more easily predictable than Edson's). The referee has to do what he has to in Edson's case *not* because he thinks that FIFA so decided (when, at the moment of enacting the replacements rule, it presented to itself the possibility of a case like Edson's), but because he has (given the nature of the game) no other alternative. In other words, the correct solution is correct, not because FIFA wanted this solution for this particular case when it was passing the replacement rule, but because, given some up to now mysterious peculiarity of games as institutions, what (the members of the relevant committee of) FIFA had in mind when the rule was passed is completely irrelevant. This becomes obvious if we notice that even if the referee happens to know that FIFA did not think of this case, his predicament is the same.

Notice how to explain the difference between Edson's and Elmer's cases on the basis of a complexity deficit must necessarily beg the whole issue. In both cases there is a complexity deficit in the sense that for each of them we might feel that there are some features of the case that should be relevant for its correct solution, though they are not picked up as operative facts by the applicable rule. In both cases we might feel that it would be better if the rule were so drafted as to include an explicit exception for the case at hand. In Edson's case, however, the fact that the rule does not contain such an explicit reference is the end of the issue, while this is not necessarily so in Elmer's.

In brief, the fact that reality is infinitely variable has in itself nothing to do with the issue discussed here, because rules are to be applied to those cases that match the operative facts of the rule only: "the legislator does not issue norms for each individual case . . .. His function consists in the creation of general norms, by means of which he resolves generic cases" (Alchourrón and Bulygin, 1971: 30).

In the strict sense, therefore, both Elmer's and Edson's cases are equally solved by the applicable rules. The difference, therefore, is not that the law has a complexity deficit that football does not have: both of them can have it. The question is rather why this complexity deficit is relevant in legal adjudication while it is not in football-adjudication. But this *is* the problem for which we are seeking an explanation.

The argument begs the question even more clearly if we were to say that Elmer's case is more complex because the law does not restrict (as games do) the considerations that can be referred to in adjudication to those explicitly contained in the rules. This is true, but correct though it is, it is not a good answer to our problem here: according to this explanation, the difference would indeed be one of complexity, but then again, the issue would be why cannot the law exclude such considerations? Or rather, why does the fact that a football rule does not mention some feature *X* count as the rule *excluding* that feature, while in the law (at least sometimes) the same fact does not necessarily imply that consequence? Thus, it turns out that the complexity deficit is not really an explanation, but a different way of describing the same problem: *why does the deficit matter in law and not in games?*

In brief, the situation is *not* that because rules of law are not nuanced enough we cannot take them to be final. It is precisely the other way around: because we expect reasonably appropriate solutions from the law, we allow for some "leeway" in the application of legal rules. Thus, Gottlieb puts the cart in front of the horses when he argues that

> What of a model that would eliminate moral judgment of any sort from the judicial role? It is hard to imagine how legal standards could conceivably reach a degree of specificity in all domains that would eliminate every moral dimension of judgment (1994: 16).

It is not because legal standards are imperfect that we need morality to step in as a corrective; it is because we expect legal judgments to display some given moral quality that we read legal standards as allowing for some "leeway". Since we do not understand the rules of games in the same way (because of their different nature as social practices), we do not have the same expectations regarding them. This has nothing to do with the intrinsic quality of the rules (their "degree of specificity"), but with our understanding of the relevant practices.

It could be useful here to consider another possible explanation, one that seems backed by common sense. According to it, the difference between games and the law is that games are not serious or important, so we don't really care about achieving the right result in games. Because we don't really care, we have such a formalist type of adjudication.

There seem to be some important truth in this explanation, but we cannot take it at face value. The reality is, many people would think that what is at stake in (say) some football matches is (for them) more important than many things that are or may be disputed in court (witness Bill Shankly).[26] I will, however, return to this point below (*infra*, 47f) because there is a sense in which an explanation of this kind can be useful.

A further explanation could be offered on the basis of the *arbitrariness* of some norms: some norms are arbitrary in the sense that the reasons for each of them are not reasons for their content, but only for their existence. They have what Atiyah and Summers (1987: 13) called *content-formality*. On the other hand, most (though by no means all) legal norms have low content-formality: the reasons for having a norm regarding murder are reasons for the content of such a norm as well (that is, to punish murder). Some legal norms are like rules of games in this sense (e.g. some traffic laws), and some rules of games are like legal norms (e.g. the rule of *dangerous play*). And it could be claimed that rules that have a high degree of content-formality cannot but be applied formalistically.

This explanation would explain precisely the point posited at the beginning, i.e. that some norms of games seem to be open-textured in the same way as norms of law. But, conversely, it would seem to imply that the application of (some) legal norms (i.e. those that have high content-formality) is beyond plausible contestation in the same way that the application of rules of games is, and this is the reason why it fails: the interesting feature of rules of games which is in need of explanation is that they are (at least *can be*) indefeasible, while legal norms are always defeasible (though of course undefeated many times). Even a legal norm with the highest content-formality, like the "drive-on-the-left" norm is defeasible.[27]

After Fuller (1958) it is difficult to believe that there are kinds of legal rules that are beyond defeasibility. Fuller taught us that regarding every (legal) rule, cases can be imagined in which doubts would legitimately be felt concerning the application of that rule. And this is the reason why the explanation we are now considering fails: it explains the defeasibility of legal rules on the basis of peculiar features of particular rules (i.e. their level of content-formality), thus implying that some other rules (i.e. those that have high content-formality) are indefeasible.

Let us try one final, alternative explanation. The difference between games and law is not one of kind, but one of degree: on one end of the spectrum one would have highly abstract and formalised games (e.g. chess), then less abstract games like football, then a highly formalistic legal system (like ancient Roman law, as we shall see), then a less formalistic one, and so on.

[26] "Law is more serious than games (the heavy view). What is one to say to that? That it overrates law? Or that it underrates games? Both answers are required" (Detmold, 1984: 160). It has even been claimed that "play" is one of a reduced number of basic human goods (Finnis, 1980: 87).

[27] Consider the problem facing an ambulance driver when he arrives to a traffic jam and realises that the opposite lane is free and nobody is coming that way (or rather the problem of the judge who has to decide if he deserves a sanction for having used that lane).

This is wrong. An intuitive reason why chess might be a better example than football in this regard is due to the fact that football is a game of physical contact, while chess is not. What relevance does this fact have for a theory of institutional facts? Consider the following: a hand ball occurs when a player (other than the goalkeeper in his penalty box) touches the ball with his hands. What is a "hand"? In the rules of football there is no definition of what a hand is, so if a mutant player touches the ball with his fifth limb there might be a problem of application after all. But a bishop in chess has nothing to do with an actual bishop, nor a knight with an actual knight, and so on. The rules of chess completely define what a bishop in chess is. There cannot be a mutant bishop. Then we should expect to find more cases of linguistic defeasibility in football than in chess.

At this point, it may be worthwhile to pay attention to Samuel Pufendorf"s criticism of Hugo Grotius. Here Pufendorf and Grotius were discussing the reason that explains the fact that mathematical knowledge is certain in a way in which moral knowledge is not. Grotius thought that the explanation for this significant difference between mathematics and morality was due to the fact that mathematical concepts are so defined that there is always a crisp and bright line to be drawn between them, while "in moral questions, on the contrary, even trifling circumstances alter the substance, and the forms, which are the subject of enquiry, are wont to have something more closely to this, now to that extreme" (1646: Book II, Ch. 23 § I, p. 557 [393]).

For Pufendorf, however, Grotius's dictum that "in moral questions, even trifling circumstances alter the substance" was ambiguous. In one sense (which Pufendorf labelled "qualitative") this is true, but it is also true of mathematics, "for it is also true that a line which varies in the slightest degree from straightness, tends to curvature", and thus this fact cannot explain the difference between the certainty of mathematical knowledge and the uncertainty of moral knowledge. If Grotius's dictum is to be understood in a different, "quantitative" sense, that is, if

> the saying means that the slightest circumstance increases or lessens the quantity of an action, we answer that this is not always true, at least in a civil court, where the judge often pays no regard to trifles. And even granting this, the fact does not lessen the certainty of moral matters, since even in mathematics the slightest addition or detraction makes a change in the quantity (Pufendorf, 1688: Book I, Ch. 2 § 10, p. 34 [23–4]).

But from this Pufendorf did not conclude that there was no difference between mathematical and moral knowledge. Indeed, he believed that "a certain latitude is found in moral quantities", but his explanation for this was different from Grotius. Pufendorf noticed that "physical quantities can be exactly compared with one another, and measured and divided into distinct parts, because they are in a material way object of our senses", hence we can "determine accurately what relation or proportion they have to one another";

> *But moral qualities arise from imposition*, and the judgement of intelligent and free agents, whose judgement and pleasure is in no way subject to physical measurement and so the quantity which they conceive and determine by their imposition cannot be referred to a like measure, but retains the liberty and laxness of its origin (Pufendorf, 1688: Book I, Ch. 2 § 10, p. 35 [24], emphasis added).

We shall shortly see that the law can attain the high level of certainty games have if it is seen as being part of the "physical" world. Insofar as the law is seen as something that "arises from imposition", as something *regulatory* in character, there is space to question the application of its rules to any particular case, and that introduces "a certain latitude". Further differences in the vocabulary should not bother us at this stage. The point is, when we leave the football-creating convention and start playing football, the rules of the game are seen by players to belong to the structure of the world in the same way in which the "rules" of bridge-building belong to the world for engineers: if you want to build a bridge, do such-and-such; if you want to score a goal, do such-and-such. But consider if you want to write a will, do such-and-such (but actually, if you don't, it might still be the case that you succeed in writing a will; if you do, it might be the case that you fail, etc.).

So one way in which we could express the distinction I have been trying to draw between two types of institution is saying that one kind is supposed to be seen by the participants as "arising from imposition", while the other is supposed to be seen as "simply the way things are". There are different ways in which things might be, and thus we should not be surprised to find out that the permeability of one game to the problem of strictly linguistic defeasibility is greater than the next (there can be mutant football players, but there cannot be mutant bishops in chess). But there is a difference of kind to be made: we shall see (in the last section of this chapter) what are the consequences for legal reasoning that follow from the fact that the law is *not* seen as "arising from imposition".

I have argued that failure to draw a distinction of this kind affects (though of course need not invalidate) John Searle's general theory of institutional facts, even though (maybe precisely *because*) Searle did not deal with the subject of defeasibility. It is about time, therefore, to consider whether (and how) the defeasibility of legal rules is a source of similar difficulties for an "institutional theory *of law*".

LAW AS INSTITUTIONAL FACT

In his inaugural lecture some twenty five years ago, Neil MacCormick put forward the thesis that "if the law exists at all, it exists not on the level of brute creation . . . but rather . . . on the plane of institutional facts". What makes propositions of law true or false, he tells us, is not "merely the occurrence of acts or events in the world, but also the application of rules to such acts or events" (1974: 51). Contracts, for example, are institutions of law. But legal institutions are not identical with rules, since Chilean contract law is one thing, the contract I have with the University of Talca is another (this point was mentioned above, at n. 22). MacCormick's claim is that institutions are "concepts", concepts that are regulated by rules in the sense that instances of them can be brought about, have consequences and be terminated according to those rules:

> The term "institution of law", as I shall use it, is therefore to be understood as signifying those legal concepts which are regulated by sets of institutive, consequential and terminative rules, with the effect that instances of them are properly said to exist over a period of time, from the occurrence of an institutive act or event until the occurrence of a terminative act or event (MacCormick, 1974: 53).

According to MacCormick, *institutive rules* are those that "lay down that on the occurrence of a certain (perhaps complex) act or event a specific instance of the institution in question comes into existence" (*ibid.* 52); *consequential* are those rules that provide for the consequences the existence of an instance of a given institution has. The existence of one instance of the institution in question is part of the operative facts of these rules. Lastly, rules are *terminative* when they provide for the termination of the particular instance of the institution under consideration (*ibid.* at 53).

Contrary to what the title of his article could make us believe, MacCormick claims that from the fact that legal concepts (or at least some of them) are "institutions" (and hence that the existence, effects and termination of instances of them are determined according to rules) it does not follow that *the law* itself is an institution: "there is an almost overwhelming temptation . . . to treat the concept "law" like the concept "contract" as denoting an institution which is defined and regulated by the relevant set of institutive consequential and regulative rules" (MacCormick, 1974: 57). This temptation must be resisted, because some legal rules elude this characterisation in terms of constitutive, consequential and terminative rules. It would, therefore, be incorrect to assume that all legal norms are "like statutes in that they can be conceived as existing "validly" in virtue of clearly statable institutive rules":

> It is at least contestable whether there are clear criteria for the existence of rules of common law. Some have indeed contended that it is a fallacy of positivism to suppose that the common law can be represented as a system or rules (MacCormick, 1974: 57).

MacCormick believes that legal norms can exist that "cannot be understood as being established in virtue of necessary or sufficient criteria of validity". This constitutes an objection to the claim that the law is an institution, at least if we accept his definition of institutions as "concepts regulated by some set of institutive, consequential and terminative rules".

But the consequences of this admission might be more important than MacCormick thinks. For consider: if there are legal norms that can validly exist without having been produced according to some institutive rule, then the existence, consequences and termination of those rules of law is not controlled by institutive, consequential, and terminative rules *alone* (this is MacCormick's concession). Because (assuming that) the institutive, terminative and consequential rules relating to the common law as a source of law do not render sufficient and necessary criteria of validity, then the common law cannot be an institution. But if that is the case, then *all* legal concepts MacCormick *is* willing to call "institutions" and whose institutive, consequential and terminative rules are (at least partly) to be found in the rules of the common law, cannot be institutions because of the very same reason, i.e. because those rules would not completely regulate the (creation, consequences and termination of instances of the) concept. Sometimes legal norms validly exist, though no institutive rule has been followed to bring them into existence. But very much the same happens concerning not only legal norms, but also instances of what MacCormick does want to call "institutions of law": a contract, for example, can exist even if the institutive rules have not been followed (*see* the example discussed by MacCormick, 1974: 68), and it can fail to exist even if the institutive rules have been followed (for an example, *see* MacCormick and Weinberger, 1986: 12) Thus it seems that either the law is an institution along with the others, or none of them is.

Later in his lecture, MacCormick returns to this subject. He accepts (as did Hart, 1948) that institutive, consequential and terminative rules are defeasible, with the consequence that they cannot specify necessary and sufficient conditions for the existence of an instance of an institution of law. Legal principles justify an "open-ended" list of exceptions, and this is "fatal" for any attempt to represent the institutive rules as stating sufficient and necessary conditions for "for valid adjudication by tribunals or whatever". Even if we were to write down a list of all the exceptions imposed by court in cases of a certain kind, "we could not be confident that we had succeeded in listing the sufficient conditions for validity of a determination or an act of delegated legislation or whatever" (MacCormick, 1974: 70).

And what he says here about institutive rules can equally be said "in relation to the other types of rules which I have mentioned, and indeed of "rules of law" generally" (1974: 73). What rules of law lay down are only "presumptively sufficient" conditions: if the law imposes certain requirements for the validity of an act in law, then the fact that an act of that sort complies with those requirements implies that the act in question "ought to be presumed to be valid unless it is challenged" (1974: 72), but challenged it might be, with the consequence that what appeared to be a clear instance of a valid act performed in accordance with clear and valid institutive rules might turn out to be invalid (*ibid.* at 72).

So the fact that institutive, consequential and terminative rules can be defeated in concrete cases does not by itself imply that the concepts they regulate are not institutions, because we can take those rules as stating "presumptively sufficient" conditions. But if this argument can do the trick for legal concepts, I cannot see why it could not do it for the law itself. In both cases we would have institutive, consequential and regulative rules that specify what is presumptively the case; and in both cases this would not prevent instances of the "institution" (i.e. a particular contract or a particular legal norm) from validly existing, even though no institutive rule has been followed to produce it.

MacCormick would not be so easily persuaded: "we neither have criteria of validity for legal principles, nor therefore a distinction between valid and invalid principles of law" (1974: 73). Though it is possible to give an account of what makes true the statement "the principle 'no one may profit from his or her own wrong' is a principle of English law", how those conditions actually work is something that cannot be understood without considering the values and purposes of the law. And to consider the values and purposes of the law is to consider the values and purposes the participants to a legal practice ascribe to them: "rules do not themselves have purposes, except in the sense that people may ascribe purposes to them" (MacCormick, 1974: 74).

The legal philosopher, according to MacCormick, has to recognise at this point that the explanation that is needed is not philosophical but sociological: "the philosopher may still pose questions, but he will have either to become a sociologist to answer some of them, or alternatively, have to wait for his sociological colleagues to give him the answers" (*ibid.*).

My objection to MacCormick's solution (treating legal concepts but not the law as an institution) is this: the lack of criteria for the validity of legal principles implies, up to the same extent, lack of criteria for the validity of instances of legal concepts like "contract" and the like. Because of that lack of criteria, we might be surprised to find that a given principle was part of the law though we did not know it. But (at least sometimes) the normative consequences of this "unexpected" (so to speak) principle will be to deny validity to some instance of the institution in question (e.g. a contract) that has been produced according to the relevant institutive rules (or, conversely, to lend validity to an instance that has not been so produced); hence insofar as we lack criteria for the validity of legal principles, we lack criteria for the validity of instances of "institutions of law"; insofar as the lack of those criteria is a reason for something *not to be* an institution, then neither the law nor contracts are institutions.

If, on the other hand, we follow MacCormick's advice and focus upon the fact that we *do* have presumptively sufficient conditions for the validity of instances of institutions of law, then could we not say that we also know what the presumptively sufficient conditions for the existence of legal principles are?

Notice again how all these complications would not in the least affect a theory of "football as institutional fact": the rule that specifies what a "goal" is does not specify "presumptively sufficient" conditions for something to be a goal, but necessary and sufficient conditions of anything to be one.

And here we can see how MacCormick's philosopher can go one step further: instead of taking it as a brute fact, she can try to explain what is it about the law that makes it so different from other normative systems in this regard. Such an explanation, we shall see, is partly empirical and partly conceptual. The argument in this chapter is (I hope) the beginning of it.[28]

TWO MODELS OF INSTITUTION

It is time to pull the threads of the argument together. To do this we can start with the distinction Searle failed to make between systems of rules (i.e. institutions) rather than rules. As was said before, this is a distinction between systems of rules (i.e. institutions) that constitute (i.e. create the possibility of institutional facts to be brought about) in order to produce some regulatory effect in the world (hence, as stipulated above, *regulatory* institutions) and systems of rules (i.e. institutions) that regulate some forms of behaviour in order to create the possibility of institutional facts to be brought about (hence *autonomous* institutions).

I think a distinction very much like the one I am trying to defend was in Wittgenstein's mind when he wrote

> Why don't I call cookery rules arbitrary, and why am I tempted to call the rules of grammar arbitrary? Because "cookery" is defined by its ends, whereas "speaking" is not. That is why the use of language is in a certain sense autonomous, as cooking and washing are not. You cook badly if you are guided in your cooking by rules other than right ones; but if you follow other rules than those of chess you are playing *another game*, and if you follow grammatical rules other than such-and-such ones, that does not mean you say something wrong, no, you are speaking of something else (1966: § 320).

[28] In his "The Epistemology of Judging" (1992), Thomas Morawetz criticises, in a way congenial to my own, the metaphor of games as "misleading" when applied to the law and other "deliberative practices" (of which he offers at 9 the following examples: "aesthetic debate, moral reasoning, historical discourse, and judicial decision-making"). But he does not offer an explanation for the fact that our deliberative practices are deliberative. The closest he gets to that is his remark that, in games, "the rules are fixed, and assumed to be known to all. But only the least important aspects of experience have this kind of simplicity. Only the least important aspects of life leave participants the option whether or not to play. In more immediate and important practices . . . we have a stake unavoidably and the shared rules-and-strategies are endlessly controversial" (Morawetz, 1992: 14–15).

This passage could be read as stating that non-deliberative practices are such either because they in some way "deal" with the "least important aspects of experience" or because they are "optional" in the sense that people can exercise an option not to play. Morawetz seems to believe that the latter is implied by the former, that is, that *because* non-deliberative practices deal with non-important aspects of experience, they allow for people to withdraw from them if they want. We have already seen that it is not "importance" that makes non-deliberative (in my terms, autonomous) practices non-deliberative (autonomous). As we shall see shortly below, Morawetz's second criterion (i.e. that those practices are in some way "optional") is, in my view, closer to the correct explanation.

The reason that, for participants, justifies the existence of an autonomous institution is the value they recognise in being able to engage in the particular kind of activity the institution sets up. Concerning institutions of this kind, it is pointless to look for an underlying activity the system is designated *to* regulate: it either does not exist, or, if it does, the point of the institution is not to regulate it, but to create a new, institutional thing *using it*. Of course, there are reasons why we want these new activities to exist but these are reasons for inventing the institution. It is not the case that we invent the institution because we want the underlying activities regulated in some particular ways: we do it because we want to be able to do something new, like playing football, or speaking a language, and so on (this is why for Wittgenstein these rules are, in a sense, "arbitrary" and speaking "autonomous").

Consider, for example the case of boxing. At first sight it might appear that rules of boxing *regulate* a fight in a way that is perfectly analogous to that in which the law regulates fights, but in the sense I have been using the expression, this is clearly inaccurate. The point of the institution of boxing is not to regulate fights (as, e.g., criminal law does), *but to create a new, institutional, form of fighting*. Of course, the creation of this institutional form of fighting called boxing is achieved (*inter alia*) by regulating the brute fact of a fight. But the *point* of (or the reason for) inventing the institution of boxing is not to regulate fights, but to *create the game*. Hence the rules are applicable only if you participate in the game, *because* you do so; if you are not boxing, then you are under no boxing obligation to apply the rules of boxing, even if you are a professional boxer (you might of course have some other reason for so doing: maybe you are better at fighting when you follow them, or you think that that is the only fair way of fighting, etc., but these are not counter-examples here).

Regulatory institutions are different: it is clearly wrong to say, regarding them, that we invent (say) the law because we want to create *ex-novo* new activities. Rather, we want to regulate in a certain way some pre-existing activities, actions, relationships, etc. (and in this sense the rules are, at least partially, "defined by their ends"). We want to be able not only to exchange goods, but also to have notions such as futurity and obligation linked to the exchange, because an exchange in these conditions (contract) seems to us more useful than a "brute" exchange (*see* Atiyah, 1982a: 1). Of course, to do this we have to invent institutional concepts like contract and the like, but the reason for so doing is our interest in the regulation of some forms of behaviour that exist outside the institution. Furthermore, it is not only not bizarre, but substantially accurate to say that because we want to regulate the killing of one human by another and economic transactions we have to invent the law.[29] Notice that if a given legal rule concerning an action φ (the celebration

[29] It goes without saying that the language I am using is in a sense particularly inaccurate: of course, "we" did not "invent" the concept of contract "because" we "wanted" such-and-such. The history of the emergence of legal institutions is more complex a subject. But I think that the

of a contract, the transfer of property, etc.) exists, then you are under a legal obligation to apply that rule every time you do φ. But you do not have a (football-) obligation not to touch the ball with your hands if you are not playing football (*see* Rawls, 1955: 164).

As an illustration, recall Bankowski's explanation of the development of an institution (quoted above at 24): "the institution grows up on the back of the substantive reasons since *the reason that it is a promise can be seen as the universalisation of the substantive reason*" (1998, emphasis added).

In this model, institutions (like promising) are (and are *seen* as) universalisations of substantive reasons. The institution is not autonomous from the reasons for it. Notice, further, that what we say here of "institutions" could very well be applied to the rules of them: legal rules are seen as universalisation of substantive reasons, as "entrenched" generalisations (Schauer, 1991). This is the reason why, though the rule might (some would say, has to) have *some* insularity from those reasons, it cannot be completely cut off from them in the way the offside rule can. Therefore, if instead of trying to explain the emergence of an institution like promising we wanted to explain that of a game like football, or that of an institution of football like the penalty kick, we would find that Bankowski's interplay between the rule and the substantive reasons behind it is quite different. Granted, there is always a sense in which football grew on the back of substantive reasons, and to see this we can avail ourselves of the distinction between "to play" and "to play a game" (Opie and Opie, 1969: 2). Once upon a time, we can say, people did not play games, because no game had been invented. They only played. In some moment, one of the players told the others that it would be much more fun if they were to kick the ball through three posts instead of just among them. So they decided. Then other players noted that it would be even more fun if there were a limited pitch, and two teams with the same numbers of players, and so forth. Sooner or later they will start playing football, or some primitive form of it.

As we saw when discussing Searle's general theory, there is an asymmetry between regulatory and autonomous institutions here. When participants in a given social practice are evolving the institution of money, they need not be aware that they are imposing on whatever they are using as medium of exchange a meaning that is not exhausted by the physical properties of it. But nothing we could recognise as football can be played if we are not entitled to assume that the "players", in one form or another, are actually aware that those three posts at each end of the pitch have meaning in addition to their physical properties: on top of their being wooden posts, they are *goals*, and if the ball crosses them a point is scored. This cannot but be transparent to the players.

argument stands any level of complexity in relation to that history, and so I am using this inaccurate language to facilitate the exposition.

Because regarding regulatory practices participants need not be aware of the fact that they are evolving them, the interplay Bankowski sees between the rules and the reasons for them is quite different. This relationship in games is, I would argue, "one way only": because of the reasons discussed above (at 9f) FIFA decided to modify the offside rule. Once FIFA so decided, and only because of it, the new rule is a rule of football.[30] There is no going back to the reasons at the moment of applying the rule, as we have seen. Because of this, a "genetic" account of the emergence of football along Bankowskian lines might be of interest for the historian of football: it shows how football was brought about. But it would not help a referee who needs to apply the rules: compare the case of promising, in which such an account would indeed help someone who has to decide whether the fact that a friend is ill is relevant to her decision to keep a promise to be somewhere else at the moment her friend needs her company. In other words, the interesting thing about Bankowski's explanation of the emergence of moral or legal institutions is that it illuminates the interplay between the rules and the substantive reasons they are supposed to advance, interplay that is in turn explained because Bankowski shows the rules as "universalisation of substantive reasons". In the case of games there is no such interplay because the rules, though they might be universalisation of substantive reasons, are not to be *seen* as such by participants. They are seen as "simply what we do" when we play football.

This last point is important because it shows why I do not have to deny that there are substantive reasons for the rules of autonomous institutions (hence they need not be wholly "arbitrary"). Imagine that we are in a convention inventing a game. We can decide, for example, that we want a game of physical ability. That would rule out any game like chess or bridge. Furthermore, we can also decide that our game is to be one of team work, so tennis is excluded, and so forth; progressively, we write down the rules of football. We might decide that we want to allow *any* physical ability, including the ability to injure the adversary if this is useful. Or we can take a more sensible approach, and decide that we do not want to allow any move that can affect the physical integrity of any player. Once we have decided that, we need to introduce the pertinent rules: even in the first case, we will have to forbid the use of weapons (at least those which do not require the exercise of some physical ability). Furthermore, we could find that we want to make the game safer, and to punish any move that can be dangerous for a player. We shall find that there are two ways of achieving this aim (Hart, 1994: 125f): we can either elaborate a list of the moves we consider dangerous, or we can give the referee discretion to determine if a given move is dangerous (of course, we

[30] Throughout, I have been referring to FIFA as football's legislative body. This is, needless to say, for ease of exposition only. Of course, many people play football without even knowing in detail the rules approved by FIFA. This, if anything, makes my argument stronger: most of the time people need not agree in advance to the rules they are going to apply. They simply rely on their knowledge of the rules. And even in these circumstances it is most uncommon to find players disagreeing as to what the rules are or how they are to be applied.

can mix these two approaches up: this is what happens today in football). We will have to decide if we want more safety at the price of discretion, or if instead we want to deny umpires discretion at the price of some safety. My point is that, given that we are deciding how to build an autonomous institution, *everything is up for grabs*, though after each decision our space of *manoeuvre* will be smaller. At the very beginning, when we decided to invent a new game, every conceivable game was the possible outcome of our convention. After our first decision, as we saw, games like chess were ruled out; after our second, tennis and the like were. The point is that many of our decisions may be fully justified by substantive reasons: they need not be "arbitrary". What makes the rules we create "arbitrary" in Wittgenstein's sense is that those rules are to be seen by players as "simply what we do" and *not* as universalisations of substantive reasons (recall the case above at 10 of the referee applying the new offside rule.)

But a legal system is in this respect different from games, and to see this it could be useful to use an example here. Recall Fuller's case of the two men sleeping at the station. If we wanted to give hard cases in law the same explanation we gave to the hard case of Ronald Fuentes' handball (that is, an explanation based on the general defeasibility of concepts), we would have to say that, insofar as the first man was doing something that it would be non-controversial to classify as a "core" instance of the word "sleeping", he (and not the second, who wasn't sleeping) must be fined. But this solution would strike any sensible lawyer (and lay persons as well) as, at best, odd. If the first man is to be acquitted, however, this is not because we can say that he was not "really" sleeping, but because we think that the rule *should not be applied* to this case. The rule is to be seen as the universalisation of substantive reasons, and the point of Fuller's example is that any participant would immediately see that no substantive reason is served by fining the first man. Now imagine that the rule is not a legal one, but the rule of a peculiar game called "staying awake in railway stations". The game consists in avoidance of falling asleep in the station, and if you do you lose five points. Here the rule is not to be seen as such a universalisation, and as a consequence of that participants can agree that the first man must pay but the second should not, *if they are playing this peculiar game.*

In other words, insistence upon *indeterminacy of meaning* as the master explanation of legal disagreement is clearly insufficient. The problem is not that we are not sure about whether the first man was or was not sleeping in the station (because his was a "penumbral" instance of "sleeping"): we know he was (anyone who is not sure has to look up "sleeping" in the OED). The problem is, rather, that we are unsure that the rule should be applied to *this particular* case to the exclusion of all other considerations, though their explicit operative facts are indeed fulfilled.

And here we can go back to the point made before, about games being somewhat less serious or important than the law. As should be remembered, this explanation was rejected because some games can be much more serious, for participants and spectators, than many legal disputes. So the point cannot be one about seriousness *simpliciter*. But if we read it in the light of the distinction between autonomous and regulatory institutions drawn above, we can reformulate it. We can say that the point of some institutions is to invent new activities while the point of others is to select, from a vast array of ways in which things can be done, those which are to be preferred. In the first case, then, the decision to participate in the activity *amounts to* a decision to abide by the rules, i.e. *not to question the application of the rules to particular cases*. If you do question that point, you fail to participate. A football player who thinks it is better to score goals with the hands will not be allowed to do so under present-day football regulations. Imagine him saying: "the point of football is to create a challenging game. If I am allowed to score with my hands, it will be more challenging than it actually is", and then going on to do it, Maradona-like. The relevant football rule should be applied, and the goal should be invalidated. His insistence on the validation of the goal for the reasons given will be taken as a signal that he did not really want to play football, but to invent another game (Rawls, 1955: 164). And if he is allowed to do so, nothing happens, except that the whole group starts playing a new game, certainly not football (some people like to say that this is how Rugby was invented). In this context, the most "serious" thing that can happen is that these people fail to play football. But there is nothing sacred (usually) about football, so they could perfectly well say, "yes, we are not playing football: we prefer to play this new game, rugby". It is in *this* sense that we can say that there is nothing *serious* about games: we can always decide to play another game.

It is for this reason that in autonomous institutions it sometimes appears that the "normative becomes, in a certain sense, descriptive" (Bankowski, 1996: 33). The rules are binding insofar as you want to participate in the activity. If you don't, the rules don't matter. Hence, the rules of an autonomous institution can be seen as descriptions of how you should behave if you want to play the game.

If the argument so far is correct, then all the considerations made about games can be applied to other institutions whose point is to invent a new activity. Consider, for example, the distinction between the rules of grammar and those of games, on the one hand, and those of style and of *fair play*, on the other (I am not implying that regulatory and autonomous institutions always come in pairs). To create the possibility of speaking English or of playing football, we need the rules of English grammar and those of football respectively. Before these rules are invented it is impossible to do one thing or the other. These rules do not exist in order to regulate the sounds or marks we produce, nor the activity of running around a ball (though indeed, in a sense, they do precisely that), but to create the very possibility of speaking (English) and playing (football). But *once* they have been created, *then* we can treat these activities as pre-existing for another purpose, and so we can think that, *given that* we can speak English or play football, we want to do so in special ways: we want to speak beautifully, or to play in an elegant and sporting manner. This is the context for the emergence of a regulatory institution: now we need a set of rules to regulate the activities of speaking and playing (i.e. norms that single out *some* of many alternative ways of speaking and playing as preferable). In other words, when we are trying not to set up the activity, but to establish normative standards for the *better* way to do something we can do anyway (like speaking English or playing football), we leave the autonomous and enter into the regulatory model.[31] And, correspondingly, we lose the certainty the rules had in the former: now it is not beyond plausible contestation what the standards of style or *fair play* demand, since now rules are (and are seen as) universalisations of substantive reasons. It is important to notice here that the rules of style and those of *fair play* are clearly not rules of language/football: you don't have to master the rules of English style/*fair play* to be able to speak English/play football, though of course your speaking/playing will be better if you do (Marc Overmars' goal is a splendid proof of that: *see* above at 11, n.8) They exist precisely because it is possible to participate in the activity of speaking English or playing football in different ways, and their point is to signal some of these ways as better than others.

THE WEIGHTIER MATTERS OF THE LAW

The distinction I have drawn above is not an empirical one: it purports to be a conceptual one, between two different kinds of institution. But the fact that the difference is conceptual does not mean that the law is, as a matter of conceptual truth, necessarily "regulatory". The model a given institution belongs to is an empirical question (though not the distinction itself), one that is settled by the way the participants understand their institution.

Consider the following analogy: it is a matter of conceptual truth (i.e. something that is settled by the concept of "mode of production") that a mode of production includes humans, raw materials and means of production. Whether a particular mode of production is capitalist or feudal or something else is an empirical question, i.e. one that is settled by the kind of production relations that actually obtains in a particular society. But *given* that a mode of production is capitalist, it is a matter of conceptual truth that, *inter alia*, proletarians are formally free; similarly with the law. I would not object if someone were to claim that the law is what I call "regulatory" as a matter of conceptual truth. This would amount to a verbal stipulation concerning the meaning of

[31] I am aware that I am stretching the meaning of the word "institution" when I say that fair play and style are institutions. The emphasis here is to be placed on the "regulatory" bit. The word "institution" could be replaced, here and elsewhere, by the expression "normative system", "practice" or the like.

the word "law", and as such would be both unobjectionable and quite unhelpful. I would prefer to claim that this is an empirical question (indeed, we shall be looking here at concrete instances of legal practices I would like to call "autonomous"). But if the answer to this empirical question were to be that a given legal system is a regulatory institution, then some consequences would conceptually follow, consequences that explain why this distinction is important.

So let us consider what a legal system conceived of as an autonomous institution would be like. The point I want to make is nicely illustrated by the way in which *formalities* can be regarded in different legal cultures. Though any formality could be used here, I want to focus particularly on the formalities required for the validity of a contract.

It seems to us completely obvious that formalities are required for some *reason*, a reason that is related to the act to which the formality is attached (in other words we are used to seeing rules requiring formalities for the validity or enforceability of a contract as "the universalisation of some substantive reason": regulatory institutions). The contract of guarantee, for example is (was) considered particularly liable to be agreed between parties of unequal bargaining power, so if the contract rerquires to be in writing the weaker party will be in a better position to counter that inequality than if it is oral. So the (English) law requires the contract of guarantee to be in writing (this is Atiyah's explanation: *cf.* 1995: 164). The formality is required because some reason of substance suggests the convenience of its existence.

This way of looking at formalities is nowadays commonsensical: "insistence on form is widely thought by lawyers to be characteristic of primitive and less well-developed legal systems" (Atiyah, 1995: 163). But the question is, *why* are (so-called) primitive legal systems more rigorously formalistic? The thesis I want to entertain here is that law has not always been regarded as a (to put it in my words) regulatory institution. The insistence upon formalities, in a way that seems so bizarre to us, is one possible consequence of the law being understood as an autonomous institution.

Here we would have to imagine a society in which officials and subjects understand the law (and the world) in ways very different to our own. We would have to imagine a society in which the law is seen not as an *instrument* used to regulate social interaction, but as a technique that rests upon regularities that pertain to the very fabric of the world, very much like the way we understand the technique of bridge-building (or cookery). They would think of "obligation" as meaning literally a (quasi-) physical bond, a bond that can only be brought about following a predetermined procedure, in very much the same way in which we take a bridge (or a prawn cocktail) to be a physical thing that can be brought about following a predeterminate set of technical rules.

This is not a purely fantastic idea. Indeed, something like this is what the ancient Romans seem to have believed, as Reinhard Zimmermann has claimed

(1990: 1f, 82f). To be able to put someone under an obligation would then mean to be able to create such a bond. This bond is thought of neither in the way in which *we* think of an obligation, nor as a relation of pure power. Precisely through the use of such formalities "the creditor's real power over the body of the person who was liable came to be replaced by a magical power over him, and it was for this purpose that a formal ritual had to be performed" (Zimmermann, 1990: 83). The function of the formalities of the *stipulatio*,[32] in this context, is quite different to the functions we are used to thinking the formalities perform. We are used to seeing formalities as protecting or promoting some value, interest etc. (i.e. as the universalisation of some substantive reason): the interest of third parties which can be affected by the transaction, the interest of the weaker party before that of the stronger, the facilitation of proof, hence the possibility of having less and cheaper controversies, and soon. But for (ancient) Roman lawyers, according to Zimmermann, all of this was beside the point. The ritual was not required for policy-based considerations, but simply because that was the *only way* of getting things done:

> it was only by means of these rituals that legal transactions could be effected: compliance with the ritual formalities brought about a *real* (but invisible and in so far magical) *change* in the relationships between the parties concerned. The slightest mistake would wreck the whole transaction: every reader of fairy tales knows that magical effects can be engendered only by a most punctilious recital of a set formula . . .. The *actual reason* for the desired legal result was not the consent between the parties but the formal exchange of the words (Zimmermann, 1990: 83–4; emphasis added).[33]

It is not part of my argument that a formalistic understanding of formalities is only possible in autonomous institutions. Some legal formalities, in some legal systems, are nowadays thought of in a very formalistic way indeed. But the formality of these areas of modern law is based upon considerations of policy: they are (seen as) universalisations of substantive reasons. Hence it is always possible, at least in special cases, to go back to the raw "policy question'"—and how "special" a case has to be is a *substantive* matter, i.e. something to be decided in the light of the policy-reasons underlying the formality (more on this later). In (ancient) Roman law, on the other hand, there was no "raw" moral (policy) question to go back to: the formalities were not required for substantive considerations, but because that was the only way in which a given effect could be brought about. This has as a consequence that the application of the rules becomes highly mechanical:

[32] The *stipulatio* was one of the most important contractual forms in Roman law. It was defined only by its form. Any obligation could be created using it (*see* Zimmermann, 1990: 68ff).

[33] The issue of the magical character of law in Rome is a controversial one: compare Hägerström (1953: 56ff), for whom the role of magic in Roman law was ubiquitous, with G. MacCormack's criticism of this thesis (MacCormack, 1969). The magic character of *ancient* Roman law is less controversial, though (*see* Kaser, 1967: 133).

> The most characteristic feature of archaic Roman jurisprudence is its tendency to endow every (sacral and) legal act with a definite form. Specific rituals had to be meticulously performed, precisely set forms of words to be uttered with great punctiliousness. The smallest mistake, a cough or a stutter, the use of a wrong term invalidated the whole act. This actional formalism corresponded to a similarly strict formalism in the interpretation of those ancient legal acts. No regard was had to the intention of the parties; what mattered were the *verba* used by them. The more rigid the interpretation, the more care was, in turn, bestowed on the formulation of the formulae. The drafters had try to eliminate every risk of ambiguity. This led to scrupulous attention to detail [and] to cumbrous enumerations . . .. Anyone who failed to employ such devices ran the risk of having to face unwelcome and unexpected consequences: as was experienced, for instance, by those who had taken the vow to sacrifice "*cuaequmque proximo vere nata essent apud se animalia*" ("whichever animated things were born in their house next spring"). Not only animals but their own children also were taken to be covered by these words (Zimmermann, 1990: 623).

To have an idea of what the law would be like in this context, we could well follow Zimmermann's advice and think of fairy tales: if you don't say the magic formula exactly as it should be said, you fail to produce the results you were looking for. Elmer's case would not have been a problem in this setting: it does not matter who (and for what reasons) gets the magic lamp, the genie will obey. In the terms of the argument presented here, there is no space for more or less reasonable interpretations of what the formalities are: interpretations are either correct or not (more strictly, one interpretation is correct and all the rest are not): *qui cadit a syllaba, cadit a causa.*

If we are to accept Zimmermann's claim about Roman law, my contention is that for ancient Roman lawyers the law was not regarded as anything like a social technique "to induce human beings—by means of the notion of this evil threatening them if they behave in a certain way, opposite to what is desired—to behave in the desired way" (Kelsen, 1934: 29) or the "enterprise of subjecting human conduct to the governance of rules" (Fuller, 1964: 106), but as a magical language that had to be mastered if some effects were to be produced, magical language that was created by the Gods and communicated to humans by priests—remember that in ancient Rome the law was administered by the Roman pontifices, who were state priests.[34] Note that there is no need for justification in this legal system: imagine one Roman farmer asking his lawyer: "why should I answer precisely '*spondeo*' to celebrate a *stipulatio*? Is it not enough to manifest my consent in any appropriate way?" The lawyer would say: "you simply cannot do otherwise if you want to celebrate such a contract". The situation is entirely similar to that of a child asking "why

[34] The main point holds even is this claim if historically false, i.e. even if the ancient Romans did not see their law as something given by the Gods: we do not think (not all of us, at least) that the laws of gravity were given by God, and that is not an obstacle to our conceiving of bridge-building as a technique that rests upon the basic structure of the world. In other words, how and why the participants came to view the world as they actually do is immaterial here.

cannot I move the king more than one space at a time?" or a naïve engineer asking "why should I build bridges in this particular way?" ("because if you don't you'll fail to play chess/build a bridge").

If I am right in this regard, then we should expect to find a different conception of legislation. Since the formalities for the validity of contracts were not universalisation of substantive reasons, policy considerations did not have any bearing on the selections of the specific forms required, nor upon the consequences of failing to follow them.

And we do find, for example, that though the Romans did have statutes forbidding the conclusion or the content of certain contracts, they used a system of statutory prohibitions that seems very peculiar to the modern observer:

> Three different types of statutes were distinguished . . .: *leges imperfectae*, *leges minus quam perfectae* and *leges perfectae*. Only acts performed in violation of *leges perfectae* were void. *Leges minus quam perfectae* threatened the violator with a penalty, but did not invalidate the act itself. Infringement of a *lex imperfecta* led neither to a penalty nor to invalidity (Zimmermann, 1990: 697–8).

The question presents itself immediately: what was the point of *leges minus quam perfectae* and *imperfectae*? If the contract was to be forbidden, why not to use a *lex perfecta*? The answer becomes clear if we take into account that "in the early days of Roman law the validity of a transaction seems to have been judged only from the point of view of the required form". A contract was defined by its form, and if the forms had been fulfilled it was simply not possible to go back and invalidate it: "that statutory prohibitions could interfere with and indeed completely invalidate formal private acts was inconceivable to the lawyers and the law-makers of the earlier Republic" (Zimmermann, 1990: 698; *see*, for a different explanation Stein, 1966).

A similar point has been made by David Daube from a different perspective. Daube was intrigued by the peculiar verbal forms Romans used, and by how those forms changed during the centuries. Roman statutes usually contained the imperative form ("shall", "shall not"); in some of them, however, the imperative form is replaced by phrases like "it is needful", "it is proper" etc. Daube focuses upon the different meaning of verbal forms of the following kind: "'if anyone damages another's property, it will be needful for him to pay' and 'if anyone damages another's property, he shall be bound to pay'" (1956: 4). According to Daube, phrases of the former type

> express, not a direct command—"I order you to do this or that"—and not even a freely formed opinion—"In my view you should do this or that"—but a reference to some higher authority—"There are compelling reasons to do this or that" (*ibid.* 8).

So the reason why these verbal forms are so common in Roman law was, according to Daube, that the legislator did not see himself as *creating* the obligation to pay damages (to use the former example). It would be odd for us to say: "if anyone wants to build a bridge (or to prepare a prawn cocktail), he or she is bound to . . ." rather than "if anyone wants to build a bridge (prepare a prawn cocktail), it will be needful for him or her to . . .". Hence, it should not be surprising by now to find out that these special verbal forms

> belong without exception to the sacred law. "If a man is killed by lightning . . ., it is not permissible to celebrate the funeral rites for him": evidently, this is not the decree of a free lawgiver, a lawgiver who might, if he liked, enjoin the opposite. It is, essentially, interpretation; It is the wise men's reading of the divine will. The priests . . . do not dictate to you. They inform you of the results of their studies of sacred things (Daube, 1956: 9).

The interesting point is that this indirect imperative form ("it is proper to . . .") is not used by republican and classical lawyers to speak of the requirements of the praetorian law (*ius honorarium*), but only to the old *ius civile*. Only the *ius civile* was understood in the magical sense with which I am now concerned: "a praetorian or aedilician obligation cannot be inferred from a search into the law or legally recognised transactions" (Daube, 1956: 15): it rests only upon the praetor's (aedile's) authority. So Daube's remarks lend support to Zimmermann's view: the law (i.e., the old *ius civile*) was not seen as a social institution created by humans to regulate their affairs, but as something that was part of the very structure of the world, something that could be mastered and put to use by humans if only they came to know it.

This is why "insistence on form is widely thought by lawyers to be characteristic of primitive and less well-developed legal systems" (Atiyah, 1995: 162): it reflects this kind of "magical" view of the law. Insistence on form, just for form's sake, is demonstrative of an understanding of law in which it is given, not made (just as the rules of chess are given to the players, not made by them). This attitude changes according to changes in the respective legal culture: "the attitude of a legal culture towards form reflects its self-image and maturity" (Zimmermann, 1990: 88). The important point is that when this attitude towards form *has* changed, controversies can arise. All formalities nowadays have been introduced to achieve some legislative purpose. That purpose, however, might be realised in different ways, even if formalities are not complied with. In these cases, "the sanction of invalidity therefore seems to overshoot the mark: it is not demanded by the policy underlying the rules requiring formality of the act . . . Equitable inroads have therefore from time to time been made in the domain of statutory forms (Zimmermann, *ibid*. 1990: 86–7).[35]

The transition from an autonomous to a regulatory conception of the law can also be seen in the Bible. Isaac's blessing of Jacob instead of Esau was valid, even though it was obtained with deceit (Gen. 27: 18–40): Jacob disguised himself as his brother and made his half-blind father believe he was

[35] *Cf*. Zimmermann (1990: 118–19), for the same point concerning the *sponsio* (suretyship): once ritual requirements have been relaxed (because there is no magic in them) "intricate problems of interpretation could arise" (concerning the *unitas actus*—the requirement of the *sponsio* to follow immediately the celebration of the respective *stipulatio*).

Esau. Because of his father's mistake, he received the blessing though he was not the first-born. The case is revealing because Esau "wept bitterly": "Bless me, too, my father", but there was no "unpicking" of the blessing, no "going back" to the raw substantive question, because there was no substantive question to go back to: "your brother came full of deceit and took your blessing" (Gen.: 35). The blessing was a (quasi-) physical thing, something Jacob had *taken* from Isaac though the former was not, under the law, entitled to it. The deception, having succeeded, could not affect the *fact* that Isaac did not have a blessing for Esau other than "by thy sword shalt thou live, and shalt serve thy brother" (Gen. 27: 40): if someone takes the prawn cocktail I am about to eat, I cannot eat it or give it to you, since I do not have it any more; Jacob took the blessing and Isaac could not go back and "invalidate" it, any more than I could "go back" and "invalidate" someone's eating my prawn cocktail and then eat it up myself.

David Daube has pointed out that "four at least of the tales of Jacob culminate in the appeal by the subtler disputant to those rigid, formalistic principles which can so often be found governing the legal or religious transactions of ancient peoples" (1944). However, he ends this piece with "a word of warning":

> no greater mistake can be made than to argue that, since the narrative here reviewed invariably leads up to the triumph of the party abusing certain formalistic principles of law, the characters described, and even the authors of the descriptions, must have been primitive men who did not see the flaws in their system. The exact opposite is true (Daube, 1944: 75).

According to Daube, "the proper question for us to pose is not, 'why did they not see that there might be an alternative to that strict, pedantic kind of law?' . . . but 'why did they apply, in some branches of the law at least, those strict, formalistic principles although they were fully aware of the possibility of unjust results?'" (*ibid.* at 75). In Chapter 6 we shall see that failure to answer the second of Daube's questions would prevent us from fully understanding Roman law. We shall also see that an answer to the first question will constitute a significant step towards answering the second. But Daube does not offer reasons for his reluctance to ask the first question. If we think of the villain's getting hold of the magic lamp in the story of Aladdin, we see that the law cannot be offered as an "alternative" to the rules governing the obedience of genies. Indeed, this might provide a clue as to the correct answer of the second question: maybe they did not see an alternative because that was simply the way the world was. "Unjust results" were simply a sad consequences of the way in which the world was ordered. What Daube considers to be obvious (that the problem of *verba* and *voluntas* as it appears in the law of contracts was "an alternative" to the rigid rules governing Isaac's blessing) was not necessarily obvious to the writer of Exodus.[36].

[36] Indeed, it is interesting to notice that Daube's arguments to show that the writer and contemporary readers of Jacob's story noticed the "flaws" in their system, that they were "wide

Be that as it may, notice the huge difference between this understanding of the law and Jesus's "new law". What was important was not the ritual fulfilment of the rules. The ruler of the Synagogue was indignant with Jesus for healing a possessed woman on the Sabbath: "there are six working days: come and be cured in one of them, and not on the Sabbath" (Luke 13: 14). This ritualistic way of understanding the law is scorned by Jesus: "here is this woman, a daughter of Abraham, who has been bound by Satan for eighteen long years: was it not right from her to be loosed from her bounds on the Sabbath?" (Luke 13: 16).

Jesus could be understood here as arguing that the substantive reason behind the law regarding the Sabbath was not affected by his healing of the woman. Since the law had to be seen as "universalisation of substantive reason", the law correctly understood was not an obstacle for his healing of the woman. But the ruler could have answered "if she has waited eighteen years, can't she wait one more day?: the law ought to be followed", implying that the law was not to be *seen* as universalisation of anything, but as "simply what we do". But he didn't: he was "covered with confusion while the mass of the people were delighted at all the wonderful things [Jesus] was doing" (Luke 13: 17).[37]

One could think from this that Jesus's law was not law at all, that his was a particularist ethics. But he clearly did not see his message in this way: "do not suppose that I have come to abolish the law and the prophets; I did not come to abolish, but to complete. Truly I tell you, so long as heaven and earth endure, not a letter, not a dot, will disappear from the law until all that must happen has happened" (Matt. 5: 17,18). Jesus's new law was regulatory law; an alternative translation of Matthew 5:18 in *The New English Bible* makes this point clearer: "Truly I tell you: so long as heaven and earth endure, not a letter, not a dot, will disappear from the law before all that it *stands for* is achieved" (emphasis added). So the message was precisely that the law was not a ritualistic–formalistic–magical set of rules that had to be fulfilled in detail (autonomous law), but something with a *point*, something that *stood for* something else (regulatory law). Later Jesus was to come back to this point:

> Alas for you, scribes and Pharisees, hypocrites! You pay tithes of mint and dill and cumin; but you have overlooked the weightier demands of the law—justice, mercy and good faith. It is these that you should have practised, without neglecting the others (Matt. 23: 23).

awake to the problem of *verba* and *voluntas* and similar difficulties" do not support his claim. The fact that these incidents "were taken note of and handed down" is, *pace* Daube, not "sufficient proof of this". The fact that we all know that Cinderella's spell was broken at midnight (though it would have been nice, wouldn't it, had it continued until the ball was over?) cannot be taken as proof that we all recognise the "flaws" in (that) system, for there is no system to begin with: Cinderella's world was one in which spells would last only till midnight, and that was it. Similarly, maybe the readers of Jacob's story saw in it simply a commentary on how useful it was to master the basic rules of the world.

[37] Jesus was constantly accused of not keeping the Sabbath: *cf.* John 7: 22–23; 9: 16, etc.

Commenting on this passage, Harold Berman has said "what the whole passage says is first, that the heart of the law is "justice and mercy and good faith", and second, that the lesser matters, the technicalities, the taxes, the "mint and anise and cumin" are also important, although they should be subordinated to the main purpose" (1993: 391).

In an autonomous institution the "mint and anise and cumin" is all that matters, insofar as you are participating in the activity the institution sets up (or, in autonomous institutions there is no distinction between the "mint and anise and cumin" and the "weightier matters"). But a regulatory institution is characterised by the fact that "justice and mercy and good faith" must be practised. This means that the "technicalities" *do* matter, but they are not (as in autonomous law) *all* that matter. Legal disagreement is explained by the fact that these two dimensions of regulatory law should be weighed up somehow: it is a disagreement about the correct way to balance them.

Jesus and the Pharisees would probably agree that they had to follow God's will. The difference was that the Pharisees believed that God's will *was* (as far as they could know it) the law. Hence, the law had to be followed blindly. To follow God's will was to follow God's law, because the law was the will: hence if you want to follow God's will, just follow the law; you need not ask what the law is really about, because it was given by God—he must know. But Jesus changed this: when the lawyer asked for a clear-cut definition (who is my neighbour?), he got a story and after that only the answer "go and do as he did" (Luke 10: 37).[38] Now to follow God's will (not only—or necessarily—the law in the formalistic–ritualistic view) was important: the (formalistically conceived) law was not enough. To the man who had followed the law since he was a boy, Jesus said: "one thing you lack; go, sell everything you have, and give to the poor, and you will have treasure in heaven. Then come and follow me" (Mark 10: 21).

Remember one of the characteristics of games, according to Huizinga:

> inside the play-ground an absolute and peculiar order reigns. Here we come across another, very positive feature of play: it creates order, is order. Into an imperfect world and into the confusion of life it brings a temporary, a limited perfection. Play demands order absolute and supreme. The least deviation from it "spoils the game", robs it from its character, and makes it worthless (1970: 29).

[38] Peter Winch has rightly emphasised that the parable of the Good Samaritan was offered as an explanation of what *the law* was. Jesus's first answer to the lawyer's question was : "what is written on the law?", and after the lawyer's answer, he said: "thou have answered right. This do, and thou shalt live". It was only when the lawyer, "willing to justify himself" asked Jesus about the *interpretation* of the law that "Jesus, answering, said, A certain man went down from Jerusalem to Jericho . . ." (Luke 10:26–30. *Cf.* Winch, 1987: 155f). Winch, furthermore, calls our attention to the fact that Jesus's answer to the lawyer's question was not linked to the latter's sharing a belief in God: "[the parable] did not appeal to the conception [of God as law-giver]: it challenges it. Or at least it commented on the conception in a way which presupposed that the *moral modality to which the Samaritan responded would have a force for the parable's hearers independently* of their commitment to any particular theological belief" (Winch, 1987: 160).

In this view, a religion (if understood as an autonomous institution) is not at all far from a game, particularly if we have in mind that in Huizinga's terms to play a game can be extremely "serious". Hence Huizinga's analysis of religion as a form of play. The same could be said of (ancient) Roman law: the least deviation from the wording of the *stipulatio* (for example, if the promissor answered the ritual question not with the word "spondeo", but with any other word, however similar or even identical in meaning) *made the whole thing worthless.* In classical Roman law (and even before) however, the raising of the *ius honorarium* and the *actiones bone fidei* changed this: it was no longer true that "the least deviation from it makes it worthless". Now some form of "justice, mercy and good faith" had to be done, without neglecting to pay "tithes of mint and dill and cumin": how these two things were served at the same time became debatable; hence the parties now had space for offering different views about what the law required, regardless of the words and the rituals used.

The distinction between two models of institution that has been put forward in this chapter is by no means new, though the labels I am using might be. Probably the clearest formulation of it, along with a realisation of its consequences for law and legal reasoning can be found in Max Weber's *Economy and Society.* For Weber, the formality of law meant that cases are decided on the basis of their "unambiguous general characteristics". Legal formalism, however, can be of different kinds, according to the nature of the general characteristics that are taken into account. On the one hand, they can be understood as "sense-data", like "the utterance of certain words, the execution of a signature, or the performance of a certain symbolic act with a fixed meaning". This is, for Weber, "the most rigorous type of legal formalism". It corresponds, if my argument is correct, to the formalism of ancient Roman law, and it is to be explained by the fact that for Romans the law was not seen as, in Pufendorf's words, "arising from imposition". The law, for example, makes the utterance of certain words (e.g. a matching word in the case of the Roman *stipulatio*: if the promissee asked, "do you *promise*?" the promissor had to answer "I *promise*") crucial to the celebration of a contract, so that if those words are not uttered there is no contract. This form of formalism, according to Weber, "exhausts itself in casuistry", because there is nothing beyond the actual fulfilment of the ritual requirement that is important for the existence of the contract. It exhausts itself in casuistry, I would argue, because no principle can control or defeat the application of the rule in the same way in which no principle of, say, "favour the most aggressive team" can control or defeat the application of the offside rule, regardless of the level of institutional support the rules of football could offer to a principle like the one mentioned.

Those "general characteristics", on the other hand, can be produced through "the logical analysis of meaning" so that "definitely fixed legal concepts in the form of highly abstract rules are formulated and applied".

This formalism views legal requirements (e.g. consent in the case of contracts) not simply taken as given, but as the product of logical rationality, because the law is indeed seen as "arising from imposition": there must be a *point* to the requirements of law, and that point is disclosed through "the logical analysis of meaning", leading to the formulation and application of "highly abstract rules". The reason why consent is important for a contract to be valid is no longer seen as inscrutable or irrelevant, hence if the promissor simply said "I do" rather than "I promise" it might well be acceptable. Thus, this second form of formalism "diminishes the significance of extrinsic elements and thus *softens the rigidity of concrete formalism*".

Interestingly enough, though Weber believed that this formalism of the "logical rationality" variety softens the rigidity of the first type of formalism, he also claimed that with it

> the contrast to "substantive rationality" is sharpened, because (substantive rationality) means that the decision of legal problems is influenced by norms different from those obtained through logical generalization of abstract interpretations of meaning.

In a system of substantive rationality, cases are solved according to, among others, "ethical imperatives, utilitarian and other expediential rules and political maxims". The formalism of the "logical rationality" variety is not substantive in this sense, because here logical rationality fulfils a "specifically systematic task", which is "the collection and rationalization by logical means of all the several rules recognized as legally valid into an internally consistent complex" (all quotations from Weber in this and the three previous paragraphs are from 1967: 61–2).[39]

Many of the themes to be developed in this book are present in Weber's remarks: law is *formal*, but this formality does not have to display the rigidity and formalism common in ancient legal systems. And yet the fact that law is not *that* formal does not imply that it dissolves into substantive reasoning. How the law can be formal-but-not-rigidly-formal and at the same time substantive-but-not-thoroughly-substantive is one of the major problems this book seeks to address.

For a completely different example, consider Hegel's criticism of mathematical knowledge (as discussed by Cohen, 1996). According to him, a mathematical explanation or proof is *external* to the subject, in so far as

> [t]he necessity does not arise from the nature of the theorem: it is imposed; and the injunction to draw just these lines, an infinite number of others being equally possible, is blindly acquiesced in, without our knowing anything further, except that, as we fondly believe, this will serve our purpose in producing the proof (Hegel, 1971: 102).

[39] Paul Amselek has also noticed that games are not analogous to law in important respects for reasons similar to those developed above. The difference, according to him, is that while in games "existence precedes essence" in law (and other institutions) essence precedes existence. *Cf.* (Amselek, 1988: 211). His remarks in this regard are, I believe, fully compatible with the argument offered in this chapter.

> *Qua* result the theorem is, no doubt, one that is *seen to be true*. But this eventuality has nothing to do with its content, but only with its relation to the knowing subject. The process of mathematical proof does not belong to the object; it is a function that takes place outside the matter at hand (*ibid.* 100–1, emphasis added).

Hegel's point, I believe, could be expressed as saying that the truth of a theorem is to be found in the definitions and rules of mathematics, not in "the object"—whatever that means. To understand a theorem is to be able to reproduce its demonstration: "if anyone came to know by measuring many right-angled triangles that their sides are related in the way everybody knows, we should regard knowledge so obtained as unsatisfactory" (Hegel, 1971: 100). But—though the result is, "no doubt" *seen to be true*—the knowing subject cannot see the *necessity* of the proof: "the proof takes a direction that begins *anywhere we like*, without our knowing as yet what relation this beginning has to the result to be brought out" (*ibid.* 102; emphasis added).

In other words, an institution like mathematics allows us to have absolute certainty with regard to mathematical knowledge, but this knowledge is in a way *defective*, because the process of proof is not internally related to the subject matter: we have to follow the process of proof in the hope that it will lead us to the demonstration we are seeking. The stages of that process are strictly determined by the (mathematical) rules, and the result is true in accordance to these rules.

The same happens, I would say, in any autonomous institution. Precisely because all that matters is the solution-according-to-the-institution, the process of finding it is *external* to the subject-matter. The justification of what (autonomous) law requires in these particular cases is *not* related in any way to the point at issue, but to the rules in question. As in mathematics according to Hegel, this understanding of law allows us to have absolute certainty about what it requires, but this absolute certainty has its price.

A SHORT PREVIEW

"What is law?" This is the central question of legal theory. "What is the law concerning this concrete case?" is the sort of question at which legal reasoning is addressed. After having shown that there is something about the nature of law as a social practice that makes the second question specially important, the chapters to come deal with the relation between these two questions. The thesis to be defended is that a theory of law implies a theory of legal reasoning; that is to say, that the second question is (at least partially) answered once the first question is answered. If this is correct, then we will be able to "read" a theory of legal reasoning into a theory of law and, reciprocally, to "read" a theory of law into a theoretical description of legal reasoning. The second central claim is that legal reasoning is formal (in the sense that it excludes substantive considerations) and yet substantive (in the sense that it cannot exclude all substantive considerations).

Chapters 2, 3 and 4 examine several traditional jurisprudential discussions in an attempt to demonstrate that a correct description of legal reasoning cannot show it to be completely formal (or exclusionary). This argument is used against the sources thesis (Chapter 2) to clear the way for an explanation of what makes legal reasoning theoretically interesting (Chapter 3). The argument presented in Chapter 3 is then used to rescue what I take to be the best reading of Lon L Fuller's original argument, both from Hart and contemporary Hartians and from Fuller himself (Chapter 4). Chapter 5 gives a fresh look to the issue of defeasibility in law and morality, trying to ascertain what are the "circumstances" of defeasibility, i.e. when and why does it make sense to say that a rule is defeasible.

Chapter 6 tries to offer an example of the argument so far by showing that we cannot really understand the law unless we understand legal reasoning. The example will be that of Roman law, and the claim will be that we cannot know what the correct solution was for a concrete case under Roman law just by learning about the Roman *rules*. Chapter 7 explores the way in which the argument concerning legal reasoning, as developed thus far, has consequences for a theory of law. Then four attempts to develop a theory of legal reasoning out of a theory of law that is, broadly speaking, positivistic, are shown to be defective. This is taken to be evidence of what is called a "tension" between legal reasoning and legal theory. Chapter 7 thus brings to completion the argument for the first thesis. Chapter 8 tries to solve the tension between a theory of law and legal reasoning diagnosed in Chapter 7 and completes the argument for the second thesis.

2

Gapless Sources

THE SOURCES THESIS AND THE PROBLEM OF AUTHORITY

We begin with an examination of Raz's "authority-based" argument for what he calls "the sources thesis". Raz's own starting point is the assumption that "law, every legal system which is in force anywhere, has *de facto* authority" (1985: 199). Having *de facto* authority implies, according to Raz, at least *claiming de iure* authority. Therefore the claim to (legitimate) authority is, according to Raz, "part of the nature of law" (*ibid.*). The notion of *de iure* authority is thus explanatorily fundamental in relation to that of *de facto* authority.

Now, in Raz's elaborated theory of authority, an authority is legitimate insofar as it complies with the three following requirements (*ibid.*, 198; *see* also Raz, 1986: 38–69):

> All authoritative directives should be based, among other factors, on reasons which apply to the subjects of those directives and which bear on the circumstances covered by the directives (the *dependence* thesis);
>
> The normal and primary way to establish that a person should be acknowledged to have legitimate authority over another person involves showing that the alleged subject is likely better to comply with reasons which apply to him (other than the alleged authoritative directives) if he accepts the directives of the alleged authority as authoritatively binding, and tries to follow them, than if he tries to follow the reasons which apply to him directly (the *normal justification* thesis); and
>
> The fact that an authority requires performance of an action is a reason for its performance which is not to be added to all other relevant reasons when assessing what to do, but should replace some of them (the *pre-emption* thesis).

According to Raz, since it is a matter of conceptual truth that the law claims to have legitimate authority, it follows (unless one wants to claim that most of the people have been deceived for most of the time regarding an important aspect of an important social institution) that the law, unlike (he says) a tree, has to be the kind of thing that can have authority. It has to have, in his words, "authority-capacity".

Authority-capacity requires, according to Raz, the presence of the non-moral features of legitimate authority (the moral features, on the other hand, being those the presence of which make a *de facto* authority a legitimate one). These features are two: (a) the authoritative directives must be presented as the authority's judgment of how the subjects ought to behave and (b) "it must be possible to identify [them] as being issued by the alleged authority without relying on reasons or considerations on which [the] directive purports to adjudicate" (1985: 202).

Note how these two features follow from the dependence and normal justification theses. If the authoritative directives are supposed to *reflect* the reasons that apply to the subjects directly, then for anything to be an authoritative directive it must at least be possible to regard it as *reflecting someone's view* of the right thing to do on the balance of reasons. On the other hand, if the authority is legitimate only insofar as its subjects are likely better to comply with these reasons if they follow the directives rather than their own judgement, then it must be possible for the subjects to follow (hence to identify and understand) the directives without relying on their own judgement. Raz's favourite example in this point is that of an arbitrator. The arbitrator's judgment is supposed to reflect the balance of the reasons that were directly applicable to the parties. Her judgment can have authority, therefore, only if it is presented as the arbitrator's view of the right balance of reasons (first condition). The decision, on the other hand, has to be such that its identification does not require going through the whole substantive reasoning again (second condition). What would a decision like "I have considered the matter and I have decided that you should do what you ought to do on the balance of reasons" be useful for? (Raz, 1985: 203. We shall see, however, that the example of the arbitrator is misleading in one crucial sense).

Raz believes that this argument holds even if his conception of authority is not accepted. All that is needed is "the claim that it is part of our notion of legitimate authority that authorities should act for reasons, and that their legitimacy depends on a degree of success in doing so" (1985: 204). This weak assumption is enough, for Raz, to "hold that only what is presented as someone's view can be an authoritative directive" (*ibid.*). Regarding the second feature, all that has to be assumed is that

> authorities make a difference, i.e. the fact that an authority issued a directive changes the subject's reasons. It follows that the existence of reasons for an authority to issue a directive does not, by itself, without the directive having actually been issued, lead to this change in the reasons which face the subjects [. . .]. The existence and content of every directive depends on the existence of some condition which is itself independent of the reasons for that directive (Raz, 1985: 204)

The upshot of Raz's argument is the sources thesis: all law is source-based law, and "a law is source-based if its existence and content can be identified by reference to social facts alone, without resort to any evaluative argument" (*ibid.*, 195). Raz argues that the traditional sources of law (legislation, custom, precedent) comply with this constraint.[1]

[1] Raz only makes casual references to custom, to say that it complies with the sources thesis (1985: 205; 1980: 214). This does not seem to me so straightforward, but I will not press the issue here, because I will argue that the sources thesis is false, at least regarding the law as it is today.

Note that the argument is not necessarily a moral argument (though *see* Perry, 1995: 131n). All it presupposes is the normativity of law, that is, that the law gives rise to reasons for action. This point being granted, the argument goes on to explain that the law makes a practical difference by way of being understood as authoritatively *reflecting* the reasons that applied to the subjects anyway. Naturally, if it is also held, as a moral argument, that the law serves, for example, the common good by solving co-ordination problems, then the sources thesis becomes stronger than before. But it does not need such a moral ground.

This ends my (very brief) summary of Raz's authority-based argument for the sources thesis. Now the first thing that should be asked is precisely *what* the sources thesis requires. If we try to answer this question we shall find two problems. In the first place, It must be remembered that for Raz the sources thesis requires that "it must be possible to *identify* the directive as being issued by the alleged authority without relying on reasons or considerations on which [the] directive purports to adjudicate" (1985: 202, emphasis added). Here, the requirement sets a condition for the *identification* of the directive. Only a directive that can be *identified* as such without relying on considerations of substance can have authority-capacity. But later the requirement mutates. "[The subjects] can benefit by [the authority's] decisions only if they can establish their existence *and content* in ways which do not depend on raising the very same issues which the authority is there to settle" (1985: 203, emphasis added. Later Raz talks of a directive's "existence and content" as subject to this requirement, *ibid.*, 204). So, is the requirement one related to the identification of law or to the determination of its content? Is it possible to make a sensible distinction between the two?

Is it the same to talk of the identification of something as a species of a certain kind and of the determination of its content? In some cases the distinction is not easy to draw. One way of identifying something as a novel is, for instance, to look at its content. But it cannot be said that the task of identifying something as a member of a certain kind and that of ascertaining its content are the same, however important connections may exist between the two. You may not know what the meaning of Picasso's *Guernica* is, but still be able to identify it as a work of art. Similarly, to know if something is a judicial decision one has to inquire if it was decided by a legally appointed court, if it was given following the appropriate procedure, etc. It is not necessary to know the content of the decision to determine if it is to count as one or not. Therefore it is not the same to say that the *content* of an authoritative directive is to be grasped without reference to substantive considerations than to say that it must be possible to *identify* it as a directive without relying upon these considerations (*see* Mitrophanous, 1998: 623). Which of these claims is Raz's?

The reason for the requirement is that authorities make a difference. If the issuing of a new law changes the subject's practical situation (if it is going to enter into their practical deliberation in any way),[2] this can be so only if they can establish both its existence *and* its content with independence of the reasons that already applied to their situation.

Raz's arbitrator (*cf.* above at 64), who says "I have reached a decision, and that is that you have to do what you have to do" has rendered a decision easily *identifiable* by its non-evaluative features, but the *content* of it is impossible to ascertain without considering the substantive reasons on which he was supposed to adjudicate. Raz thinks this to be an example of an authoritative directive that fails to have authority-capacity: the parties in the example "were given a uniquely identifying description of the decision and yet it is an entirely unhelpful description" (1985: 203). Therefore, he has to claim that his requirement applies not only to the identification of a directive but also to the determination of its content.

The second ambiguity in Raz's argument concerns precisely what this requirement rules out. Looking back to more or less the same paragraphs (with different emphases) we can see that the formulation changes in each of them. Originally, what could not be done was to identify a directive (and its content) "*relying on* reasons or considerations *on which* [the] *directive purports to adjudicate*" (202), but later the requirement mutated to exclude the "*raising* [of] the *very same issues* which the directive is there to settle" (203) and sometimes it is very broad indeed: "a law is source-based if its existence and content can be identified by reference to social facts alone, without *resort* to *any* evaluative argument" (195), or "without resort to *moral* argument" (218; all these emphases are added). These statements contain different requirements (I will identify them according to the pages in which they appear). Statement 195 is the strongest: it excludes any evaluative consideration whatsoever. Depending on the meaning of "moral", of course, 218 could be equally strong or weaker than 195 (Raz switches the meaning of "moral" in different places: *cf.* 1994: 88 n.6, 244 n.12). On the other hand, 203 is the weakest: it only excludes the raising of the *very same* substantive issues the directive is there to settle. Statement 202 is somewhere in between: it allows the use of some moral (or evaluative) considerations, but it excludes those among which the directive is supposed to adjudicate. Hence, we could distinguish various versions of the sources-thesis: the *strongest* version requires 195, while the *weakest* requires only 203. Raz appears to hold the strongest version, since his was presented as an argument against what has been called "inclusive" (or "soft") positivism, i.e. a form of positivism that allows moral standards to be part of the law insofar as they are entailed by the source-based law.

In fact, the only version of the sources thesis that could do justice to Raz's argument is, in my view, 195. To see why we must ask: how is one suppose to decide whether a particular rule "purported to adjudicate" on a given reason?

[2] That is, either as a protected reason for action, as Raz would claim, or as an "ordinary" first-order reason. *See* Marmor (1994: 117f).

Consider Pufendorf's case: did the directive purport to adjudicate on the relative merits of having clean public squares and assigned it a great value, or was that reason not considered at all? One can see how this train of thought could prevent subjects from being able to benefit from the authority's directives: did the arbitrator take into account the fact that I, the losing party, am poor and needy? If I conclude she did not, I could still raise an objection against the execution of the decision, and that would not count as my challenging the authority. And if I had to decide on which reasons the directive purports to adjudicate and on which reasons it does not, then I would not be able to benefit from the authority's directives. It follows that the correct reading of the second condition has to be 195, since 202 or 203 are too weak to fulfil the function the second condition is supposed to fulfil.

I am not interested in the details of Raz's argument here. But note how weak the premises of the argument are: if the law is normative, it makes a normative difference; if it makes a normative difference it follows that it *can* make a normative difference; if it can make a normative difference, it must be the case that you can identify, understand and apply it (at least in normal cases) without considering the reasons for it (more on whether the sources thesis covers the application of the law below). Note further that the thesis is *not* that the subjects have, even in normal cases, a moral duty to apply the law. It is only that they will be able to do so. The same argument could be grounded in Alexy's notion of "discursive possibility". The rules and forms of general practical discourse, Alexy tells us, define procedures which would not, in many cases, lead to certain results: a given statement and its negation might be justified according to those procedures. Thus, "the need for legal discourse arises out of the weakness of the rules and forms of general practical discourse" (Alexy, 1989: 288).

If legal discourse is to provide a solution for that weakness of general practical discourse, it seems that the sources thesis has to be true. In other words, it has to be possible to identify the law and ascertain its content without reopening the questions of general practical discourse that the law was supposed to answer (the existence of law as a social institution is explained by the fact that general practical discourse is insufficient to settle issues that have to be settled). If the need for legal discourse arises out of the weaknesses of general practical discourse, then it cannot be the case that legal discourse mirrors those weaknesses.

The point to be discussed is not, then, that of the plausibility of a positivistic conception of law, though the argument will have same impact on that: it is, rather, that some features of legal reasoning, as I will try to show, seem to imply that the law is structurally dependent on what Alexy called "general practical reasoning". If this is true, it would seem as though legal discourse cannot "improve" general practical discourse, for it reproduces, instead of settling, Alexy's "discursive possibility". This concern is not restricted to members of the so-called positivistic tradition (indeed, Alexy can hardly be considered a positivist; *cf.* Alexy, 1994: 26ff). Looking outside that tradition, for example, we find that Lon Fuller was well aware of the risk of the law becoming pointless once evaluative arguments are allowed in the identification of the law:

> Fidelity to law *can* become impossible if we do not accept the broader responsibilities [. . .] that go with a purposive interpretation of law. One can imagine a course of reasoning that might run as follows: This statute says absinthe shall not be sold. What is its purpose? To promote health. Now, as everyone knows, absinthe is a sound, wholesome and beneficial beverage. Therefore, interpreting the statute in the light of its purpose, I construe it to direct a general sale and consumption of that most healthful of beverages, absinthe (Fuller, 1958: 670).

This passage shows Fuller's awareness of the tension between his own ideas on "purposive interpretation" and his conception of the law as the enterprise of "subjecting human behaviour to the guidance of rules". And the tension is, what do we have rules for, if in every case we will have to discuss the issue all over again? The sources thesis could be said to specify the "broader responsibilities that go with a purposive interpretation of law": the point of the law is to provide for the common good (or to subject human conduct to the guidance of rules), and this cannot be achieved if the law cannot settle controversial moral questions. Hence the plausibility of Raz's authority-based argument for the sources thesis: if at the moment of applying the directives the subjects have to go back to the "raw moral question" then the advantage of having an authority (i.e. the advantage of having the law) is lost. If Raz's sources thesis is wrong, then the law appears to be pointless.

Raz made this point in order to justify the sources thesis: "the authoritative nature of law gives a reason to prefer the sources thesis" (1985: 214). In the rest of this chapter I want to argue that this is indeed true, but it does not stop the sources thesis from being false, and this is shown by the fact that it cannot explain legal reasoning without distortion.

Before answering that question, it is important to be clear about what I am calling "legal reasoning". This will lead us to Raz's distinction between what he calls the "narrow" and the "wide" sources theses, and to the problem, mentioned above, of whether or not the sources thesis covers the application of the law. This issue will be rather important for the argument to be developed in the following chapters, and we shall come back to it every now and then. First, the distinction:

> Let us distinguish between what source-based law states explicitly and what it establishes by implication. If a statute in country A says that income earned abroad by a citizen is liable to income tax in A, then it only implicitly establishes that I am liable to such tax. For my liability is not stated by the statute but is inferred from it (and some other premises). Similarly, if earnings abroad are taxed at a different rate from earnings at home, the fact that the proceeds of export sales are subject to the home rate is implied rather than stated. It is inferred from this statute and other legal rules on the location of various transactions.

> The two examples differ in that the statement that I am liable to tax at a certain rate is an applied legal statement depending for its truth on both law and fact. The statement that export earnings are taxed at a certain rate is a pure legal statement, depending for its truth on law only (i.e. on acts of legislation and other law-making facts). The sources thesis as stated at the beginning can bear a narrow or a wide interpretation. The narrow thesis concerns the truth conditions of pure legal statements only. Pure legal statements are those which state the content of the law, i.e. of legal rules, principles, doctrines, etc. The wide thesis concerns the truth conditions of all legal statements, including applied ones. It claims that the truth or falsity of legal statements depends on social facts which can be established without resort to moral argument (1985: 214–5).

Using Raz's distinction, we can say legal reasoning is reasoning about which "applied legal statements" follow from true "pure legal statements" given some factual premisses. It follows that even if the argument I am about to develop is correct, that would not affect the validity of the narrow sources thesis, which is silent concerning the application of the law. The thesis (in this version) does not claim that what the law is for a particular case (for *any* particular case) is something that can be established according to social facts alone, at least not before a court has so decided (*see* Raz, 1980: 212). I believe, however, that if Raz's authority-argument is an argument for the sources thesis, it has to be for the *wide* sources thesis (and the argument is similar to the one used to prefer 195 over other readings of the second condition, above at 66f). But Raz is cautious concerning the wide thesis:

> All the arguments so far concern the narrow sources thesis only. Nothing was said about its application to applied legal statements. I tend to feel that it applies to them as well, since they are legal statements whose truth value depends on contingent facts as well as on law. If one assumes that contingent facts cannot be moral facts, then the sources thesis applies here as well. That is, what is required is the assumption that what makes it contingently true that a person acted fairly on a particular occasion is not the standard of fairness, which is not contingent, but the "brute fact" that he performed a certain action describable in value-neutral ways. If such an assumption is sustainable in all cases, then the sources thesis holds regarding applied legal statements as well (1985: 218).

We can now see that the example of the arbitrator is misleading, since it hides away this important qualification. "You should do what you should do on the balance of reasons" is useless, but "the buyer ought to transfer ownership of the goods" is *equally* useless unless the parties to a contract of sale can *apply* the decision to their particular case, that is to say, unless they can get, from the (pure) legal statement quoted above, an (applied) legal statement like "Jones ought to transfer ownership of his copy of *The Concept of Legal System* to Watson". It follows that the very same considerations Raz used to support the sources thesis against the "coherence" and the "incorporation" theses can be used to support the wide against the narrow version of it.

Indeed, what are we to make of Raz's statement (*ibid.* 218) that "all the arguments so far concern the narrow sources thesis only"? The "arguments so far" were advanced to claim that only if the law complies with the sources thesis does it have authority-capacity. The reason for this was that authority-capacity required the two features we have been discussing, and that they in turn required the sources thesis. Let us focus upon the second feature, that authoritative directives can be identified and their content ascertained without using evaluative considerations. Why was this condition required? The answer is, because if it were not met the would-be directive would fail to be able to fulfil its function (let alone actually to fulfil it!), and subjects would fail to be able to be benefited by the existence of the authority: the subjects "can benefit by [the authority's] decisions only if they can establish their existence and content in ways which do not depend on raising the very same issues which the authority is there to settle" (Raz, 1985: 203). Only if this condition is met would an allegedly authoritative directive be able to comply with the normal justification thesis. But now we are told that the "arguments so far" concern the narrow version only, with the obvious implication that authority-capacity requires only the *narrow* sources thesis. This means that the argument turns out to be that the law can have authority-capacity even if the wide sources thesis is untenable, that is, even if subjects can *never* get *any* "applied legal statement" without raising all the moral considerations that were pre-empted by the authoritative directive, *even if the authority is fully legitimate.*

This is an important point, so it might be advisable to re-state it: if the authoritative nature of the law is an argument for the sources thesis at all, it has to be for the wide sources thesis. For consider: Raz claims that "a decision is serviceable only if it can be identified by means other than the considerations the weight and outcome of which it was meant to settle" (1985:203). Serviceable *for what*? For the subjects to be able to *act* upon the decision rather than their own judgement. But to be serviceable in these terms what is required is the *wide* sources thesis, i.e. that we can stop thinking about the substantive problem behind the authoritative directive and simply do as it commands. If this cannot be done no authoritative directive can ever comply with the normal justification thesis, which makes reference to the fact of the subjects *complying* with the authoritative directives, i.e. acting according to them in concrete cases.

But maybe I have just been labouring the obvious, since Raz believes that, if we are prepared to grant one further point (that moral facts are not contingent) then the wide thesis follows from the narrow thesis. I think the point should readily be granted. Therefore, if the distinction were used as an objection to the argument to follow, we could easily answer: since the narrow version plus the extra premise of moral facts not being contingent implies the wide version, if the wide version of the sources thesis is defeated by reasons other than the rejection of that extra premise, the narrow version would be defeated by implication. On this assumption I shall proceed.[3]

[3] As a matter of fact I do not think that this is an instance of labouring the obvious. Raz's last-minute restriction of his argument to the narrow sources thesis only stems, I will claim later

LEGAL INDETERMINACY

We all know and have known for centuries that the law is often controversial. This means that it is often the case that informed people, lawyers and judges, disagree about what the law is in particular cases. Can the sources thesis explain why and how the law is controversial?

To succeed, a sources thesis-based explanation of legal disagreement has to meet two conditions: on the one hand, it has to show that legal disagreement is disagreement of *fact*, i.e., about the social facts that constitute the content of the law. On the other hand, it has to offer an explanation that makes sense of the *explanandum*, i.e. one that shows as controversial at least most of those cases that are seen by participants to be controversial.[4]

The first requirement is a direct consequence of the sources thesis, so it must be asserted if that thesis is to be defended: if all law is source-based, it follows that disagreement about the law can only be disagreement about some source-based entity. The explanation, that is to say, has to proceed more or less along the following lines: if only social facts can determine the existence and content of a law, when these sources exist the court has to apply them (i.e. apply the norms the validity of which is grounded upon such sources). But given the kind of social facts that determine the content of the law, it will often be the case that they are silent or vague as regarding some particular cases. In those cases there is no source-based law on the subject, and since all law is source-based, there is no law.

Naturally, it would not affect the sources thesis (in any of its versions, strong or weak, broad or narrow) to recognise that the application of source-based law can be defeated for moral reasons. The description the sources thesis gives to this situation would have to be that the *legal* obligation of the court is to follow (i.e. to apply) the source-based law, but the court might,

(below, at 188ff), from his unwillingness to draw the conclusions that his theory of law implies for a theory of legal reasoning.

[4] Raz's main argument for the sources thesis was that, since the law claims to have authority, it has to belong to the kind of thing that can have authority. But, strictly speaking, from the fact that I claim *X* it does not follow that I can have *X*. Raz, of course, knows this: "since the law claims to have authority it is capable of having it. Since the claim is made by legal officials wherever a legal system is in force, the possibility that is normally insincere or based on a conceptual mistake is ruled out . . .. Why cannot legal officials and institutions be conceptually confused? One answer is that while they can be occasionally they cannot be systematically confused. For given the centrality of legal institutions in our structures of authority, their claims and conceptions are formed by and contribute to our concept of authority" (1985: 201). I think that Raz is right in thinking that to claim that most of the people are conceptually confused most of the time concerning an important aspect of an important social institution is not plausible. This very argument constitutes the second condition for any explanation of legal disagreement: it cannot be committed to claim that most of the people most of the time are insincere or conceptually confused. If we were allowed to assume this to be the case concerning legal adjudication, then the reasons for believing otherwise concerning the law's claim to authority (a crucial step in Raz's argument) would be greatly weakened.

because of moral reasons, find that its *moral* obligation is not to apply the law. Since according to the sources thesis the fact that the law ought to be different does not imply that it actually is different, the court's having the moral duty not to apply the source-based law would not affect the existence of the court's legal duty. The argument proceeds, therefore, on the assumption that, unless otherwise stated, we are concerned only with the question "what is the law (as opposed to 'the morally correct solution') for this case?".

We shall soon see that this is a crucial point, so let me emphasise this stipulation: unless otherwise explicitly stated, hereinafter words like "ought", "should" or "must" and the like will be used in a legal sense. Thus, "the court ought to *X*" will mean "the legal obligation of the court is to *X*" (or, "legally, the court ought to *X*"), whatever the morality of X. Since I am following Raz in assuming that a legal obligation does not necessarily imply a moral one, this stipulation is of no moral consequence at all.

According to the sources thesis, then, there can be disagreement about what the law *is* (disagreement that can only be disagreement of *fact*), or disagreement about what the law ought to be. Hard cases, as usually discussed in the jurisprudential literature, are of the second kind: in hard cases the law is unsettled, hence there is no law in the matter, hence what is really going on in a hard case is a discussion about the best way to use the court's discretion, i.e. about what the law *ought* to be.[5]

Though in solving these (hard) cases the courts will have to use sourceless evaluative arguments, this is not an argument against the sources thesis, *insofar as it has been previously established that there is no law in these matters*. In hard cases the court is not trying to identify a source-based rule nor trying to ascertain its content, but deciding how best to use its law-making powers. Given that most legal systems nowadays contain a *non liquet* rule or principle, this is not surprising at all. Hence, for analytical clarity, in hard cases two stages can be distinguished: in the first stage, the court examines the (source-based) law, and arrives at the conclusion that the law is unsettled, i.e. that there is no law on the matter. In the second stage, the court is allowed to use its discretion to "fill in" the gap just discovered (NB: *discovered*, not created). Two points are important in this regard.

First, this analysis of hard cases in two stages is required by the sources thesis. What courts are supposed to do is one thing if they are using their discretion, and quite a different thing if they are applying the law. And they ought (remember the stipulation) not to use their discretion (or, they do not have discretion) unless the source-based law fails to provide an answer to the case, while at the same time it requires the court to decide it. This does not mean that in any ruling it will be easy, or even possible, actually to distinguish these two stages. But the *conceptual* possibility of drawing such a line is essential to the sources thesis: the operation of deciding whether a case is clear has

[5] The *locus classicus* of this argument is Hart (1994: Ch. 7).

to be grounded in non-evaluative considerations. Legal rules, if the (wide) sources thesis is right, can be applied without evaluative considerations. This is possible only if the cases to which the rules apply can be distinguished from those to which they do not without using the considerations the rules are, according to Raz's argument, supposed to pre-empt.

Secondly, it has to be said that the sources thesis is meant to be a conceptual explanation of law as we know it. So Razians have the burden of proving that there is an independent conceptual base for this qualitative distinction between creating and applying the law in this sense (i.e, independent from the sources thesis itself. If the only reason we have for accepting the distinction is the fact that if we don't the sources thesis would be wrong, then the thesis would be a stipulation of the meaning of the word "law"—and I don't think that this is the way in which Raz expects us to see the thesis).

HARD AND CLEAR CASES

The distinction between hard and clear cases, though common in modern jurisprudence, is not uncontroversial nor clear itself (one telling cause of this is the fact that legal positivists, with the remarkable exception of Neil MacCormick, to be discussed in Chapter 7, do not usually give actual examples of hard or clear cases: they simply acknowledge the possibility of their existence). In the sense the sources thesis needs the distinction it refers to cases covered or not covered by the law. As such, however, the distinction is question-begging, since what needs to be explained is when a case is or fails to be covered by the law, and the ancillary question of how we are to find that out. An answer to this problem provides the criterion that differentiates clear from hard cases.

One possible answer that should, however, be screened out from the outset is "when the law is controversial the case is hard, otherwise it is clear". This may sound odd, since the distinction itself was introduced in order to explain disagreement in legal reasoning. But upon closer examination, I hope, it should be rather obvious why the criterion that distinguishes clear from hard cases cannot be the brute fact of (dis)agreement. First, people may disagree concerning all sorts of things: they may differ about what is the meaning of the law, what are the proven facts of a case, what the court should do, etc. (this time in the moral sense of "should"). It could be said that since we are trying to find an explanation for legal disagreement that is compatible with the sources thesis only the first problem should concern us, i.e. disagreement about the meaning of the law. But here we find a different reason why the brute fact of (dis)agreement cannot be what characterises a case as clear or hard: people may disagree because of all sorts of reasons. To focus on the obvious example, some people may disagree simply because they are mistaken. Hence it cannot be the sheer fact of disagreement that makes a case hard. And conversely, a case is not clear when people mistakenly think that the law is settled in its solution for it.

In other words, a theory has to explain when disagreement is "true" and not mistaken disagreement. Thus a theory could, without violating the second condition as discussed above (at 71), classify some controversial cases as clear cases and some non-controversial cases as hard.[6] Nevertheless, and unless an argument is offered to claim that lawyers (or, generally, people when discussing what the law is) are particularly prone to make mistakes, the cases that are hard according to whatever criterion the theory offers, and the cases that are in reality controversial, must overlap over a significant range of instances (this was the second condition). This is the single most important test we could possibly have to evaluate the adequacy of a theory of law and legal reasoning.

That clear cases exist is a truism. The problem is how they are to be characterised (*see* Stavropoulos, 1996: 12). Some authors seem to believe that Dworkin's critique of Hart was based upon the fact that hard cases were significant in a statistical sense, i.e. that there was a huge number of them. Thus Matthew Kramer, for example, claims that

> once we apprehend the extent to which the ordinary workings of a legal system must be regularized if the system is to be viable as a regime of law—an extent which varies from system to system, but which is always considerable—we can see that Dworkin's attack on the rule of recognition is untroubling for the positivist (1999: 142).

In truth the problem has nothing to do with *how many* cases are controversial or uncontroversial. I do not see any reason to believe that Dworkin claims that legal systems can exist without substantial agreement among participants. One of the most significant differences between Hart and Dworkin is how precisely to characterise that substantial agreement, and what is its function regarding the existence and operation of the legal system. To put it bluntly (and therefore rather inaccurately), is a case clear because the applicable rules were considered by all those involved to be just and fair, or is it clear because the state of affairs that constitute it fall into the core of the meaning of the applicable rule? Obviously the *sheer number* of hard cases will not make any difference here, and hence the positivist Kramer is defending should be troubled by Dworkin's argument unless she can offer a reason to prefer her description of legal practice rather than Dworkin's.

For the purpose of the following discussion I want to distinguish three (in fact, as we shall see, two) ways in which the distinction between clear and

[6] Example: one *might* want to classify Pufendorf's case as a hard case, based on the fact that the correct solution is correct because of substantive reasons, even though it is the opposite to what its literal meaning indicates (of course, one's wanting to do so depends upon having a theory of hard cases that focuses on these two features). One could then go one and explain that this is a hard case even though there is no disagreement (because everyone agrees that the barber should not be fined), because it displays the features that make disagreement common (i.e. substantive reasoning).

hard cases can be drawn (with no claim whatsoever to exhaustivity: *see* Bengoetxea, 1993: 185ff for a much longer list):

In a *semantic* sense, the distinction is grounded upon the fact that laws are expressed in words, and sometimes words are not clear, i.e. sometimes their meaning is elusive. But since to know the meaning of a word is to be able to produce standard examples of its application to some cases, there must be cases in which there is no doubt about their meaning. Sometimes at least it must be possible to understand and apply a rule without having to interpret it, because "interpretations still hang in the air along with what they interpret" (Wittgenstein, 1958: § 198). This is, however, no reason to think that it will never be necessary to interpret it. When interpretation is thus necessary the case is said to be *hard*. In a semantic hard case, arguments are needed to specify the precise meaning of ambiguous terms in the canonical formulation of the applicable rule.

In a *regulative* sense, the distinction between clear and hard cases is one between regulated and unregulated cases. When a case is regulated by the law, the decision-maker has to apply the solution provided by it. When it is unregulated, there is a gap in the law, and the applicator has discretion to solve it (*see* Raz, 1979a: 181). In a *regulative* hard case the problem is that the law does not settle the issue, so arguments are needed to show how the law ought to be: judicial decisions in regulative hard cases are creative decisions.

In an *evaluative* sense a case is hard when there is a rule that is prima-facie applicable, but that for some evaluative reason (because it would be too unfair, or too absurd and the like) the application of that rule to the case can be disputed.

An evaluative hard case is one in which the law *could* be applied without any argument beyond semantic ones. In other words, the case fits the explicit operative facts of some valid rule in a clear and straightforward manner. The problem is that even though the operative facts are fulfilled, given the nature of the particular case, what is in need of justification is the application of the rule itself (i.e. the solution provided by the rule is clear, but what is unclear is whether or not *the rule* should be applied).

What are the relations between these different ways of drawing the dividing line between clear and hard cases? We shall see that the important distinction is that between the first and the third way to draw the line. Thus, for authors like Raz and Hart they are basically the same, or at least the regulative is the *genus* and the semantic the species. This is so because for them the content of the law is given by the meaning of the legal rules. The fundamental criterion is, a case is hard if there is no applicable law. If the meaning of the prima-facie applicable rule is unclear, then that rule does not provide a solution for the case, hence there is no law for the case.

Examination of this question will force us to pay some attention to that old chestnut of continental legal theory, that of the possibility of gaps in the law. I will be claiming that the sources thesis would force upon us an unpalatable alternative: either regulative hard cases do not exist (beyond strictly so-called semantic hard cases, in the sense identified above) or they crop up everywhere. Both of these options will prove to be untenable. If the sources thesis is rejected, however, we shall be able to offer a more sensible explanation for the possibility of regulative hard cases.

This last point will prove to be important because, I will try to show, a reasonable explanation of legal reasoning must be able to reduce "evaluative" hard cases to regulative ones. This is because a (non-evaluative) regulative notion of hard cases can explain *why* in hard cases judges have discretion, but it is unable to explain *when* judges will have discretion, while a (non-regulative) evaluative notion of hard cases can explain *when* judges have discretion, but it cannot explain *why* they do. A correct explanation will have both notions overlapping. In what follows, evaluative hard cases will be the important ones and regulative hard cases will be the object of the dispute: while the sources thesis would claim the label "regulative hard cases" for semantic hard cases only, I want to reclaim it for evaluative hard cases.

ON GAPS IN THE LAW

There are three answers that a theory of law could possibly give to the problem of the (in)existence of gaps in the law:

(i) Legal systems are necessarily gapless.
(ii) Legal systems necessarily have gaps.
(iii) Whether or not a particular system is gapless is an empirical question.

Let us begin with (i), the most famous defender of which was Hans Kelsen. Kelsen believed that, for any conceivable case,

> either the court ascertains that the defendant or accused has committed the delict as claimed by the plaintiff or public prosecutor and has thereby violated an obligation imposed on him by the legal order; then the court must find for the plaintiff or condemn the accused by ordering a sanction prescribed in the general norm. Or the court ascertains that the defendant or accused has not committed the delict and therefore has not violated an obligation imposed on him by the legal order; then the court must dismiss the action or acquit the accused—that is, the court must order that the sanction ought not to be directed against the defendant or accused (1967: 242).

The law is always applicable: a so called gap in the law is not a *legal* gap, but a situation in which the application of the law as it is to the particular case is so absurd and unjust that the judge assumes that the law is not to be applied to the case. In Kelsen's words:

> the existence of a gap is assumed only when the absence of such a legal norm is regarded as politically undesirable by the law-applying organ; when, therefore, the

> logically possible application of the valid law is rejected for this political reason, as being inequitable or unjust according to the opinion of the law-applying organ (*ibid.*, 246).

According to Alchourrón and Bulygin (1971), Kelsen's case is instructive because he tried to support his argument for the inexistence of legal gaps in two different ways. Alchourrón and Bulygin maintain these are *the* two ways in which such a claim could be justified. We shall consider them in some detail.

For a system to be gapless (or closed), it has to contain some closure rule according to which if no deontic property can be ascribed to a certain action, a deontic property is ascribed to that action. The obvious candidate for such a closure rule (or principle) is what Alchourrón and Bulygin call the "principle of prohibition": everything that is not prohibited is permitted. According to the meaning of "permitted" in it, Alchourrón and Bulygin distinguished two versions of this principle, one *weak* and one *strong*: in the strong version, "permitted" means positively permitted, while in the weak version it means simply not prohibited. In its weak version (when "permitted" is understood as meaning simply "not prohibited"), the principle of prohibition "is analytic and therefore necessarily true", because it states that if action is not prohibited it is not prohibited (1971: 125).

Thus, though the weak version of the principle of prohibition is necessarily true (i.e. it is logically true to claim that it is part of every conceivable legal system), for Alchourrón and Bulygin its existence in every system is compatible with those systems having gaps, "for it does not close any normative system and hence does not exclude the possibility of incomplete systems" (*ibid.*, 126). In fact, they said, "a gap is a case in which there is an action *p* such that it is weakly permitted (and is not strongly permitted) by the system" (*ibid.*). The strong version of the principle of prohibition, on the other hand, is strong enough to close any system, but "far from being necessary, is a contingent proposition" (*ibid.*, 127). Since Kelsen did not offer any argument to show how and why a norm could have "the mysterious property of belonging to all legal systems" (*ibid.*, 132), they can be closed or open according to whether or not they contain, as a matter of empirical fact, a strong principle of prohibition. This would amount to a rejection of (i), Kelsen's thesis, and an endorsement of (iii).

In Kelsen's early work, according to Alchourrón and Bulygin, the completeness of legal systems was based upon the strong version of the principle of prohibition. But precisely to avoid having to claim that there was a norm that existed in all conceivable legal systems, Kelsen abandoned the strong and adopted, in the second edition of *The Pure Theory of Law*, the weak version of the principle of prohibition. For Alchourrón and Bulygin, having made this move, Kelsen could not maintain the completeness of legal systems, and had grudgingly to accept the possibility of gaps:

> the permitted behaviour of one individual is opposed by a behaviour . . . of another individual—a behaviour that likewise is permitted. Then . . . a conflict of interests is present which the legal order does not prevent; no legal order can prevent all possible conflicts of interest (Kelsen, 1967: 243).

Alchourrón and Bulygin see in this an implicit recognition of the existence of legal gaps, because "what else are gaps if not "conflicts of interests which the legal order does not prevent"?" (1987: 187).[7] *This* is very implausible indeed. Consider the following case: there is no rule of Scots law that specifies where a recently married couple has to spend their holiday. Imagine that he wants to go to France, but she wants to go to South Africa. They have a conflict of interests, because (imagine) both of them have to and want to travel together. Imagine further that he sues her, and asks the judge to find in his favour that they have to go to South Africa. What will the judge do? She will probably say that there is no existing rule, so that she must dismiss the suit.[8]

This example shows that there are two different questions that Alchourrón and Bulygin fail to distinguish: (a) what is the law in Scotland concerning married couples' holidays?; and (b) what is the correct legal solution for this case? In Raz's terms, (a) is a question about a pure legal statement, while (b) is one about an applied legal statement. Alchourrón and Bulygin believe that an answer to (a) *is* an answer to (b):

> When there is a gap, what ought the judge to do? Should he find against the defendant or reject the petition? The answer is clear: if the primary system says nothing at all about the action under dispute, *the judge has no specific obligation* either to find against the defendant or to reject the suit. He has only the generic obligation to decide the case and he fulfils his obligation by deciding in one of two possible ways: finding against the defendant or rejecting the petition (provided that these are the

[7] I have not been able to trace this sentence back to the original 1971 English edition. The quotation is taken from the 1987 Spanish edition (Alchourrón and Bulygin, 1987: 187). In the original English version this passage seems to correspond to the following: "Kelsen himself seems to admit that there may be a conflict of interests which is not solved by legal order, because no legal order can solve all possible conflicts of interests" (1971: 131).

[8] For a similar position, *see* Ruiz Manero (1990: 43): "according to Kelsen, if no norm provides a deontic qualification for the defendant's behaviour, the judge does have a specific obligation: that of finding for him. Kelsen certainly distinguishes between prohibition in a negative [i.e. weak] and a positive [strong] sense, but this does not imply, in his view, that the judge has the obligation to find for the defendant only when his behaviour is positively permitted, and only the generic obligation to decide the case when that behaviour is negatively permitted. In other words, the absence of a rule that deontically qualifies the defendant's behaviour has for Kelsen . . . exactly the same consequences as the existence of a norm that permits it" (*ibid.* at 42). It is not clear, however, whether Ruiz Manero agrees with Alchourrón and Bulygin concerning the possibility of gaps in the law. He claims that "Alchourrón and Bulygin are right when they claim . . . that gaps are "conflicts of interests which the legal order does not prevent", but they seem not to notice that it is possible to allow for the existence of "conflicts of interests which the legal order does not prevent" without implying in any way an acknowledgement of the possibility of gaps". I fail to see how Ruiz Manero can square these two propositions: if gaps *are* "conflicts of interests. . . (etc.)", then surely nobody can believe in the existence of the latter without believing (at least implicitly) in the existence of the former. As will be clear shortly, in my view the correct solution is to recognise that the existence of conflicts of interests which the legal order does not prevent is not enough for the existence of a gap.

> only two ways of deciding it). In other words, the judge has the obligation to decide, that is, to admit or to reject the suit, but he has neither an obligation to admit it nor an obligation to reject it (1971: 156–7).

Alchourrón and Bulygin's mistake, in my view, stems in part from their characterisation of judges and other jurisdictional organs.[9] Without offering any arguments, they take the "solving of conflicts of interests" to be their "primary function" (*ibid.* 147). If this is assumed, then a strong case can be made for their claim that a conflict of interests not solved by the legal order is a gap. In other words, an arbitrary definitional fiat is Alchourrón and Bulygin's link between (a) and (b).

I do not want to claim that judicial decisions do not, as a matter of fact, solve conflicts of interests most of the time (an idea, incidentally, that has overwhelmingly been developed out of theoretical reflection on private law adjudication in capitalist countries). But from a conceptual or logical point of view, which is Alchourrón and Bulygin's, this is the wrong way of characterising the function of courts. They mistake the role courts have in the context of modern liberal societies with the structural role they play in the working of legal systems as such.

Indeed, not even in modern Western legal systems is it always the case that judicial decisions solve conflicts of interest, if not for other reasons, because there is not always a conflict waiting to be solved. In many jurisdictions, for instance, a judicial decision is needed in order to convict a criminal, even when the latter has confessed to the offence: the fact that the defendant is willing to be punished does not always make the judicial decision superfluous. But even if in some way one could claim that there is a conflict in those situations, that would not be enough to warrant Alchourrón and Bulygin's claim. Mirjan Damaska, for example, has argued that the link between jurisdiction and conflict-resolution is strong in liberal countries but less important in systems where the law is seen as a means of public policy (1986: 84; *see* below at 216f).

How should we characterise judicial activity, if not upon the basis of conflict-resolution? One plausible alternative is to characterise it as Hart did when he introduced his notion of secondary rules of adjudication. On this view, what is distinctive of jurisdictional activity is not that it solves conflicts of interests but that it provides "authoritative determinations of the fact of violation of the primary rules" (Hart, 1994: 97). On this view, conflict-resolution will appear as the characteristic activity of the courts only if that is taken to be the main point of the rules courts are supposed to apply. But if those rules are understood as having as their main point a different one (implementing public policy, maximising utility, and so forth), then conflict-resolution might well be regarded as a mere by-product of the application of the rules.

[9] I say "in part" because even if this point is granted to Alchourrón and Bulygin there would, I believe, be space to reject their conclusion. But if their characterisation of jurisdictional organs is mistaken, as I believe it is, (at least if offered as a *logical* characterisation) their failure to distinguish (a) from (b) is more evident.

If this is correct, then there is no warrant for Alchourrón and Bulygin's move from (a) to (b), at least not without further argumentation not provided by them. To see this, let us consider Alchourrón and Bulygin's own example, as commented upon by Aleksander Peczenik:

> Assume that a statute stipulates that (1) the restitution of real estate is obligatory, if the transferee is in good faith, the transfer is made with consideration, and the transferor is in bad faith; and (2) the restitution of real estate is obligatory if the transfer is made without consideration. Assume now that the transferor is in good faith and the transfer is made with consideration but the transferee is in bad faith. Is the restitution of real estate obligatory? The norm does not answer the question. A gap occurs. One can establish such gaps in an objective, "value-free" manner but to fill them up, one must complete the statute with an additional norm, such as the following one: An action is permitted, if it is not explicitly forbidden by the law . . .. Such a norm may be established in a statute or another source of the law. If it is not, then filling up the gap demands that one makes a value judgment (Peczenik, 1994: 25).

As regards question (a), we can safely say: Argentinean law was (at least in 1971) silent concerning the restitution of real estate by the possessor when the possessor (the transferee) is in bad faith (call this property of the case *A*), the transferor is in good faith (*B*), and the transfer is made with consideration (*C*). We can, indeed, as Peczenik claims, "establish such a gap in an objective, value-free manner".

Things are, though, quite different concerning the second question, (b). Here the problem is, "what ought the court to do?".[10] The generic answer is, apply the law. Assume the rightful owner is suing the possessor for restitution. There is no applicable rule, in the Alchourrón–Bulygin–Peczenik case (this was our conclusion regarding the first question). Therefore, the judge has to say "there is no rule to be applied", that is, there is no rule whose application is triggered by properties *ABC*. But this is precisely what the defendant will be claiming, that he is under no obligation to restitute the property since there is no rule whose application has been triggered by properties *ABC*. Given that the court is supposed to "provide authoritative determinations of the violation of primary rules" the court has to say that in a case like the one now under consideration there is no rule to apply, i.e. that it has to find for the defendant (this was *precisely* Kelsen's point). It follows that the existence of a gap in the law is not enough to establish that the court has discretion to solve the case. Hence, it is not necessarily the case that "filling up the gap demands that one makes a value judgment".

I am not claiming that legal systems are necessarily complete, only that the existence of a "normative" (as opposed to an "axiological") gap is not enough to explain the court's having discretion.[11] Recall the case of the married

[10] Remember my stipulation before (at 72) in virtue of which "what is the correct legal solution for this case?" becomes identical in meaning to "what should the court do?".

[11] The distinction between axiological and normative gaps is introduced by Alchourrón and

couple in Scotland. That might well be called a gap, since the answer to question (a) has to be that Scots law is silent on that issue (at least in 1998). And this is what, I believe, Alchourrón and Bulygin would indeed say (*cf.* Alchourrón and Bulygin, 1971: 161ff). My point has merely been that if this is a gap, then the distinction between regulated and unregulated cases turns out not to have anything to do with hard and clear cases: can we really say that this case is *hard* because it is "unregulated", meaning that the court has, according to the law, discretion to solve it? If it finds for the plaintiff, shall it not be breaking the law? Of course it will: the case is a regulated case, and the answer to the legal problem posed by it is: "the law does regulate the case, instructing the court to dismiss the claim" (*cf.* Machan, 1979: 125, on what he calls decisions that "prevail by default").

Ronald Dworkin has also argued that a conception of law as an institutional fact (his argument is clearly designed to apply also to a sources thesis-based conception of law) necessarily implies the existence of gaps. He also collapses Kelsen's distinction between a legal gap and a "conflict of interests not regulated by the law", because

> the internal logic of a rule is one that allows three truth values because it allows for a distinction between what the logicians call "internal" and "external" negation. That is, there's a difference between saying "There is no rule permitting me to take my bicycle into the park" and "There is a rule not permitting me or forbidding me". Since that is a logical feature of rules, if we think of law as institutional fact, we will think there are many cases in which it is true neither that a rule has been created permitting me to enter the park nor that a rule has been created forbidding me to do so, and in those circumstances that the proposition "I am permitted to do so" is neither true nor false (Dworkin, 1991: 86).

This view suffers from the same defect as Alchourrón and Bulygin's: it considers only what Dworkin calls the "internal logic of rules", but not the effects that the existence of law-applying organs have upon such an "internal logic". A law-applying organ has the role of applying legal rules once their operative facts are fulfilled. If no rule's operative facts are fulfilled, no rule can be applied. This will mean that many conflicts of interest will not be solved by the law, but it does not mean that the courts will have discretion. If no rule concerning bicycles in the park exists, then Dworkin cannot be fined by law-applying organs if he takes his bicycle into the park. If he is prosecuted

Bulygin in the following passage: "The expression "gap in law" is often used in legal language (and specially in judicial parlance) to refer to situations in which there is a solution (so that these situations are not normative gaps in our sense), but one that is axiologically inadequate. However, not every bad or unjust solution is regarded as a gap; jurists speak of gaps—in this new sense which we are trying to characterise—when the solution is inadequate *because* the legislator did not take into account some distinction which he should have taken into account. This type of gap presupposes the existence of some relevant property (relevant in the prescriptive sense), which is, nevertheless, irrelevant (in the descriptive sense) for the system in question. In other words: a property which ought to be relevant is irrelevant for the system.

This type of gap will be called *axiological gap*, in order to distinguish it from normative gap . . ." (1971: 106–7).

because of his cycling in the park, there is one right legal answer: he should be acquitted. In both cases what the court must do follows from its characterisation as a law-applying organ.[12]

According to the position under criticism here, an Argentinean judge in 1971 would have discretion to solve a case characterised by properties *ABC*, because the law did not offer a solution for that case. I submit that their position is made plausible because, as Kelsen said, to apply the law according to its literal meaning is (assuming that the rightful owner is suing the possessor) deemed to be morally–politically objectionable. I would follow Kelsen in saying that if in a case like this the judge has discretion, it is *not* because there is a "normative gap", but because there is an "axiological gap". In support of this claim I would simply point out the very many cases (like the case of the Scottish married couple) of "normative" gaps in which, because there is no gap in the "axiological" sense, we would not be inclined to think of the judge having discretion. In brief: *it is impossible to discriminate, without evaluative arguments* (of the sort the sources thesis rules out), between cases that are to be treated as legal gaps and those that are to be treated simply as cases in which the plaintiff did not have a legal ground for his claim. How can it be said (without using such arguments) "if the law does not punish the theft of electricity[13] that is a gap" and at the same time "if the law does not punish drinking orange juice that is not a gap"? A normative gap (what is common to the theft-of-electricity case and the drinking-orange-juice case, i.e. the fact that none of these actions figures on the operative facts of any valid legal rule) is not enough for the court to have discretion. Only axiological gaps can be a source of discretion for the court. But according to the sources thesis axiological gaps are not legal gaps, since they are defined, as we saw, as cases in which "there is a solution but one that is axiologically inadequate" (*see* above, 80, n. 11). Hence, the existence of gaps cannot provide an explanation of legal disagreement compatible with the sources thesis.

Let us now consider the reasons why Raz believes that legal gaps exist. In fact, he thinks that they *must* exist. Raz's case is interesting because he does not make the mistake of believing that an answer to (a) is an answer to (b): "contrary to much popular imagining, there are no gaps when the law is silent" (1979b: 77). But this does not mean that the law is gapless. Indeed, Raz seems to believe that gaps are an unavoidable consequence of the sources thesis:

A dispute is regulated if questions of the form "In this case should the court decide

[12] Needless to say, I am assuming that no norm exists in the system that grants every person a general right to do whatever is not prohibited by the law. If this is the case (as it is in most legal systems today) the answer to Dworkin's point is even simpler: the logical distinction between "internal" and "external" negation holds only if there is no rule in the system that makes an external negation equivalent to an internal one.

[13] This is Kelsen's example: *cf.* Kelsen, 1967: 246. German law made it a crime to steal movables, but electricity is clearly not movable and even more clearly not unmovable. Was the theft of electricity a crime?

> that p?" have a correct legal answer. It is unregulated if some of these questions do not have a correct answer, i.e. if there is a gap in the law applying to the case (1979a: 181).
>
> Are such gaps inevitable? It seems that the sources thesis makes them unavoidable since it makes law dependent on human action with its attendant indeterminacies (1979: 73).

According to Raz, there are three independent situations in which the sources thesis "makes legal gaps unavoidable":

1. *Open texture.* "A cause of legal gaps [...] is the indeterminacy of language, of intention and of other facts" (1979a/b: 73) The first kind of legal gaps that the sources thesis makes unavoidable is explained by the open texture of language. I hope that by now it is clear why this explanation will not work as an explanation of legal disagreement: on the one hand, open texture (in the first of the two senses in which Hart used the expression that will be distinguished below, at 89f) does not by itself imply the kind of uncertainty that is characteristic of legal disagreement, as was argued in the previous chapter and Hart himself recognised (see Hart, 1967: 106, discussed below at 113f). Indeterminacy is not an interesting problem in autonomous institutions (e.g. chess), hence, the fact of an institution being what I called "regulatory" makes a difference that an open texture-based solution cannot explain. The same could be said about the indeterminacy of intention: who cares, when applying the offside rule, what the intention of FIFA was?

2. *Conflicting laws.* The second kind of gap is due to the possibility of conflict between laws. Raz distinguishes two types of conflict. On the one hand there can be a conflict because two conflicting legal reasons are balanced: "they cancel each other and it is false that there is a conclusive reason for the act and false that there is a conclusive reason for its omission . . .. This kind of situation involves no unresolved conflict nor any legal gap" (1979a/b: 75). Completely different, however,

> is a situation of unresolved conflict. It arises when conflicting reasons fail to override each other, not because they are equally matched, but because they are not matched at all: for whatever reason, the conflicting reasons are incommensurable as to strength. In such a case it would be wrong to say that the agent is permitted to perform the act. But it would be equally wrong to say that he is not permitted to perform it (1979:a/b 75).[14]

Is this situation at all possible? Note the special vocabulary Raz is using here: he is not talking of conflicting "laws" but conflicting "legal reasons". I will take them, however, to be the same (*cf.* 1979a/b: 65–6).[15] How can two (or more) laws be incommensurable?

[14] Ronald Dworkin has drawn a very similar distinction between these two cases of conflicting laws: *cf.* 1991: 89. As he rejects the sources thesis, however, his argument is not liable to the objection presented below against legal incommensurability.

[15] "Two common answers to "Why ought one to *f*?" are "Because there is a new law to that effect" or "Because last year Parliament decreed so". Both come much to the same thing" (1979a/b: 65).

In *The Morality of Freedom*, Raz gives three independent sources of incommensurability: 1) the "'incomplete' definition of the contribution of criteria to a value" (1986: 326);[16] 2) the "vagueness and the absence of sharp boundaries which infect language generally and therefore apply to value measured by a single criterion as well" (1986: 327);[17] and 3) the fact that "value is often determined by the probability that the option will produce certain effects. Judgments of probability are infected by considerable incommensurabilities of their own" (*ibid.* 327).

If the sources thesis is true, the existence and strength of a legal reason will depend upon its source only. Hence the first and the third sources of incommensurability are of no use here: the first because there will be only one criterionæthe relevant social sourceæto the determination of valueæthe correctness of a legal answer, the third because if the sources thesis is true, then the test to determine the existence and content of any law will be backward-looking: it will look for a social source in the past, not for the consequences in the future. Only the second could explain why legal reasons (i.e. legal rules, laws) could be incommensurable. Unfortunately, the second sense is the most doubtful of all. In the first place, it is not clear at all that the situation in the second is to be regarded as one of incommensurability. In Raz's signpost example, it seems to me that the proper way to describe the situation would be to say that if the signpost is too small it is not visible (or barely visible) while if it is too big it is difficult to see as well. Some of the sizes in between will be better than others, but many of them will be equally visible. This description would involve no incommensurability, since different sizes are definitely more, less or equally visible than others (Raz did not think an argument was needed to show why the contrary was "likely to happen").

Nevertheless, even if I am wrong in this respect, and the situation with the visibility of the signpost is one of incommensurability, as an explanation of legal gaps it amounts to a repetition of the argument of open texture: if there is incommensurability in the second case it will be due to the "vagueness and the absence of sharp boundaries which infect language generally" (Raz, 1986: 327). Hence the possibility of conflicting laws involves no new reason for us to think that the sources thesis makes legal gaps unavoidable.

3. *Discretion.* The last kind of gap that the sources thesis makes unavoidable also arises "out of conflict situations" (1979: 75):

[16] "This is most obvious where a value is a function of several criteria, so that a good novelist, for example, might be judged by his humour, his insight, his imaginativeness and so on. It is possible that our weighting of the different criteria does not establish complete ranking of all possible combinations" (1986: 326).

[17] "Suppose one is judging how good a signpost is by its visibility. Its visibility depends, let us simplify, on its size only. The bigger it is the more visible it is, until it reaches a certain point beyond which its visibility declines . . .. There is likely to be a range of sizes regarding which it will be neither true nor false both that different signs are of equal visibility and that one is more visible than the other" (1986: 327).

> The law may make certain legal rules have prima facie force only by subjecting them to moral or other non-source-based considerations. Let us assume, for example, that by law contracts are valid only if not immoral. Any particular contract can be judged to be prima facie valid if it conforms to the "value-neutral" conditions for the validity of contract laid down by law. The proposition "It is legally conclusive that this contract is valid" is neither true nor false until a court authoritatively determines its validity (1979: 75).

As a matter of fact, however, the proposition "It is legally *conclusive* that this contract is valid" is false: the court can decide otherwise, because "by the sources thesis courts have discretion when required to apply moral considerations" (1979: 75). If the courts have discretion in this case, then it is true that the contract is not (conclusively) valid (of course, it is also true that the statement "it is legally conclusive that this contract is invalid" is false). Anyway, this case is not interesting, for it is far too contingent. It would explain only those hard cases in which the law *explicitly* refers to moral standards. Recall that we were looking for a reason why the sources thesis made legal gaps *unavoidable*, not only possible.

No gap can make a case hard if the sources thesis is true. There are no "regulative" hard cases in chess, for example; that is the reason why autonomous institutional systems can be formalised (a computer can "play" chess).[18] So, while it might true that "on any matters left open by the rules of chess, a scorer can fix the prevailing standards through his own patterns of decisions, and he can adjust those decisions if he becomes convinced of the wisdom of such a move" (Kramer, 1999: 148) the point about games is that matters are not left open only because they have not been explicitly closed: no rule of football allows, nor specifically permits, players to dye their hair yellow. Was the case of the Romanian team in their 1998 World Cup match against Croatia "unregulated"? Did the referee have discretion? Was the matter "left open"? Yes, no, no. An autonomous institution strictly complies with the sources thesis: the existence and content of the rules of chess can be *completely* determined without using evaluative arguments. *But precisely because evaluative arguments are out of place* in chess- or football-adjudication, there are no unexpected hard cases in football or in any other autonomous institution.[19]

[18] Indeed, attempts to formalise legal rules as games have been formalised have been less than successful: "our attempts to handle legal rules in computer programs make us more careful about believing that rules can have existence outwith a framework of political and/or social factors. If Hart was correct in believing that rules can be easily handled entities and which have an obviousness to both the group and the individual, then it would be possible to believe that rules could simply be valid or not valid and that there were no policy, social or political factors involved in their construction. But that is not the case: if it was so, then we should easily be able to computerize our clear rules of law" (Leith, 1988: 114).

[19] "Unexpected": the attentive reader will remember a hard case in chess like the one discussed by Dworkin (1977: 101ff). I call that an *expected* hard case because it was made hard by the rule's use of a verbal formulation ("*unreasonable* annoyance") that had the precise point of giving the referee some discretion, like the dangerous play or advantage rules in football. This point was dealt with above, at 29f.

In short, legal gaps produce a dilemma for the sources thesis: either they do not exist, and then all cases are regulated by source-based rules, or they exist in an amazing quantity: not only stealing electricity, but also gardening, wearing dark clothes, sleeping at night, sleeping during the day, and an enormous number of other actions which are not explicitly forbidden nor explicitly allowed would constitute, if brought before a court, "unregulated cases", meaning that the court would have discretion to solve them in the most appropriate way.[20] Thus, when looked at from the point of view of legal reasoning, the sources thesis implies either formalism or rule-scepticism.

[20] The list, of course, is jurisdiction-relative (replace as appropriate).

3

Meaning and Application

I have argued in Chapter 2 that the sources thesis cannot explain why, to use Pufendorf's expression, "some latitude" is to be found in legal reasoning. In this chapter I want to offer an explanation for that "latitude", based upon the distinction between the meaning and the application of rules. The way in which this distinction works in law, or so I will argue, cannot be explained by a theory of law that emphasises the distinction between law and morality, but the full argument for this latter claim will have to wait until Chapter 4.

PLAYING ON RAILWAY STATIONS

Let me go back to the "staying awake in railways stations" game mentioned above in Chapter 1. Imagine that you are playing it. The winner is the player who scores the maximum number of points. Points are won in different ways, but players who fell asleep in railway stations suffer a penalty and lose some points:

(1) It will be a fault, punishable by a fine of 5 points, to sleep in any railway station.

Let us now replay Fuller's case. We have seen that if you are a referee your decision has to be in some sense *mechanical*, i.e. you have nothing to do except to apply the rule. As we saw in the first chapter, if you are playing the game you cannot avoid applying the rule; if you don't apply it, you are caught in a performative contradiction: the propositional content of the presuppositions of your action contradicts what you are saying or doing (for the idea of a performative contradiction, *see* Habermas, 1993: 55–6; for a similar idea, called by him "performative inconsistency", *see* Finnis, 1980: 74):

(2) We are playing the game "staying awake in railways stations";
(3) "Staying awake in railways stations" is defined (inter alia) by rule (1) above;
(4) This player was found sleeping in a railway station;
(5) It is not the case that this player should suffer a penalty of 5 points.

It is obvious that, for a number of reasons, (5) can indeed be true (*see* below, 93 n. 1). But it is not possible to accept (2) and (5) *at the same time*: if you accept (5) you have to reject (2), because part of the content of (2) is the negation of (5) when (4), as specified in (3). In other words, a player cannot say: "I am doing something that is defined by the fact that *for all p's, if p then q*, and I am faced with a *p*, but *q* is not the case". Or, better, he can decide not to *q*, but if he does so he is giving up the game (or playing a new game).

In other words, the special circumstances of Fuller's two defendants are, insofar as the application of (1) is concerned, irrelevant. Nothing in the example introduces the least complication. The application of (1) does not become "hard" because the first man was sleeping while waiting for his delayed train. This is perfectly compatible with (we could even say, this *is*) Hart's thesis concerning the open texture of language: the reasons why the man fell asleep (and what *else* he or the second were doing at the moment of their arrest) are immaterial to the classification of his behaviour as "sleeping in the railway station". Since that classification is the only important issue for the application of the rule, everything that has no bearing on how to classify their behaviour has equally no bearing on how to apply the rule. Recall the reasons why the "complexity deficit" of rules was rejected (above at 33ff) as an explanation of the difference between games and the law. We see these reasons at work here: the game does not allow for any "complexity deficit", and that's simply the way games are.

But imagine now that *it is the law* that

(6) It shall be a misdemeanour, punishable by fine of £5, to sleep in any railway station.

Now, if we simply look at (6), we shall not see any significant difference. Its operative facts are the same, hence the application of (6) should be triggered by the same facts as the application of (1). But, interestingly, its application is much less straightforward. For a start, we can say that there are two different descriptions of the problem Fuller's example poses. On the first version, it does not raise a legal, only a moral, problem for the judge:

(4) This man was found sleeping in the station
(7) The law is that this man should be fined.

On this description, the facts of Fuller's example might well justify the judge saying

(8) Because of substantive (moral) considerations I should break the law.

but this is scarcely of interest, since we have stipulated that we are not concerned with the *moral* question of what the judge has to do, but only with the *legal* question of what the law requires him to do. We will see that this is the description positivists have to offer of cases of this kind (*see* below, at 101ff).

Compare this description with the one following, which is Fuller's preferred one (or my version of it):

(6) It shall be a misdemeanour, punishable by fine of £5, to sleep in any railway station.
(4) This man was found sleeping in the station.
(9) Because of substantive (moral) considerations, and without denying the truth of (4) nor the validity of (6), it is the law that this man should not be fined.

Under both descriptions, what the judge ultimately has to do is not to fine the man. According to the second, however, that is the *legal* obligation of the judge, while according to the first the judge would be breaking the law in not fining him, however justified he might be from a moral point of view. The question is, of course, whether (9) can be uttered without performative contradiction. If this is answered in the affirmative, as I think it can be, the question of which description is the correct one will then have to be addressed.

I will not, however, address these issues directly. Instead, in what remains of this chapter I will try to approach the first issue from different angles, in order to show that the reason why (5) cannot be uttered without performative contradiction is that in autonomous institutions getting the meaning right is all there is to rule application, while in regulatory institutions this is not necessarily the case. If this conclusion is correct, there will be some conceptual space open to discuss how best to describe the application of rules like (6) to cases like Fuller's, whether in terms of (8) or (9). This will be undertaken in the next chapter. Now I want to begin with a careful reading of Chapter 7 of Hart's *The Concept of Law*, in order to distinguish two different (I believe incompatible) versions of the "open texture" thesis, one that would imply (8) and one that would imply (9).

HART ON OPEN TEXTURE

In this section I want to argue that, if Chapter 7 of Hart's *The Concept of Law* is read carefully, the contrast between his views and those of Fuller on the subject of legal adjudication becomes less obvious than it is usually thought to be (the contrast I have in mind is made bright and sharp in, e.g. Marmor, 1994: 129ff).

I will not offer here a full exposition of Hart's open texture thesis, which has already been touched upon in the first chapter. Suffice it to say that he tried to strike a middle way between what he called "rule formalism" and "rule scepticism", and that to do this he borrowed from F Waismann (1951) the idea of open texture. To make an often-quoted passage even more often quoted,

> If we are to communicate with each other at all, and if, as in the most elementary form of law, we are to express our intentions that a certain type of behaviour be regulated by rules, then the general words we use . . . must have some standard

> instance in which no doubts are felt about [their] application. There must be a core of settled meaning, but there will be, as well, a penumbra of debatable cases in which words are neither obviously applicable nor obviously ruled out (Hart, 1958: 63).

So understood, Hart's is a thesis about the limits of certainty that general classificatory terms can have in natural languages: "[open texture is] a general feature of human language; uncertainty at the borderline is the price to be paid for the use of general classifying terms in *any form of communication* concerning matters of fact" (1994: 128, emphasis added). It is an inescapable feature of natural languages as we know them, and hence is part of the human predicament: if we are to communicate with each other using natural (rather than artificial) languages, then it is pointless to strive to achieve complete certainty. *There is nothing we can do to exclude open texture*, at least insofar as we also want to use general classificatory terms:

> my view was (and is) that the use of any language containing empirical classificatory general terms will, in applying them, meet with borderline cases calling for fresh regulation. This is the feature of language I called 'open texture'" (Hart, quoted by Bix, 1993: 24).

On this first reading of it, the open-texture thesis is one about language, and only derivatively about the law. "Open texture" is not a feature of law but, as Hart explicitly says, one of natural languages. Needless to say, since (or only because) legal rules are expressed in natural languages, the open texture of the latter communicates, so to speak, to the former. Thus it is not surprising at all to hear from Hart that, for example, "whichever device, precedent or legislation, is chosen for the communication of standards of behaviour, these, however smoothly they work over the great mass of ordinary cases, will, at some point where their application is in question, prove indeterminate" (Hart, 1994: 127–8). In this account, since what makes hard cases hard and clear cases clear is "(semantic) uncertainty at the borderline", Fuller's example has to be described according to (8). What the first man was doing was as "core" an instance of the concept-word "sleeping" as it could possibly be.

Immediately after presenting the notion of open texture, and in an apparent effort to cheer the reader up, Hart explains that uncertainty at the borderline is certainly nothing to be afraid of. But in the course of this consolation the nature of the open-texture thesis switches: it ceases to be a thesis about one of the inescapable features of natural languages as we know them, to become one about the *convenience* of having open-textured (i.e. not completely certain and predictable) rules. It ceases to be a feature of language to become one of the law (or, in general, of "regulatory" institutions).

Of course, there is no reason why you cannot argue that *X* is the case and then go on to argue that *X* is also desirable, which is the usual way in which the relevant passages on *The Concept of Law* seem to have been read. But Hart did something more: when arguing about the desirability of open texture, and contradicting his statements quoted above (and many others) Hart conceded that *it is possible*, for us here and now, to eliminate the uncertainty at the borderline, i.e. "to freeze the meaning of the rule so that its general terms must have the same meaning in every case where its application is in question" (1994: 129).

He even explained to us how:

> To secure this we may fasten on certain features present in the plain case and insist that these are both necessary and sufficient to bring anything which has them within the scope of the rule, whatever other features it may have or lack, and whatever may be the social consequences of applying the rule in this way (*ibid.*).

And if we were to follow his advice,

> we shall *indeed succeed* in settling in advance, but also in the dark, issues which can only reasonably be settled when they arise and are identified (*ibid.*, 130, emphasis added).

Suppose, then, that we *do indeed succeed* in settling in advance the outer limits of the law. Then, the explanation of their uncertainty must lie in the reasons why it is not convenient for us to do so, i.e. the reasons why these cases "can only reasonably be settled when they arise and are identified". In other words, if we *can* eliminate the uncertainty at the borderline, then it is simply wrong to say that the reason why the law is uncertain at the borderline is because the uncertainty at the borderline *cannot* be eliminated; the reason why the law is uncertain at the borderline is *not* some inescapable feature of general classificatory terms in natural languages, but the very different one that it is *unreasonable* to try to settle "in advance, but also in the dark" issues we cannot yet identify.

Following this second line of argumentation, Hart explains that he is dealing not with a limitation on the levels of certainty imposed on human beings by the language they (we) happen to have, but with the very different issue of striking a correct balance between two competing "social needs", namely

> the need for certain rules . . . and the need to leave open, for later settlement by an informed, official choice, issues which can only be properly appreciated and settled when they arise in a concrete case (*ibid.*).

And furthermore, this tension is one that "*in fact*, all legal systems, in different ways" solve reaching some kind of compromise (*ibid.*, emphasis added). Open texture, then, is not an external limit that language imposes on the levels of certainty human beings can achieve, but the *consequence of a normative decision*, i.e. a decision about how best to balance the requirements of certainty with those of appropriateness. Given this alternative account, then, the correct description of Fuller's example might very well be (9), assuming that, as a matter of fact, the case was one of those "left open" for future settlement.

(Some stipulations will be of use here: (a) I will call "certainty" the first of the social needs Hart distinguished and (b) "appropriateness" the second; (c) I will talk of "application" when referring to the problem of how a rule should be applied to a particular case, and (d) of "meaning" when referring to that of grasping a rule's meaning).

It is important to emphasise that, as we have seen, what a hard (clear) case is varies according to each of these interpretations of the open-texture thesis. On the first interpretation, a case will be hard when the facts are such that they do not fit naturally and uncontroversially one or more of the general classificatory terms of the relevant rules, i.e. when it is what I have called a "semantic" hard case (when, for example, the rule forbids you to go into the park with a vehicle and you want to use a toy car in it). On the second interpretation, however, the point is not uncertainty at the borderline. As we can "indeed succeed" in having clear and certain rules (regardless of the features of natural languages), a case will be hard because what is at issue is *not the classification of particulars in the world*, but the very different one of whether or not *this* case was one of those left "open, for later settlement by an informed, official choice" even if it is covered by the semantic meaning of the rule in question (was the case of the veteran's memorial settled when the "no vehicles" rule was issued or was it "left open"?). The second explanation of open texture contained in *The Concept of Law* is thus based on the idea of an evaluative, not a semantic, notion of the clear/hard cases divide.

We now go back to the case of the man sleeping in the station. According to the first Hartian explanation of open texture, the case is clear insofar as what the man did is a core-instance of the term "sleeping". In Fuller's example this is true by stipulation, hence the case cannot but be clear. But on the second explanation the situation is different. Though the man was indeed sleeping in the station, it is possible to think that this case is not covered by the rule, in the sense that it was "left open for future settlement" (indeed, many would say something stronger than this, that the case wasn't really left open: the rule does not apply, obviously, because in this case the requirements of appropriateness are much stronger than those of certainty).

We can link this conclusion to the first chapter's main argument: this is what makes the law so different from games. *In games there are no evaluative hard cases*, because in autonomous institutions there are no issues that are "left open for future settlement" unless they are explicitly left open (*see* the dangerous play rule, quoted above at 31, n. 23). So all we will have to do is to determine the meaning of the rules, and then, *providing that we are participating in that activity*, the rule will be, in a sense, self-applying. The rules define what you have to do to participate in the activity: if you do participate, your doing so implies your not questioning the application of the rules. If you do question that, you will simply fail to participate in the game (or make a mistake or—which amounts much to the same thing—violate the rules of the game). You can't be a participant if you don't participate; hence the performative contradiction.[1]

Regulatory institutions, in which the norms that make them up are (and, more importantly, are *seen as*) universalisations of substantial reasons, are always open-textured in the second Hartian sense, in the sense, that is, that the solution to the problem of application is not solved by them. The regulatory direction of the institution (i.e. the very feature that distinguishes it from autonomous institutions) creates the possibility of reasonable rules producing inappropriate results: creates, in other words, conceptual space for the problem of application. This is why the institution requires a solution to the

[1] Let me insist on one point, to prevent misunderstandings: the argument does not imply that participants have an all-things-considered duty to apply the rules of the institution: "You can make a dying parent happy by the acclaim that will come to you from appearing to win a game. Will you do so by secretly breaking a rule? This is a moral problem requiring an ultimate decision about which the rules of the game give an unequivocal answer, which you can only reject by rejecting the game (preferring to play your own secret game in order to achieve what you conceive to be a moral purpose)" (Detmold, 1984: 49). There is no reason to think that, because he is refereeing a match of football, an umpire has an overriding or all-things-considered moral duty to apply the rules, and plenty of reasons to believe that he can indeed have a (moral) duty not to do it. Imagine that the match up to then is a tie, and that a member of the local team commits a foul inside his penalty box. The referee knows that if the local team loses it is highly likely that there will be violent riots, and he also has (good) reasons to believe that if there are riots there will be many casualties, perhaps even deaths (unfortunately, this is not too fantastic an example). Imagine, in short, that the situation is such that the correct thing to do for the referee is not to award the penalty kick. Imagine further that the referee fulfils his moral duty and refuses to award the penalty kick. One way of describing the situation would be to say that they are not playing any longer, but of course this is, in a straightforward sense, not necessarily true. What (I think) we would say is that, however justified the referee's action, he was in breach of his duty as referee. If the rule is not applied we know that, *inside the game*, he was definitely wrong, *wrong beyond plausible contestation*. To contest this would be "most kindly taken as a joke" (Rawls, 1955: 38). If they are playing football at all, the rules have to be applied. If, for whatever reasons, the rules are not applied by the referee, then he is either wrong or not refereeing a football match.

This is the reason why, even though we have seen that in autonomous institutions "the normative becomes descriptive" (Bankowski, 1996: 33), this does not imply that no criticism is possible. Remember Wittgenstein's point: "You cook badly if you are guided in your cooking by rules other than the right ones; but if you . . . follow grammatical rules other than such-and-such ones, that does not mean you say something wrong, no, you are speaking of something else" (Wittgenstein, 1967: § 320; the full passage was quoted above). But of course, if I (here and now) follow rules other than those of English grammar (saying for example, "he have thought a lot about it") nobody would think that I am writing in a language of my own invention, but that I made a mistake. This points out the obvious fact that, when we are dealing with autonomous institutions, our criticism of other participants is based on the assumption that they are playing as well. This assumption will be natural in many contexts; but I *could* say, couldn't I, that I wasn't writing in English after all (and then what you will say is that I am wrong in writing in this peculiar language without making that clear; your complaint will not be that I violated the rules of grammar—I wasn't trying to apply them in the first place—but that I failed to do what, for a number of reasons, I had to do: either to write in English or to say that I was not doing so).

Thus we can follow MacCormick and Weinberger's advice and avoid being "saddled with the thesis that the rules of games (e.g. of chess) can never really be broken. For someone who does not conduct himself as the rules requires (e.g. by making diagonal moves with his knight) is by definition failing to play this game, viz., chess. So cheating at chess would be impossible" (MacCormick and Weinberger, 1986: 24). The distinction between failing to follow the rules of chess and cheating at chess is not internal to the rules of chess, so to speak, but external to them: it depends on whether one is wanting to play chess, intentionally misapplying a rule to get an advantage, etc.

competition between certainty and appropriateness, but the norms *are not in a position to give that solution*; the problem is how formally these norms are to be applied, and on this issue these norms cannot but be silent—in Hart's terms (1967: 106), "rules cannot provide for their own application".

PRINCIPLES, RULES AND EXCLUSIONARY REASONS

This point is clearer if we consider the third of Raz's theses about authority, what he calls the "pre-emption thesis". According to it, rules are exclusionary (or "protected") reasons. This means that the rule X, which is a universalisation of substantive reasons *A*, *B*, *C*, to *M*, is not to be *added* to *ABC* to form *ABCX* (in the process of deliberation previous to the decision to *M*), but that it *replaces ABC* and excludes them from consideration. Hard cases, in the evaluative (Hart's open-texture thesis's second) sense, are cases to which the norm applies according to its meaning (the man *was* sleeping in the station), and what is discussed is precisely whether or not the norm should be applied as a rule (i.e. as an exclusionary reason). *Regarding this particular issue, it is clear that the norm itself cannot provide any guidance.* In fact, if the norm is a rule (i.e. an exclusionary reason), we would not have had any problem in the first place. To see the problem we have to consider the substantive reasons. If we are prevented from looking back at them, no problem can arise. It is clear, though, that the problem of ascertaining whether or not (6) should be applied as a *rule* (i.e. an exclusionary reason) has to be answered before any application of it is possible. And it has to be answered for every application of it. And where, if not in the rules, will the answer be found?

I will have something to say on this issue in the final chapter. What, for the time being, is important to notice is that we do have different answers for different instances of the application of the same rule. An argument designed to show the correct legal solution for each of Fuller's men would be recognised by most lawyers as deserving its day in court: the first man, so the argument might go, should not be fined, even though he was actually sleeping, even though his case was literally covered by the rule. But the case of the second man is different. Here the fact that he was not doing that to which the literal formulation of the rule refers (to wit, sleeping) would be an important consideration not to fine him: *nullum crimen sine lege*. The criminal law protects every potential sanctionee by limiting the state's punitive power only to those cases and circumstances in which the sanction was previously intimated. Therefore the second man, who was not sleeping cannot be punished. But it is clear that if we do not fine the first man, the literal meaning-based argument will be rather weak to exclude the second. The explanation for this asymmetry is based on the different position in which the balance between certainty and appropriateness is struck in different situations: because of substantive, moral (or political) reasons, we might regard the case of the first man as a (evaluative) hard case and that of the second as a clear one.

Hence it is misleading to speak of laws as rules, at least if by "rules" one understands something like an exclusionary reason. The fact is, the issue of ascertaining the content of a norm can and should be distinguished from that of establishing how it should be applied: norms can be more or less formal*(ly applied)*. If (6) is applied as an exclusionary reason, the substantive merits of the case will cease to be relevant once it has been shown that the man was sleeping in the station. But (6) could be applied in a less formal way, assuming that *some* of the substantive merits of the case are to be taken into account, but not all of them (hence, for example, neither the first nor the second man should be fined) or with a very low degree of formality, saying that the first man should not be fined but the second should (this decision is even less formal than the previous one because not only in the case of the first, but also in the case of the second man the decision-maker has gone directly towards the substantive reason of which the norm is a universalisation). The *concept* of law does not imply any of these solutions. The solution is not a conceptual one: as Hart said, "in fact all systems, in different ways, compromise" (1994: 130) between form (certainty) and substance (appropriateness). Legal norms might indeed be exclusionary reasons, but if this is offered as a conceptual explanation of what (to follow) a rule is, the problem of application is begged. This is so because in this sense, "rules" are "norms with built-in application procedures" (Habermas, 1996b: 220).

We can now see that the choice between (8) and (9) is not one that a theory of law has to make: it is a *legal* choice. Imagine that I were to say: "if (6) were a rule of Chilean law, and the facts had occurred at Santiago's Central Station, neither the first nor the second man should, according to Chilean law, be fined". This *looks* like an ordinary legal claim. If it is interpreted as a legal claim, however, we would expect a theory of law to be silent about it, in the same way in which a theory of law has nothing to say about the question of whether a particular defendant is guilty as charged (if you were the defendant, would you choose a Chilean lawyer or a legal theorist as your lawyer?). But if we were to claim that legal rules are exclusionary reasons, reasons that (from the legal point of view) should be applied "to the exclusion of all conflicting reasons", would we not be implying that the theory does settle the question of which is the correct description of Chilean law, (8) or (9)? So the claim that rules are exclusionary reasons is a legal claim, as indeed is the pre-emption thesis itself. This is important, because a theory of law that forces upon us solutions that might, for a given legal practice, turn out to be legally wrong is a defective theory of law.[2] This ambiguity between the conceptual and the

[2] This is the sense in which I interpret Dworkin's claim that "jurisprudence is the general part of adjudication, silent prologue to any decision at law" (1986: 90). We can remain agnostic as to a somewhat stronger reading, according to which no decision at law can be rendered without the decision-maker actually invoking such a jurisprudential theory (*see* below, at 170f).

substantive is, I believe, what Fuller was getting at when he complained, regarding the Hartian claim that law and morality were conceptually different, that

> At times [Hart] seemed to be saying that the distinction between law and morality is something that exists, and will continue to exist, however we may talk about it . . . At other times, he seemed to be warning us that the reality of the distinction is itself in danger and if we do not mend our ways of thinking and talking we may lose a "precious moral ideal", that of fidelity to law (Fuller, 1958: 631).

To illustrate this point it would be useful to have a look to what Patrick Atiyah and Robert Summers have to say about formality and formal reasoning. According to them, reasons can be formal or substantive. A substantive reason "is a moral, economic, political, institutional or other social consideration" (1987: 1). A (legal) formal reason "is a legally authoritative reason on which judges and others are empowered or required to base a decision or action, and such reason usually excludes from consideration, overrides, or at least diminishes the weight of, any countervailing substantive reason arising at the point of decision or action" (*ibid.* 2). In these terms, Atiyah and Summers's concept of formal reason is close to that of a rule for Raz (an "exclusionary reason") or Hart (a "content-independent reason": *cf.* Hart, 1982). But Atiyah and Summers do not argue that a rule is, by definition, an exclusionary reason (though they do argue, at 70, that legal rules must be treated as generating reasons with *some* degree of formality). They distinguish amongst four senses of "formality" and then suggest that a rule *can score differently in each sense.*[3]

There is, however, a crucial difference between Raz's exclusionary reasons and Atiyah and Summers's formal reasons. I think, in fact, that they stem from the same basic idea, but are very dissimilar indeed. In particular, I do not think that Raz would be at ease speaking of "higher" and "lower" formality. Since something cannot be "half-excluded", he would, I suppose, argue that formality ("exclusionary-ness") is an all-or-nothing feature: the fact that he

[3] Atiyah and Summers's four types of formality are: authoritative formality, content formality, interpretive formality and mandatory formality. *Authoritative* formality is divided into two ideas: the *validity* formality of a rule (a rule has a high degree of validity formality if its validity is determined only with reference to its sources) and its *rank* formality (its level inside the legal hierarchy of the respective legal system). A rule's *content* formality is determined by two factors: "the extent to which the rule is shaped by *fiat* and the extent to which it is under-inclusive or over-inclusive in relation to its objectives, that is, the extent to which cases which the purpose of the rule would embrace are omitted from the rule's coverage, and cases which the purpose of the rule do not embrace are in fact covered by the rule" (1987: 13). *Interpretive* formality refers to the process of interpretation of the rule. This process can be less formal and more substantive in two ways: it "may be substantive to the extent that the interpreter searches for and gives effect to underlying purposes and rationales which are implicit in the text or which can be ascertained from other sources (such as legislative history). Sometimes no such purposes or rationales can be identified, but interpretation can still be substantive to the extent that the decision-maker then relies on substantive reasons . . . drawn from other, non legal, sources" (*ibid.*, 15). Finally, *mandatory* formality is a function of the "extent to which otherwise relevant substantive considerations are . . . excluded, overridden, or diminished in weight" (*ibid.*).

allows for discussion as to what the *scope* of an exclusionary reason is (*cf.* Raz, 1992: 46ff) is not an objection to, but a proof of this point, for given whatever scope the rule happens to have, it is exclusionary, in Raz's view, inside these boundaries. In fact, Atiyah and Summers explicitly reject Raz's and Hart's analysis in this regard.[4]

In Atiyah and Summers's view, the level of mandatory and interpretive formality of a rule *is not determined by the rule itself.* If we are trying to know how the rule should be applied, a reference to the rule itself is quite unhelpful. But here we come full circle to the question we by-passed before: once we have grasped the meaning of the rule, should it be applied regardless of other considerations of substance? One answer that will not do is if the rule is a rule (i.e. an exclusionary reason), it should be applied regardless of any substantive consideration, because these substantive considerations are pre-empted by the rule. From Atiyah and Summers's point of view (as for Hart in the second interpretation of his open-texture thesis), this would not be so straightforward. Sometimes, when presented with a case in which the application of a rule has unexpected consequences, the correct solution might well be to disregard those consequences because of considerations of predictability (certainty). In other cases, the right solution will be to look for the appropriate norm to be applied, regardless of the literal meaning of the rule. But what is interesting in Atiyah and Summers's model is that it makes clear the point noted above, i.e. that "formality" is not something that is attached to some normative standards (therefore called rules) but a *mode of reasoning* (Klaus Günther has made a similar point: *see* 1993b: 269). When facing a problem, the decision-maker will have to *decide* if the norms to be applied are to be *applied as rules* (i.e. exclusionary reasons). To decide that they are to be so applied is to assume that predictability's (rule of law's, etc.) requirements are more important in the case than those of appropriateness.

What kind of factors affect the formality recognised to a legal norm? A full answer to this question is bound to be jurisdiction-relative, for the reasons offered in Chapter 8. We can consider, as an illustration, Patrick Atiyah's claim about the reasons for what he calls "the decline of formal reasoning":

> a will, for example, or a contract required to be in writing, may be declared void or unenforceable if the formalities are not observed. In such cases we do not stop . . . to ask whether the failure to comply with the formal requirements is outweighed by some other substantive reason in favour of giving legal force to the will or contract. Once the legal rule of ineffectiveness for lack of form is clearly established, the application of that rule shuts out from consideration the substantive arguments in favour of validity or enforcement (1984: 94).

Interestingly enough, Atiyah acknowledges not only that legal reasoning is both substantive and formal, but also that there has been a trend "in contract

[4] "Here in particular we depart from Raz, Hart and others who see mandatory formality as categorical or on–off rather than a matter of degree" (Atiyah and Summers, 1987: 17n. *See* also 408).

law and, indeed, perhaps in all of the law" towards substantive to the detriment of formal reasoning (1984: 93). The reason Atiyah gives for this change of attitude towards form is that one of the presuppositions of formal reasoning is that "substantive reasons either will be, or have been, or at least could have been, more appropriately and satisfactorily dealt with another time, or in some other manner, or by some other person" (*ibid*, 118). The same point is stressed by Bankowski, who claims that "the implication is that at some time the substantive problems were solved rationally and thus we can now afford to use formal reasoning" (1993: 13).

And this presupposition is deemed to fail each time more frequently: "one of the reasons why formal reasons are today less favoured in contract law may stem from increasing doubts as to whether the reasons of substance which bear more directly on the result have ever been properly weighed by anyone" (Atiyah, 1984: 119). Given these "increasing doubts", says Atiyah, each time judges are more prone to "unpick the transaction, to open it up, as it were, and go behind the formal reasons, and look at the substantive reasons for the creation or the negativing of obligations" (*ibid*, 116).

In other words, "ruleness" (if by "rule" anything like "exclusionary reason" is meant) is not a feature of a normative standard (therefore called *a rule*) by virtue of what that norm *is*, but in virtue of the peculiar (exclusionary) features of the application procedure the decision-maker uses when deciding what to do. Recall Habermas's claim that rules are "norms with built-in application procedures" (1996b: 220). Thus the distinction, for example, between principles and rules is not a classification of legal *norms*, but a typology of *legal reasoning*: what a decision-maker has is a set of legal norms, and the question of whether they are rules or principles is a first-order legal question not to be answered by a theory of law, but a first-order legal claim.

Now consider Peczenik and Hage's characterisation of principles:

> In their purest form, principles are one-sided in that they refer to only one aspect of the case to which they apply. For instance, the principle that one should not hold political prisoners generates a reason to release the leader of some secession movement. It does not take into account that this leader may cause much social upheaval, the prevention of which (another goal) may provide a reason to keep this leader imprisoned. Both goals, the avoidance of political prisoners and the avoidance of social upheaval are one-sided in that they only refer to one side of the case. They generate colliding reasons, corresponding to different sides of the same case. In order to give a balanced judgment on the case as a whole the contributing reasons generated by the different goals must be balanced (2000: 309).

But the problem is, we can understand the "principle" that one should not hold political prisoners as a rule if we understand it precisely as *not* one-sided: we can say that the *rule* that one should not hold political prisoners *does* take into account the increased risk of social upheaval we might be running, only to declare that the value to be served by the government's not being allowed to hold political prisoners trumps it in all cases. Both this claim and the opposite one, that it is a *principle* and therefore is one-sided and subject to negotiation in the light of competing values, are possible interpretations of the directive "no governmental official shall be allowed to hold political prisoners". The norm itself will not tell us which interpretation is correct. In the same spirit, we could understand Pufendorf's Bolognese norm as a rule (because it reflected not only the (negative) value attached to streets fights but also the (positive) value of cleanliness in public places, in such a way that these two values together would trump any other value or constellation of values) or as a principle (because it does not assume such a balancing of values. It simply declares the values behind it to be important, but it says nothing about *other* values: this is something that is "left open for later, official settlement when the issue arises and is identified"). Maybe this is Peczenik and Hage's point when they claim that "the logical distinction between rules and principles does not answer the question whether some rule-like entity is a rule or a principle" (2000: 313).

Thus, legal norms can be applied as rules, i.e. as exclusionary reasons, but there is no reason to think that only because they are *legal* norms they have to be so applied. If legal norms were exclusionary reasons by virtue of their being legal, then we could not distinguish between cases in which the rules can be applied "without fresh official guidance or weighing up of social issues" and those that were "left open for future settlement". The distinction can only be made on the basis of the reasons of substance that apply to the case, reasons the legal norm (if understood as an exclusionary reason) would exclude from consideration. Because we can and do distinguish, to say that a given norm—say, (6) above, at 88—is to be applied as a rule (i.e. an exclusionary reason) *is to offer a solution to the tension between certainty and appropriateness*, a solution the correctness of which will not be established by any amount of conceptual argumentation, because it is not a conceptual question. Hence,

> the artificial conventionalization of legal norms as positivized "rules" requires an additional justification. It is only on this premise that one can justify, from an internal perspective, why situational context may be left unconsidered when applying norms as rules (Günther, 1993: 270).

These remarks are not meant to be taken as stipulations like those offered above at 92. Their point is to note that the concept of an exclusionary reason hides away a crucial problem for legal reasoning: if rules are exclusionary reasons, then *there is no conceptual space for the problem of application.* If, on the other hand, I am correct in saying that the property "ruleness" (or exclusionary-ness) cannot be attached to legal norms, then there is no such hiding away: how rule-like (exclusionary) the application of a norm like (6) must be in a case such as Fuller's example is *the* issue that makes his an example of a hard case. But if a rule is an exclusionary reason this problem *would never appear*, because to see it we would have to consider precisely the kind of reasons that the "rule" was meant to exclude.

Hence, though (6) is not a rule (an exclusionary reason), it can be applied *as* one. The point I have been arguing for in this section is that this can be done only after having decided that, in the case, certainty outweighs appropriateness. It can be the case, however, that no good substantive reason to treat (6) as a rule can be found, and hence that it has to be treated as (say) a principle. In that case, (6) will be taken as *evidence* for the existence of some substantive reason that deserves the court's attention. Maybe the substantive reason behind (6) is to keep railway stations clean; maybe the first man's behaviour did not affect the reasons behind (6), while the second's did. Maybe in this case the correct (legal) solution for the case is to fine the second man and release the first, even though only the first was "sleeping".

Now we are in a position to see, I hope, where the problem of Hart's open-texture thesis (in its first interpretation) lies: it assumes that interpretive problems are problems of ascertaining the precise meaning of a given rule. On this (first) interpretation of the open-texture thesis, Hart has to assume that *legal norms settle their own status* (i.e. that rules can do precisely what Hart would later deny they can do, to wit, "provide for their own application"—*cf.* Hart, 1967: 106), that we only need to read (6) to know that it is a rule, and we need only to know that(6) is a rule in order to know how it should be applied (i.e. as an exclusionary reason). Only if it is assumed that (6) *is* (as opposed to "is—or can be—applied *as*) a rule (meaning an exclusionary reason), Hart's open-texture thesis (on its first interpretation) can be accepted.

In fact, if legal norms are considered to *be* exclusionary reasons, the lack of clarity in the meaning of the norm will be the only explanation available for the fact of legal disagreement. This is so because, as we have seen, to say of some norm that it is a rule (meaning an exclusionary reason) *is to solve* the problem of application. It is to say that you should not consider any other relevant feature of the case than those enumerated by the rule: That is (they say) what *following a rule* means.

I think that an argument like the one presented in this section is the real gist of Fuller's criticism of Hart and because of this I think it would be useful to turn to that debate and to some recent answers that have been offered on Hart's behalf. This will be the subject of Chapter 4.

4

Fuller v. *Fuller*

In a nutshell, Fuller's objection to Hart's distinction between core and penumbra was that it is not possible to understand the meaning of a rule without inquiring into the rule's purpose. Meaning, said Fuller, is context-sensitive in a way that Hart seemed to neglect. If this is the case, it follows that no straightforward distinction between clear and hard cases is available. In every situation it will be necessary to ascertain the purpose of the rule to know its meaning: it will never be the case that rules can be clearly applied without any inquiry into their purpose. In what follows, I will discuss Fuller's critique of Hart's distinction in terms of the defeasibility of legal rules. His point, in a way, was that legal rules, however clear their literal meaning, might always turn out to have implicit exceptions, exceptions that can be ascertained only by looking into the rules' "purpose". The ripostes we shall be considering in this chapter amount, in different ways, to the claim that the defeasibility of legal rules is not an interesting issue for legal theory, either because it is a moral rather than a legal problem (in the first section), or because it is a contingent feature of contemporary rules, hence it is as theoretically important as the fact that sometimes judges wear wigs (in the second section). Here we shall not only be concerned with the particular authors to be discussed, but with a proper explanation for the defeasibility of legal rules. Indeed, I tend to think that the two options that we are about to consider (i.e. defeasibility either as a moral rather than a legal problem or as the consequence of a contingent decision) are the only plausible candidates for an explanation of that feature of legal rules that wants to be faithful to the alleged "conceptual" distinction between law and morality.

IS DEFEASIBILITY A NON-LEGAL, MORAL PROBLEM?

In his *Interpretation and Legal Theory*, Andrei Marmor has tried to show the feasibility of a positivist distinction between clear and hard cases. This led him to consider a position like Fuller's, which negates the possibility of such a distinction. He called Fuller's the "objection [to the clear/hard cases distinction] from defeasibility", and answered it with the argument to be criticised below. Though Marmor's arguments clearly fail, in my view, to defeat Fuller's objection, in a way his argument is clear and uncompromising, and that makes it worthwhile to consider it in some detail. This I will do in the second subsection below, while in the first I will use Marmor's criticism of Fuller to rescue Fuller's argument from Fuller himself.

Clear cases and mechanical jurisprudence

During his sustained defence of a Hartian theory of law, Marmor found that he had to defend the distinction between clear and hard cases. He (rightly, in my view) thinks that positivism needs that distinction, understood as one "between (so-called) easy cases, where the law can be applied straightforwardly, and hard cases, where the issue is not determined by the existing legal standards" (1994: 124). This led Marmor to consider Lon Fuller's criticism of Hart's position, based as it was upon a denial of that distinction. The purpose of Marmor's argument concerning clear cases, he tells us, is to determine "whether the distinction between easy and hard cases has any conceptual basis which is independent of the legal positivist doctrine" (*ibid.* 125). But before beginning the main argument, Marmor sets aside two "crude miscontruals" regarding clear cases:

> First, one cannot overemphasise the warning that the terms "easy" and "hard" cases are potentially misleading. The distinction has nothing to do with the amount of intellectual effort required in order to decide a legal case . . .. Nor is there any intended implication here that application of the law in easy cases is in some way "mechanical" or "automatic" as it is sometimes suggested. There is nothing mechanical about the application of a rule to a particular case, nor is there necessarily anything complex or difficult about solving most of the hard cases (*ibid.* 127).

The first remark is both true and important. The intellectual effort I would have to use to solve a complex mathematical operation is enormous (most likely beyond *my* capabilities), but this does not stop mathematical operations from being "easy" in this sense (that is the reason why, following Hart, I am using "clear" instead of "easy"). The second is more opaque. "Mechanical applicator of rules" might not be a fashionable job description, but *if* a clear case exists, then the person called to solve the case *is* performing an activity which in some sense can be called "automatic" or "mechanical", just as in the situation of a referee: if you see a foul, (automatically) award a free kick, don't think about it. It is this "don't-think-about-it-ness" that justifies the label "mechanical". The operation is automatic because the only thing that the referee should do is to apply a pre-existing rule to a set of facts that fits the rule's operative facts, without considering any other feature of the case. This follows from Marmor's definition of a clear case ("where the law can be applied straightforwardly"). A computer can "play chess" only because rules of chess can be applied "mechanically". This is something Hart saw when he contrasted "deciding cases in an automatic and mechanical way" with "deciding cases by reference to social purposes" (1958: 68) The fact that

Marmor does not see anything "mechanical" in the positivistic description of the application of a rule to a clear case seems to suggest that he did not understand the point of the metaphor. When you are mechanically applying a rule, you only have to check whether or not the operative facts of the rule are fulfilled: if they are, apply the rule; if they are not, do not (next case). In fact, it seems difficult to see how an exclusionary reason can be applied at all if not in a mechanical or automatic way.[1]

But let us not pause for long in minor skirmishes. Marmor's argument is that Hart's distinction between "core" and "penumbra" provides the "independent conceptual basis" for the distinction between clear and hard cases both of them are anxious to establish. Cases that fall into the core of a law are clear, cases that fall into its penumbra are hard. I will try to clarify this using Hart's famous example of the rule "no vehicles shall be taken into the park".

In using that example, Hart's point was that, while we may disagree about the application of the word "vehicle" to many particulars in the world, we would not have understood the *meaning* of it unless we are able to distinguish the kind of objects that are plain instances of it. Our grasping of the meaning of that word *is* our acquiring the ability to recognise such instances. This is clearly something Fuller did not agree with:

> What would Professor Hart say if some local patriots wanted to mount on a pedestal in the park a truck used in World War II, while other citizens, regarding the proposed memorial as an eyesore, support their stand by the "no vehicle" rule? Does this truck, in perfect working order, fall within the core or the penumbra? (1958: 663).

Hart would have to say that a truck is a standard case of the word "vehicle" (Hart, 1994: 126). Fuller's point could be read (though he did not put it in such a way) as amounting to the fact that the understanding of the meaning of a law is only part of what the judge has to do when solving a case. Once he has learned that there is a norm against vehicles in the park and that the memorial has been proposed, he has to ask himself, "how formal should the application of this legal norm be? Which substantive issues are pre-empted by it?".

But Fuller, as a matter of fact, did argue that Hart's views were mistaken because Hart's theory of meaning was mistaken. When Fuller claimed that "the most obvious defect of [Hart's] theory lies in its assumption that problems of interpretation typically turn on the meaning of individual words" (1958: 662) his complaint was that Hart focused on the meaning of *individual* words, not that he focused on the *meaning* of individual words. In other words, Fuller conceded Hart's unstated premiss that all that there is to application is getting the meaning right:

[1] Maybe Marmor is just saying that there is nothing mechanical here, because in any case a human being has to apply the rule. I find the idea that human beings cannot do anything that is mechanical rather bizarre (I shall come back to this point, when discussing the relevance of deductive reasoning for an explanation of Hartian clear cases: *see* below, at 172f).

> I have stressed here the deficiencies of Professor Hart's theory as that theory affects judicial interpretation. I believe, however, that its defects go deeper and result ultimately from a mistaken theory about the meaning of language generally. Professor Hart seems to me to subscribe to what might be called "the pointer theory of meaning", a theory which ignores or minimizes the effect on the meaning of words of the speaker's purpose and the structure of language (*ibid.*, 668-9).

Fuller's main objection to Hart's theory of meaning is that it does not account for the speaker's intention and holds that meaning is "context-insensitive" (I think this is what Fuller had in mind when he wrote about "the structure of language": the fact that meaning is context-sensitive, something he thought Hart would deny. That this interpretation is faithful to Fuller's idea seems to follow from his comment on Wittgenstein's *Philosophical Investigations* (*ibid.*, 669), which he quoted as giving support to his own view: "[it] constitutes a sort of running commentary on the ways words shift and transform their meanings as they move from context to context").

Wasn't Fuller, fighting windmills here, however? Hart could easily accommodate these two objections without having to give up his core/penumbra account of meaning (and of legal interpretation). This point has been persuasively argued by Marmor (1994: 129–35), who argued that "either a word has a meaning, in which case it can be used, and hence it must also have standard examples, or it is devoid of meaning, in which case it simply cannot be used" (*ibid.*, 134–5). We cannot understand a word if we are not able to recognise something as a standard instance of it. These instances are said to constitute the "core" of the meaning of the word. But words also have a "penumbra" of meaning, i.e. the application of a word to some facts will prove controversial or uncertain.

Marmor then goes on to link Hart's argument to a "highly sophisticated conception of meaning and language, namely, that of Wittgenstein" (1994: 125). His point in doing this was (as I understand it) to give further support to the idea that there must be cases in which no interpretation is needed for the application of a rule:

> if a rule could not determine which actions were in accord with it, then no interpretation could do this either. Interpretation is just another formulation of the rule, substituting one rule for another, as it were. Hence it cannot bridge the gap between rule and action (Marmor, 1994: 149; commenting on Wittgenstein, 1958: § 198).

This argument might eventually be enough to accept Marmor's claim that Fuller was wrong in thinking that *the meaning* of a norm can only be understood in the light of its purpose. We do not need *any* information about the purpose of the modification of the offside rule, nor about the purpose, if there is such a thing, of the rule about the correct tense-formation in English. Even in the case of legal rules Fuller's claim is, I believe, often false. Indeed, *we know the meaning of* (6): we know the kind of cases that would accord with the rule and the kind of cases that would not. But the strength of Fuller's point (and conversely that of Marmor's criticism of Fuller) changes radically if it is taken to be about *application* rather than *meaning*. In this reading, Hart's account is insufficient not because his theory of meaning is wrong, but because he thought that problems of legal interpretation were problems of getting to the *meaning* of the relevant legal norms, while legal interpretive problems (at least *also*) arise when it is unclear how formal the *application* of the norm has to be, when it is not clear whether or not some substantive consideration prompted by some features of the case are excluded or pre-empted. Fuller, no doubt, had this problem in mind, but he mixed it up with that of getting the meaning of a legal norm "really" right:

> If a statute seems to have a kind of "core meaning" that we can apply without a too precise inquiry into its exact purpose, this is because we can see that, however one might formulate the precise objective of the statute, this case would still come within it (1958: 663).

Note that Fuller is not saying something here about an abstract example taken to be in the core of the meaning of the norm. He is talking of a *particular* and *concrete* case; he is saying that *this singular case* is covered by the norm. In my reading of Fuller, we should read the passage just quoted as follows:

> If a statute seems to have a kind of "core meaning" that we can apply without a too precise inquiry into its exact purpose, this is because we can see that however one might formulate the precise objective of the statute, this case does not display any feature giving rise to substantive considerations not pre-empted by the rule.

If I am right, Marmor's objections to Fuller's conception of meaning are correct, but he hit the wrong target. No doubt it is possible to understand a rule without even knowing the purpose of it, no doubt the military truck was a core-instance of the word "vehicle". We saw that no appeal to the purpose of the law was necessary in ancient Roman law, because legal norms were not seen as universalisations of substantive reasons. You did have to answer *spondeo* and not another synonym, not because that was the correct way to serve some substantive reason, but because there was no other way of contracting. The possibility of legal systems like Ancient Rome's shows that no general statement about legal norms being impossible to apply without grasping their purposes can be true, but this is not to say that legal norms in the twentieth century can be equally applied. For this you would need an additional argument, an argument that Marmor, who did not see the point, was not in a position to provide.

To clarify the argument so far, consider the following sets of theses:

(10) The meaning of a rule determines its application; problems of legal interpretation arise only because of the ambiguity, uncertainty or vagueness of the meaning of a rule; hence

(10.1) If the meaning of a legal rule is not ambiguous, uncertain or vague, the case is clear; but

(10.2) Because of structural features of natural languages (open texture in its first interpretation), it is not possible to get *any* rule with a completely certain, unambiguous and precise meaning; hence

(10.3) Whenever rules (*any* rule) are expressed in natural-language words, problems of interpretation are bound to arise.

(11) Meaning is use: to know the meaning of a word is to be able to produce on request standard instances to which the word applies; Hence

(11.1) To know what a rule (*any* rule) means is to be able to identify cases to which the rule plainly applies without interpretation; Hence

(11.2) As we *are* able to understand the meaning of legal rules, there *must* be legal cases to which rules apply without question.

Marmor, following in Hart's footsteps, found (10) too obvious to offer any argument for it. If (10) is correct, (10.1), (10.2) and (10.3)) are correct insofar as we accept Hart's plausible remarks about meaning, (11), a view I will not question.

In fact, it appears that once (10) has been granted the rest follows more or less naturally, if "meaning is use", that is, if (11) is true. My argument is that throughout his article (1958, *passim*) Fuller mistakenly accepted (10) and felt that Hart's mistake was in (11). That is to say, given his acceptance of (10), the only way in which he was able to object to Hart's view was to argue that (11) encapsulated a wrong theory of meaning, hence both (11.1) and (11.2) were false. Marmor's arguments are (I believe) enough to prove that Fuller was wrong here, that his arguments failed to disprove (11) or (11.1). I have no quarrel with this. But (my reconstructed version of) Fuller's argument has been based upon a rejection of (10), such that I do not need to reject (11). If (10) is rejected, (10.2) and (10.3) become groundless. The crucial point here is that (11) and (11.1) are incapable of rendering (11.2) without the support of (10.).

The rejection of (11.2) is a consequence of the distinction, offered in Chapter 1, between two models of institution (or, strictly, is the consequence of the rejection of (10), which is a consequence of such a distinction). So allow me to insist, without (10), (11) and (11.1) still hang in the air along with (11.2), and cannot give it any support.

We can see how the distinction between two models of institution offered in the first chapter is crucially related to this issue. Marmor is right when he argues that

> unless it can be shown that there is something unique to adjudication . . . we have no reason to doubt that legal rules can often be simply understood, and then applied, without the mediation of interpretive hypothesis about the rules' purposes (1994: 154).

But he failed to see that there is indeed something special to legal adjudication: modern legal systems are regulatory institutions, and concerning the rules of regulatory institutions (10) is false.

Defeasibility and morality

Marmor's formulation of the "objection from defeasibility" is:

> [s]ince it is the case that any legal rule—if construed literally—might, under certain circumstances, have utterly immoral or otherwise absurd results, a judge must always ask himself whether the case before him is one in which the results would be unacceptable if the rule were thus applied (1994: 135).

Now, I do not believe this is the best way to put it, but for the time being it will do. For Marmor the argument is such that "immediate reflection" should find it "puzzling: it seems to hold that since any rule, if construed literally, *can* result in absurd consequences, it follows that no rule can be construed literally, which is an obvious fallacy" (1994: 136). As will be clearer later, it is Marmor here who is mistaken. It is difficult to deny that rules *can* be applied literally: the point is whether a literal application (of a legal rule) is, as a matter of conceptual truth, a *correct* application (i.e. correct in legal terms). Marmor also tries to downplay the "objection from defeasibility" by making it appear rather dull: what can result in obvious absurdities is the application of a rule *literally construed*. But this is just a rhetorical move: the whole point of Hart's views on meaning was that, however context-sensitive (as opposed to "literal") meaning is, we are bound to find plain instances of (concept-) words (see Marmor, 1994: 30). If this is correct, the application of a legal rule to states of affairs that constitute such plain instances of its operative facts is equally bound to produce, in some cases, these absurd consequences, however context-sensitive (again, as opposed to "literal") we take meaning to be.

Be this as it may, and to solve his puzzlement, i.e. to "save" the argument from being "obviously fallacious", Marmor modifies its conclusion, replacing the (descriptive) "must" in its formulation for a (prescriptive) "should" (1994: 136).

After his charitable rescuing of the argument, Marmor is free to say that "it cuts no ice in the dispute with Hart", because it confuses "the question of what *following a rule consists in* (which interested Hart) [with that of] *whether a rule should be applied in the circumstances*" (1994: 136). Marmor immediately continues:

> Even if we concede that judges should always ask themselves the latter question (which is far from clear), it does not follow that rules cannot be understood, and then applied, without reference to their alleged purpose or any other consideration about what the rule is there to settle (1994: 136).

In terms of the example we have been using, Marmor is claiming that the question of whether or not the first man should be fined (i.e. the question of whether or not the rule should be applied in the circumstances) is not the relevant point, which is, rather, what following a rule consists in, i.e. what the court must do *if* it is to follow the rule (or what *the law*—rather than the court's all-things-considered duty—is for the case). And I believe it is only fair to Marmor if we understand him as saying that *if* the court is to follow the rule, the first man should be fined. Maybe, we could continue along Marmorian lines, a legal rule can *never* be applied in a morally justified way without judges asking themselves whether or not there are moral reasons requiring them in the instant case not to apply the rule (though this is "far from clear"), but then they are asking themselves whether they should follow the rule as a matter of moral duty (and, we could even say, as "ought" implies "can", the fact that judges can ask themselves the question whether or not they ought to apply the rule shows that rules can be applied without reference to their alleged purpose, etc.).

Marmor rightly points out that Fuller (1958) collapsed the two questions. We have already seen why he had to: he believed in the truth of (10), i.e. that *the meaning of a rule determines its application.* Since he also wanted to claim that no application of the rule is possible without grasping its purpose, he had to claim that in order to understand the meaning of a rule its purpose had to be ascertained. This is the reason why he felt compelled to subscribe to a "purposive" account of meaning (1958: 668), when a purposive account of *legal* rule-application would have been enough. When the meaning of a rule determines its application (e.g. in chess), rules need not be defeasible. Here, again, we came across Bankowski's observation of the normative becoming, in a certain sense, descriptive.

I have argued in Chapter 3 that the application of legal rules is not determined by their meaning. If I am right in this regard, we can restate what Marmor called "the objection from defeasibility" without having to collapse Marmor's two questions as Fuller did. We are concerned here only with the first one, i.e.

(12) What does following a rule consist in?

Marmor's answer to (12)) is Wittgenstein's rule-following considerations. He thinks that if he can connect Hart's distinction between clear and hard cases to Wittgenstein's considerations an "independent conceptual basis" would have been found for the former, a basis that would be strong enough for him to reject most of the criticism such a distinction has attracted. This answer to (12) is, however, problematic. For one thing, Wittgenstein considered only what I have called "autonomous institutions", hence he did not address the problem of the exclusionary character of rules. Wittgenstein was well aware of (someting very close to) the distinction between what I call "regulatory" and "autonomous" institutions (*see* the passage quoted above, at 43). It cannot therefore be a mere coincidence that all the examples he discussed were of (what in that passage he called) "arbitrary" rules. And though rules of, say, football are indeed exclusionary reasons, the fact that a non-exclusionary account of them fails to make sense at all (this was Rawls's point, discussed above, at 3ff) makes this feature of rules of games uninteresting. As was said above, the defeasibility of rules is not an interesting fact about the rules, but about the institution they belong to. If the focus is placed on the rules, this feature does not come to light.

Following Wittgenstein we could remark that following a rule is a practice, and the practice of (for instance) football defines how rules of football are to be applied: acknowledge them complete exclusionary force. Nothing but the rule counts. The referee should not consider any substantive issue whatsoever, unless he is explicitly authorised to do so by the rule (if we wanted to express this point in Wittgensteinian terms, we could say: this is what "rule" means in the language-game of games. Marmor is, then, committing the very mistake Wittgenstein was so anxious to warn us against: he is assuming that concepts—like "rule"—remain the same across different language games). A referee can answer "this is simply what we do" to explain his application of the rules of football, while a judge is supposed to do precisely what Wittgenstein said was useless, to offer an interpretation. Generally speaking, then, I think we can safely say: in what Wittgenstein called "arbitrary systems" (and I am calling "autonomous institutions"), *because* they are "arbitrary" (autonomous) the answer to the question "why is the rule such-and-such?" can only be "this is simply what we do". In "teleological" (i.e. "regulatory") systems, (part of) the answer is a justification in terms of the goals the system is supposed to advance.

In his discussion of Wittgenstein, Marmor was anxious to show that once the subject has got the meaning of a rule she follows it *acting* according to it (to the rule, i.e. the meaning she has got[2]). Once the view that the application of a rule is determined by its meaning is rejected we can see that there is something else that, along with the meaning of the rule, has to be grasped before any application of it is possible. And that "something else" is the determination of how formal the application of the rule should be, of how many (and which) substantive issues or reasons are pre-empted by the rule. This question is as much a part of a full answer to (12) as the grasping of the meaning of the rule.

Marmor did not address this possibility. His argument is designed to show that given that Fuller accepted that the meaning of a rule determines its application, his criticism of Hart was mistaken. Doubtless, he was right in this. But

[2] Here I am collapsing the rule with its meaning. *Cf.* Schauer (1990: 55ff). This not terribly important, though some authors might disagree. Thus Aarnio, criticising Schauer, claims that "a linguistic formulation of a rule (rule formation) may cover several possible "rule candidates" (rules) i.e. ways to interpret the formulation. In this very sense, rule formulations are only *prima facie* expressions calling for contextual interpretation, and further, being interpreted a rule formulation refers to the rule all things considered. From this point of view, the rule-based and the particularistic model can be combined" (Aarnio, 1998: 25). The discussion is, I believe, irrelevant for my purposes: it does not matter whether we equate the rule with its meaning and say that after the legal rule has been understood there is still a problem of application, as I am doing, or that the rule's meaning is "just" a rule-formulation, compatible with several rule-candidates, the correct one to be chosen at the moment of application, as Aarnio does. In my view, the approach adopted here has the advantage that it allows us to know what the law is before the concrete case comes up.

given that it is Fuller's unstated premiss, rather than his criticism of Hart, which has to be abandoned, it remains to be seen if Marmor's point can still be sustained. An affirmative answer to this question can only be given if it is the case that conceptual considerations can show not only that legal norms are formal (i.e., that they exclude from consideration *some* substantive reasons), but also *how* formal these norms are (i.e. *which* substantive issues are excluded from consideration). Whoever wants to claim that rules can be applied without evaluative considerations has to claim not only that *some* evaluative considerations are to be disregarded, but also *which* considerations are those that have been pre-empted. The need to answer these two separate questions also seems to have been overlooked by Raz:

> [Primary organs, i.e. courts] are institutions which are bound to act on certain reasons even if they do not think that on the balance of reasons they ought to do so. That means that primary organs are institutions which ought to act on certain reasons *to the exclusion of all others*, namely institutions which are subject to an exclusionary reason not to act on certain reasons . . . .Let us again use the law as our paradigmatic case. If a man is legally required to do *A* in C then the courts are bound to hold that he failed to do what he ought to have done if he fails to do *A* in C. They *will refuse to listen* to arguments to the effect that failing to do *A* in C is really what he ought to have done since there were extralegal reasons which override the reason that the legal requirement provides (1992: 142f, emphasis added).

But will they? Of course they will if "extralegal reasons" are defined as those reasons the courts will refuse to listen to. Though Raz does say that "if the primary organs do not regard themselves as bound to apply a certain norm it does not belong to the system" (1992: 142), he rapidly rejects the claim "that the law consists of all the standards which the courts do in fact apply" (*ibid.*). Hence, Raz's point is not a tautology: he is not first defining "extralegal reasons" as those the courts will refuse to listen to and then saying that courts will refuse to listen to extralegal reasons. The question, then, presents itself, will the courts refuse to listen to (independently defined) "extralegal reasons"?

Raz is right in claiming that courts ("primary organs") are required to act on certain reasons even if they think that on the balance of reasons they should not. But from this it does not follow (and he did not offer any additional argument for this) that *all* the norms of the system exclude *all* possible conflicting considerations, that courts are required to decide on legal reasons "to the exclusion of *all* others". All of these "all's" are taken for granted on the basis of the (true) fact that courts "are bound to act on certain reasons even if they do not think that on the balance of reasons they ought to do so". This seems to place too much conceptual weight on a premiss that, though true, is of much more limited consequences.

Consider a case like *National Insurance Commissioner, ex parte Connor* (1981 All ER at 769), in which a woman applied for a widow's allowance under s 24(1) of the Social Security Act 1975. However, she had previously been convicted (and put on probation) for the manslaughter of her husband. Section 24(1), the (at least) prima facie applicable rule, stated that

> A woman who has been widowed shall be entitled to a widow's allowance at the weekly rate specified in relation thereto in schedule 4, part 1, paragraph 5, if— (*a*) she was under pensionable age at the time when her late husband died, or he was then not entitled to a Category A retirement pension (section 28); and (*b*) her late husband satisfied the contribution condition for a widow's allowance specified in schedule 2, part 1, paragraph 4 . . ..

If we insist on separating the questions of what following a rule consists in from that of whether a rule should be applied in the circumstances, we would have to say that if the court was to follow the rule, Ms Connor should have been given the pension (no other grounds for denying her the pension were invoked), but that, because of moral reasons, the rule should not be applied in the circumstances (assuming that, as a matter of morals, this is the case). The court, Raz would have to claim, would have to "refuse to listen" to arguments to the effect that denying the pension is what (morally) ought to be done.

But the court did not engage in "raw" moral debate about whether or not the rule had to be applied. What was under consideration was, rather, whether the correct understanding and application of s 24(1) of the Social Security Act 1975 implied that the court had to apply it as a completely formal reason (i.e. excluding *all* the elements that were not part of its explicit operative facts) or instead, as a formal-and-yet-not-completely-formal reason.

To put it another way, the court accepted that some substantive considerations were pre-empted by the rule. The facts of the case, however, gave rise to a substantive consideration that is not *normally* present in cases in which the application of s 24(1) is in question. For the court, the problem was whether this substantive consideration was among those pre-empted by the rule. In *normal* cases, the fact that some features of the case are not listed in the rule's operative facts is enough to conclude that they are irrelevant:

> Counsel for the applicant points out that nowhere in the wording of the Act is there any provision disentitling the widow to her widow's allowance by reason of the fact that she may have been responsible in some degree for her own widowhood (Lord Lane CJ, in *National Insurance Commissioner*, at 772).

But in *this* case this consideration was not necessarily all there was to it, and the question was how important the fact that the applicant had been convicted for the manslaughter of her husband was, whether it was *important enough* to be relevant. The crucial point for the court was precisely whether this particular case was one of those, to use Hart's words, "left open for later, official settlement when the issue arises and is identified". If it was not one of them, the court would not have any discretion: "there is no doubt that those two conditions are satisfied and that had the situation been a normal one she would have been entitled to the widow's allowance under that section" (Lord Lane CJ at 773).

According to Marmor's argument, in this moment Lord Lane would have had to continue with something like this: "after conclusively having shown that the applicant is entitled, according to the law, to the widow's allowance, it remains to be decided whether this conclusion is morally sound". This is, however, not the way in which the problem was presented. For the court, the question was to ascertain whether the fact that the rule did not explicitly include a reference to public policy was enough to exclude public policy as one consideration to be taken into account when applying the rule. It was not up for discussion that the rule had *some* degree of formality, nor that if the solution turned out to be one that the court did not like it would have to adopt it regardless. The point was how "exclusionary" the rule was, i.e. whether or not its application had to be *formal enough* to exclude public policy.

The judges, in other words, accepted that they were, in Raz's words, "bound to act on certain reasons even if they did not think that on the balance of reasons they ought to do so", but they did not accept that that meant they had to act *to the exclusion of all others*.

And this is a problem that s 24(1) of the Social Security Act 1975 could not be expected to solve. Conceptual considerations about what following a rule consists in leave open *both* the argument that

> because this particular Act with which we are concerned . . . is . . . a self-contained modern Act the rules of public policy do not apply and that whatever may have happened . . . nothing that the applicant did can alter her plain entitlement under the words of s 24 (1) which I have read (*ibid.* at 773–4).

and the argument (eventually the court's view) that

> the fact that there is no specific mention in the Act of disentitlement so far as a widow is concerned if she were to commit this sort of offence and so become a widow is merely an indication . . . that the draftsman realised perfectly well that he was writing this Act against the background of the law as it stood at the time (*ibid.* at 774).

The problem of Raz's argument, which is shared by Marmor's, is that he selects one way of applying the rule (complete formality) and claims that it is the only way in which the rule can be applied, if it is to be applied at all. There is no conceptual warrant for this move, which is, in the end, completely arbitrary.

The same problem appears in Schauer's criticism of Fuller. According to Schauer, Fuller was wrong because he confused the problem of whether a case is covered by a given rule with the problem of whether the results produced by the application of the rule to the case are too absurd or otherwise immoral. This is the argument we have been rejecting in this section, but from it Schauer extracts two particular criticisms of Fuller's argument. In the first place, the fact that we sometimes think that the application of a given rule to a particular case is absurd shows, instead of refutes, that there are clear instances of application of the rule (we can think that the result is absurd only after we have understood that the rule applies); in the second, sometimes judges are authorised not to apply a rule when these results are absurd (or unjust, etc.) enough. How absurd or unjust they have to be, *and* whether or not judges will be so authorised, is a contingent matter that varies from time to time (this second of Schauer's arguments will be discussed in the next section).

Note that Fuller could not accept the first of Schauer's points because he, as was said, seemed to accept the thesis that interpretive problems in law were problems of getting the meaning right. Given this concession, he could not grant, without conceding defeat, that the rule can have a meaning that is independent from its purpose. If you hold

(13) It is not possible to *apply* a rule without determining its purpose,

and

(10) The meaning of a rule determines its application,

then the only way in which you could harmonise these two beliefs is having a notion of meaning that is itself dependent upon that of purpose. This is because once the truth of (10) is granted, then (13) becomes equivalent to

(14) It is not possible to *understand the meaning* of a rule without determining its purpose.

Now, as I argued in the last section, Marmor (and others) was right in claiming that (14) is plainly false. As Fuller's criticism relied on (10) and (13), he had to claim (14) by implication. Given that (14) is false, it follows that (13) is false as well. And the Fullerian case against Hart is closed.

What neither Marmor nor Schauer realised was that from the falsity of (14) all that follows is the impossibility of holding *both* (10) *and* (13). I take (13) to be the real gist of Fuller's claim. I accept that (14) is obviously false, hence I have to deny (10). Once (10) is rejected, (13) does not imply (14), and Fuller's case can be reopened. In this reading, Fuller's crucial mistake was to accept (10). Once this mistake is corrected, the rejection of (10) implies that neither I nor this somewhat reconstructed Fuller are committed to denying what are *core* meanings of rules; it also implies that from the existence of *core meanings* the existence of clear legal cases does not follow. As with Marmor before, Schauer needs (10) for his argument to stand, because he explicitly assimilates *core* meanings to clear cases: "there are *core* meanings of rules (clear cases under the rule)" (1991: 213).

As before, it is interesting to note that Hart himself was aware of this complication:

> it is a matter of some difficulty to give any exhaustive account of what makes a "clear case" clear or makes a general rule obviously and uniquely applicable to a particular case. Rules cannot provide for their own application, and even in the

> clearest case a human being must apply them. The clear cases are those in which there is general agreement that they fall within the scope of a rule, and it is tempting to ascribe such agreements simply to the fact that there are necessarily such agreements in the use of the shared conventions of language. But this would be an oversimplification because it does not allow for the special conventions of the legal *use of words*, which may diverge from their common use, or for the way in which *the meanings of words may clearly be controlled by reference to the purpose of a statutory enactment* which itself may be either explicitly stated or generally agreed (Hart, 1967: 106; emphasis added).

Here Hart, faced with cases in which the correct legal solution is not that dictated by the meaning of a rule, seems to accept some version of (14) instead of questioning (10). The problem with this strategy is that once (14) is conceded his distinction between core and penumbra cannot hold (what the core is is controlled by reference to the purpose of the rule, hence there are no cases to which the rule obviously applies without reference to its purpose). In other words, this passage of Hart's has to be read in the light of the second interpretation of the open-texture doctrine (*see* 90f), and the italicised phrases must be taken as an attempt to make the two readings of the open texture thesis compatible. But it does not work, as Schauer, who thinks Hart was right in his doctrine of core and penumbra, insists (commenting on the same passage of Hart's):

> Hart need not have conceded even as much as he subsequently did to Fuller. In acknowledging the function of purpose in constituting the very idea of the rule itself, Hart too was incorporating what is but a contingent choice made by most contemporary legal systems (1991: 213).

If we understand Schauer's (rather cryptic) reference to "the very idea of the rule itself" as a reference to the meaning of the rule, I think he is undeniably right, which is only a different way to say that (14) is false. Both (10) and (13) cannot be true without (14) also being true. Schauer and Marmor opted for a rejection of (13), which is surprising, given that they did not offer any argument in favour of (10). And it is indeed (10), not (13), which is false.

I do not have to deny, of course, that courts sometimes do face Schauer's or Marmor's problem. Some laws are unjust, and it might very well be (indeed, it is) the case that sometimes courts have the moral duty not to apply them because of this very reason. In cases of this kind the court has to say "this is the law, but it is too unfair to be applied". The Chilean Constitution, for example, gave General Pinochet the power to drive political opponents into exile without due process of law (article 24 transitory). Think of a Chilean judge having to solve a case of judicial review of one such decision. It is, I believe, a strength of my argument that I do not need to collapse the case of the Chilean judge with that of Lord Lane. The argument we are now considering would imply that, in both cases, it was clear what the law was, but the court (might have) had the moral duty not to apply it. The court in *National Insurance Commissioner* did not believe that it was putting forward a moral critique of the law. They were discussing the appropriate way of applying a reasonable piece of legislation. If the Chilean judge, on the other hand, is to fulfil his moral duty, he has to break the law and invalidate Pinochet's decision even though it has been produced according to a constitutional power-conferring rule. Only the first case is one of an application problem.

Be that as it may, the last part of Schauer's last-quoted remark ("Hart too was incorporating what is but a contingent choice made by most contemporary legal systems") links up with his second criticism of Fuller to be discussed here, i.e. the claim that the case of the first man in the station is hard because as a matter of contingent truth modern legal systems empower courts not to apply the law when its consequences are absurd. This claim of Schauer's is to be discussed in the next section.

"MY CODE IS LOST"

Schauer notices that it is odd to say that the no-vehicles-in-the-park rule forbids the memorial, and that the no-sleeping-in-the-station rule applies to the businessman. But he also acknowledges the oddness of saying that the military truck to be used in the memorial is not a "vehicle", or that the first man was not really "sleeping". His solution for this problem is simple and straightforward:

> an intolerance for absurdity has produced a legal environment in which judges are commonly *empowered* to set aside the result indicated by the most locally applicable rule-formulation when that result would be absurd. But that approach . . . is contingent and not necessary. Moreover, it is by no means clear that the seemingly distasteful alternative has nothing to be said of. Wary of empowering judges to determine purpose . . . some system might instruct judges simply to apply the rule, even if the result seemed to them inconsistent with its purpose, or even if the result seemed to them absurd. Such an approach would reflect a decision to prefer the occasional wrong or even preposterous result to a regime in which judges were empowered to search for purpose or preposterousness, for it might be that such empowerment was thought to present a risk of error or variance of decision even more harmful that the tolerance of occasional absurd results. The question, therefore, is not only whether a result is absurd, but whether decision-makers should have the jurisdiction to determine which results are absurd and which not. When so recast, the argument for what is often pejoratively referred to as "formalism" may still not be persuasive, but is far from absurd . . .. What we see, therefore, is a persistent tendency, especially in judge-centred legal theorizing, to take the contingent empowerment of judges as demonstrating the incompatibility of a rule with the tolerance of an absurd result (Schauer, 1991: 214).

What are we to make of this argument? To begin with, it must be noticed that the idea of being empowered by the "legal environment" is ambiguous, because "legal environment" can mean either "the (social) environment *of* the law" or "the environment constituted *by* the law (as it constrains or empowers judges)". In the former case, it would mean that the environment in which *the law* exists is such that, regardless of the content of the rules, judicial organs have the power not to apply the rules when the results they would produce are too absurd or otherwise unfair; in the latter, that the legal environment in which *courts* have to justify their decisions contains legal rules granting them such power. In the first sense Schauer's point would be perfectly compatible with the perspective argued for in this book: given that the law is (understood as) a regulatory institution, legal rules are (necessarily) defeasible. In this explanation, it is a contingent fact that the law is a regulatory institution, but given that it is one it is not contingent that rules are defeasible (and hence, that courts have the power to declare them to be defeated in concrete cases). Notice that in this sense of the expression "legal environment" the law cannot deny courts that power, since the power is a consequence of the environment in which the law itself exists (and every law would exist in the same environment, including the laws denying that power). In this sense, therefore, the fact of legal rules being defeasible because of the legal environment is something that is, so to speak, beyond the reach of the rules of the system to modify.

Therefore, if "legal environment" is to be understood as "social environment in which the law exists" Schauer's question ("not only whether a result is absurd, but whether decision-makers should have the jurisdiction to determine which results are absurd and which not") is not a question that the legal system can answer, and Schauer's power would not be a source-based legal power, but a power derived from the "social environment" or, as I would prefer, from the way the subjects conceive of the law and legal practice (i.e. as a "regulatory" social institution). In this sense, the fact that judges are so empowered would not "reflect a decision to prefer" non-application of rules when doing so would result in absurd outcomes.

But this conclusion would imply that (in "regulatory" legal systems) legal rules are defeasible even if the legal system does contain rules denying courts those powers, even if rule-makers positively want to do so. Schauer wants to claim precisely the opposite, that defeasibility is a contingent feature of some legal systems because they happen to give courts more power. We cannot, therefore, understand his reference to the "legal environment" in this particular way.

So we had better return to the second possibility, and understand the reference to the "legal environment" as the environment *of the court* (not that of the law). In this second sense, the thesis is that it happens to be the case that modern legal systems have rules granting courts the power not to apply the law when the result would be too absurd. If the reason why legal rules are defeasible is that further rules of the system empower judges not to apply the rules when that would produce too absurd a result, then of course Schauer would be right, and from the fact that rules are defeasible nothing would follow about "the incompatibility of a rule with the tolerance of an absurd result" (the situation would be entirely similar to the advantage rule in football, in which the referee has some discretion explicitly given by the rule).

The main objection to Schauer's thesis of the defeasibility of legal rules as being explained by the contingent empowering of judges is that it flies in the face of historical evidence. Granted, there are legal systems that contain rules of the kind Schauer had in mind. Consider article 9 of the Louisiana Civil Code:

> Art. 9. *Clear and unambiguous law.* When a law is clear and unambiguous and its application does not lead to absurd consequences, the law shall be applied as written and no further interpretation may be in search of the intent of the legislature.

The fact that laws of this kind exist is only half of the proof Schauer's argument needs. He has to show that we (and also, but not only, judges) are inclined to think that in some cases covered by the meaning of a rule (i.e. those in which the results produced by the application of the rule are absurd) the rule should not be applied because our systems contain rules like article 9 (this is a point Hart convincingly levelled against Kelsen's thesis of the unity of international and municipal law, *see* Hart, 1968a). In other words, it must be the case, for Schauer's argument to stand, that if a rule so empowering judges were not found, and in its place we had a rule denying those powers, then we (and the judges in such systems) would think that, because they do not have that power, rules should be applied regardless.

One of the cases quoted by Schauer (1991: 213) as one of the situations in which the application of a rule is absurd is the case mentioned in the first chapter:

> there was a law of Bologna, that whoever drew blood from another person in a public place should suffer the most severe penalties. On the basis of this law a barber was once informed upon, who had opened a man's vein in the square.

But Schauer does not quote Pufendorf's very next sentence:

> And the fellow was in no little peril because it was added in the statute that the words should be taken exactly and without any interpretation (Pufendorf, 1688: Book V, Ch. 12, § 8, pp. 802–3 [547]).[3]

In Schauer's view, then, this should be a clear case: what the barber did constituted a "clear case under the rule" and according to the rule the words should be taken exactly and without interpretation. Schauer's theory apparently implies that the correct legal solution, according to Bolognese law, is to punish the barber, while Pufendorf's opinion is the opposite. So how are we to interpret the disagreement between Schauer and Pufendorf? Schauer intends his thesis to be part of "a philosophical examination of rule-based

[3] There are some minor differences between Pufendorf's example and Schauer's (e.g. a surgeon instead of a barber), because Schauer seems to be quoting from *United States* v. *Kirby*, 74 US (7 Wall) 482, 487 (1967).

decision-making in law", and if we read it as such the disagreement will be a philosophical disagreement. But we can see that the disagreement might very well be a first-order legal dispute, and then we should understand Schauer's thesis as an ordinary legal claim (Schauer, counsel for the prosecution, and Pufendorf, counsel for the defendant). If it is a legal claim, one that might be true or false in different legal systems, it cannot be true as a matter of conceptual truth. And of course, in a sense, we know that the latter is the case: it makes perfect legal sense to argue, as did Pufendorf, that rules should be "flexibly" interpreted even in the face of rules demanding strict interpretation, because those rules should also be interpreted.

More generally, a brief look back to nineteenth-century Western legal development is enough to show that, though it was common for legal systems undergoing processes of codification to have rules denying courts such powers, problems of application did not disappear.

The Louisiana Civil Code seems to be a good starting point, given its seemingly completely Schauerian article 9. The fact is, that article dates back to only 1987. The original article (then art. 13) of the 1870 Civil Code was significantly different:

> Art. 13. When a law is clear and free from all ambiguity, the letter of it is not to be disregarded, under the pretext of pursuing its spirit.

Note the crucial difference between the two enactments: only the first gives the courts the power Schauer had in mind, the second cannot have any sense except to *deny* it, as clearly as it possibly can.

If Schauer is right, then, there must have been a huge difference in judicial practice in Louisiana before and after 1987, but this is not the case. In fact, the difference between the two is classified, by the commentators of the Code, as "changes in phraseology and terminology [which] do not change the law" (Yiannopoulos, 1989: 4). And however that might be, it is simply not the case that the Civil Code transformed the courts into mechanical applicators of the law (Kilbourne, 1987, esp. chs 3 & 5).[4]

More decisive cases can be found in eighteenth- and nineteenth-century Europe, in the heyday of the movement of codification. It is a known fact that in France the judicial establishment was not trusted by the revolutionaries, neither was it held in high regard by Napoleon himself. The *Code Napoleon* purported to be a complete statement of the private law applicable in France, and the ideology behind it was clear and uncompromising:

> it is possible that the law, which is clear-sighted in one sense, and blind in another, might in some cases be too severe. But as we have already observed, the national judges are no more than the mouth that pronounces the words of the law, mere

[4] For the sense in which I am using the expression "mechanical applicator" *cf.* above at 102f. Kilbourne studies the impact of the 1808 Louisiana Digest and the 1825 Civil Code. Article 13 of the 1870 Civil Code, however, was introduced in 1825.

> passive beings, incapable of moderating either its force or rigour (Montesquieu, 1756: Bk. 11.6, p. 172).

In fact, we are told, "Napoleon had tried legislatively to prohibit tampering with [his] sacred text, outlawing those commentaries that, as one Bonapartist jurist lamented, "destroy the Code"" (Kelley, 1984). But Napoleon's wishes could not make the *Code Civil* indefeasible, because the reason the *Code Civil* was defeasible was not that Napoleon wanted it to be so, but that it was a law (i.e. a rule of a regulatory institution) and as such it was necessarily defeasible. When he saw how commentaries on the Code were growing in number, Napoleon is said to have cried "mon Code est perdu".[5]

A similar situation happened in Prussia and in Austria during the codification. In the latter, the *Codex Theresianus* could not be more explicit: "we forbid all judges to deviate in the least from the clear precept of our law under the void pretext of some equity that differs from the sharpness of the law" (*see* van Caenegem, 1991: 182). The Prussian *Algemeines Landrecht*, we are told,

> is typical in its all-embracing scope. It contains sixteen thousands provisions . . .. They prescribe with mathematical precision what is right and what is wrong, and cover many matters which would be regarded today as quite inappropriate for legal regulation. Thus there is a detailed statement of the circumstances in which a wife is excused from her obligation to accord her husband his marital right, for example, when she is breast-feeding (§§178–80) (Stein, 1980: 53).

In general, it does seem true to say that "codification was historically a weapon against the judiciary" (van Caenegem, 1987: 152): what was intended was ***precisely*** to tie the courts up, not to let them adjust the law. French courts, for instance, were instructed to apply the law, and when a difficulty arose, they had to refer the problem back to the legislature. French, Prussian and Austrian legislators, among others, were indeed "wary of empowering judges to determine purpose and instructed judges simply to apply the rule, even if the result seemed to them inconsistent with its purpose, or even if the result seemed to them absurd". But they could not do it: every rule they passed to that effect existed in the same legal environment, i.e. as part of a regulatory institution. Conversely, judges nowadays have that power even in the face of rules like the old article 13 of the Louisiana Civil Code. As the Louisiana Civil

[5] Consider some of the examples discussed by Marcel Planiol: according to art. 1382 Code Civil, "every act of what nature soever, which occasions damage to another, obliges him through whose fault it has happened, to repair it". Planiol rightly points out that this provision is "much too sweeping. If an exception were not introduced for acts which are the exercise of a right, but which cause damage, there would be a great addition to the number of cases to which this provision would be rightly applicable" (Planiol, 1939: § 216). Notice how effortlessly Planiol moves from the fact that the law ought to make a distinction to the fact that it *does* distinguish, without being troubled by the obvious meaning of art. 1382. Other cases discussed by Planiol are art. 2194f *Code Civil* (it reads "the date of the marriage contract" but it *should* say—hence it *does* say—"the day of the marriage") and art. 408 (it reads to the effect that widows of ascendants should be summoned to family meetings, but it *should* read—hence it *does* read—the ascendant widows).

Code commentator rightly said, rules granting those powers "do not change the law" (Yiannopoulos, 1989: 4).

Indeed, we know that there are many cases in which what is (considered by participants to be) the correct result is not the one most obviously intimated by the meaning of the source-based rules (*see* Tunc, 1986, *passim*). So the question has to be, who is a theorist of law to tell practitioners they are legally wrong? Schauer would seem to be forced to do precisely that, insofar as those legal systems contain rules that bar judges from "deviat[ing] in the least from the clear precept of our law under the void pretext of some equity that differs from the sharpness of the law". Therefore, the point is not how prone French or Prussian or Austrian courts and commentators are or were to break the law, but rather to show how, even when judges are denied powers not to apply the law because of substantive considerations, even when most judges accept a version of the doctrine of the separation of powers, problems of application, in the sense defined before, do not disappear and rules are still defeasible:

> Legal history teaches us that whenever there is an attempt to confine private law to codes (as if to keep it within an invincible fortress capable of defying the passage of time) it arises as a reaction to the opposite phenomenon: that is, when the state has not monopolized the production of law, but rather allowed it simply to flow from many sources, including the opinion of jurists. In its turn, the idea of removing the law from state control appears promptly after each codification, as an insuppressible need to adjust statute law to historical events (Manfredini, 1994:16–17).

And the claim *here* is that this fact teaches us something about the nature of the law.

CONCLUSION

So let us retain the main conclusion of this chapter, and to do so recall Schauer's and Marmor's mistake: they assume that (10), (the claim that the meaning of a rule determines its application) is obviously true. They think that the point is one about whether or not *core meanings* can exist. They believe that once it has been established that it is possible to understand a rule without reference to its purpose Fuller's objections fall to the ground:

> [T]he thesis that one always needs to determine the purpose of the rule in order to be able to specify which actions are in accord with it, amounts to contending that the application of a rule always requires its translation into another rule, which is an obvious absurdity (Marmor, 1994: 153).

> [U]nless we embrace an implausible particularist theory of meaning, under which the notion of meaning collapses into what a decision-maker in a particular environment should do on a particular occasion, it appears that Hart was correct. There *are* core meanings of rules (clear cases under the rule) (Schauer, 1991: 213).

Schauer's argument explicitly assumes that a clear case under the rule is a case that is covered by the "core" meaning of the rule, *because* it is covered by the "core" meaning of it (a position that is only reasonable if (10) is accepted). Similarly, Marmor's confusion of the problems of meaning and application is patent, once (10) is distinguished from (11): the argument is *not* that one always need to "determine the purpose of the rule in order to be able to specify which actions are in accord with it". You can specify which actions are in accord with (6) without any enquiry into (6's) purpose. This is but a repetition of Hart's argument: you can't understand the meaning of a rule if you cannot determine which actions are in accord with it. But one thing is to "specify which actions are in accord with a norm" and another is to determine whether it should be applied as a rule. This point cannot but be missed if the focus is kept upon the *concept* of a rule (an exclusionary reason), a concept that has been taken from autonomous institutions (games and the like. Raz introduced his concept of exclusionary reason in *Practical Reason and Norms* which contains an extremely interesting discussion of games; the title of Schauer's book makes this clear as well). In autonomous institutions the relation between a rule and its application is indeed a grammatical one; this is taken by Marmor to follow from what following a rule means: "to follow a rule, one needs to understand and act according to it . . .. [T]he relation between a rule and its application is a grammatical one, that is, internal to language" (1994: 153). If this follows from anything, however, it follows from what following a rule in autonomous institutions is; in regulatory institutions, on the contrary, there is more to the application of a norm than understanding its meaning. Marmor seems to have been misled by the fact that the superficial grammar of law and games is similar, while their deep grammar is notoriously different. An important part of the solution for this problem is to follow Wittgenstein's advice: "don't *think*, but look!" (1958: §66).

These remarks clarify the sense in which I have argued for Marmor's "obvious absurdity": should the rule "no vehicles may be taken into the park" be translated into the norm "this military truck may not be used in this memorial" or in the norm "this military truck can be used in this memorial"? The problem cannot be grammatically settled: that would beg the question, because we know that grammatically the first "translation" has to be preferred. The real question is that of determining how formal the application of the norm has to be. And it is obvious that the norm itself cannot settle *that* problem.

Note that to select the second "translation" is *not* to say that the norm contributes nothing to the decision. This would be the case only if we had previously and independently decided that the norm forbidding vehicles in the park was a *rule*, i.e. an exclusionary reason *and* that the reason for preferring the "second" translation was that the truck is not a vehicle. There are other possibilities. The norm could be taken as evidence of some substantive reason that deserves attention: the court could authorise the memorial only, for example, insofar as it is designed and built in such a way that the substantive reasons of which the "no vehicles" norm is a universalisation are not greatly affected:

> if we accept, for example, that the norm "speed limit 100 km/h" has an exception in cases of emergency, then sometimes to drive faster than 100 km/h will be allowed. This does not mean that any speed is allowed; here the norm works as a principle (Prieto, 1992: 48).

Only if Prieto's rule is an exclusionary reason will this not be the case: the only reason an exclusionary reason is defeated by first-order reasons is that given the scope of the former the latter were not excluded in the first place (in truth, it is incorrect to say that the exclusionary reason was "defeated", since it was not applicable in the first place).[6]

[6] There is one further argument that could be used to give a source-based account of the existence of implicit exceptions. The argument looks at legislative intentions, and would have us recognising exceptions only when the legislator would have granted one, had they thought about the case now under consideration (*see* Alchourrón, 1995: 16ff, and what he calls a "dispositional" analysis of defeasibility). I will not go into this argument because the answer looks obvious to me: "What is said, of course, is that Parliament "cannot" have intended so unjust a result. But the grounds for the imputation of intention are the evaluation of the implications of the rejected interpretation; no independent recourse is available to the otherwise mysterious concept of "legislator's intention" (MacCormick, 1984: 240). *See* the case discussed by Michael Moore, who imagines a law-maker who, after being successfully lobbied by butter-producers who wanted to avoid competition, passes a statute requiring margarine-makers to dye their product red: "Suppose that dyeing margarine red in fact causes a real good to be achieved, perhaps the prevention of its consumption by those deathly allergic to it. Purposive interpretation of such a statute would then not be guided by the purpose (motive) of the legislature that passed the statute. Rather, such interpretation would ignore that psychological question and engage in moral reasoning: how can the moral good that is the purpose (function) of the statute best be served?" (Moore, 1994: 227). Of course counsel for one of the parties might put forward Alchourrón's thesis and claim that the statute has to be interpreted according to the actual intentions of the law-maker (i.e. to shield butter-producers from competition). But here, as before, we find that what appeared to be a theoretical claim (i.e. Alchourrón's dispositional analysis of defeasibility, or Moore's moral reading of purpose) turns out to be an ordinary, first-order legal claim.

5

Nothing at all or Nothing Exceptional

Rules typically function by ascribing a normative consequence to the occurrence of some "operative" facts. We have seen that a curious feature of the law (probably what led Celsus to say *ius est ars boni et aequi*, law is the art [NB, *art*] of goodness and fairness: D. 1.1.1.*pr*) is that *legal* rules are not so well-behaved: sometimes, on the face of the occurrence of the operative facts, the normative consequence is not due. Legal rules are defeasible.

Still, what exactly does it mean to say that rules are defeasible? And, more importantly, in which circumstances can rules be defeasible? One answer is that rules are defeasible when they belong to regulatory institutions; in this chapter, I will approach the issue from a different perspective, so the argument here, if correct, will provide independent support to the claims made in Chapter 1.

EXCEPTIONS AND RULES

A norm is said to be defeasible when the requirement it expresses is to be followed generally, though it can be defeated in some cases. Defeasibility is a property of (some) general norms. In MacCormick's words,

> [l]aw has to be stated in general terms, yet conditions formulated generally are always capable of omitting reference to some element which can turn out to be the key operative fact in a given case (1995: 103).

Though this seems to be clear enough, it is not always easy to distinguish two different situations which must, however, be distinguished. It is only too obvious that a rule is not defeated if the reason why it was not applied is that it was not applicable. A rule is only defeated if it was not applied even though it was applicable:

> We do not speak of an action as an exception to the rule, of course, unless we believe or assume that the rule applies to the action. If the rule does not apply, there can be no question of an exception; if the rule applies, there could be a question about an exception and if the rule applies but we are justified in not following it, an exception is allowed (Miller, 1956: 262).

Notice that we could not use Marmor's argument here, even if it were correct. Miller is not talking of a legal rule that applies but we which are morally justified in not following; he is speaking of a moral rule that applies but which we are morally justified in not following. In other words, he seems to be claiming that the rule applies, but it is not (morally) the case that it should be applied. And what does it mean to say that a (moral) rule applies if not that (from the moral point of view) it should be applied? The only solution is, I believe, to understand that a rule applies when, according to its meaning, it should be applied. To say that a rule is defeasible is to say, then, that there are (or can be) cases covered by the (meaning of the) rule to which it does not apply. It must be clear, then, why legal rules cannot be legally defeasible once (10), that is, the view that the meaning of a rule determines its application (see Chapter 4), is accepted.

Notice that the expression "legal rules cannot be legally defeated" is not a pleonasm: the qualification "legally" is important in this context. Miller was considering the issue of exceptions to moral rules, hence his test to identify an exception: "if the rule applies but we are justified in not following it, an exception is allowed". I think it is fair to Miller's point, and it is at any rate important when discussing legal defeasiblity, to stress that the justification must stem, so to speak, from the same kind of normative consideration as the applicable rule: if a *moral* rule is to have an exception, it is because though the rule applies, we are *morally* justified in not following it; if a *legal* rule is to have an exception, it is because though the rule applies, we are *legally* justified in not following it, and so on (this points back to our stipulation at 72 above). The fact that the *moral* rule applies, but the law commands me not to apply it hardly implies that the moral rule has been defeated, in the sense of a (moral) exception having being incorporated to it.

To talk of "exceptions" might, however, be misleading in one important sense: exceptions are clauses that limit the scope of a rule, hence by definition if there is an exception the rule is not applicable. So it seems that exceptions are impossible according to Miller's criterion: for an exception to a rule to exist the rule must be applicable, but if an exception exists the rule is not applicable.

The solution to this puzzle is rather obvious, and to see it, two different moments should be distinguished (it is an important fact, to which I will come back shortly below, that the distinction holds more easily in legal than in moral discourse). There is a *legislative* moment, in which the rule (and later its modifications, etc.) is posited, and then an *adjudicative* moment, in which it is applied. There is nothing particularly interesting about exceptions introduced at the legislative moment: they are simply part of the rule, and, as was said, limit its scope. The interesting problem (and the problem Miller had in mind) was that of exceptions introduced to the rule at the moment of application: consider a rule like (6), but add to it an exception of the first kind:

(6') It shall be a misdemeanour, punishable by fine of £5, to sleep in any railway station, except if the defendant fell asleep while waiting for a delayed train.

In this situation, it is obvious that Fuller's case would not be interesting in the least. The problem posited by Fuller's example was precisely that there was no explicit exception: the rule was (6), not (6'). It is in this context that Miller's test is useful: if, according to its meaning, the (legal) rule does not include an exception for the case at hand, but we are nevertheless (*legally*) justified in not following it, then we can say that the rule is defeated (in Miller's terms, the rule has an *exception*—that is, an exception which was introduced at the moment of applying the rule, not at the moment of creating it). We can thus see why a claim like Hart's "a rule that ends with 'unless . . .' is still a rule" (1994: 139) cannot but miss the whole point: what we are dealing with is rules that *do not*, as a matter of fact, end with "unless . . .".

Further more, it is important to notice that though what are defeated in concrete cases are legal *norms*, if my argument is correct that is not an interesting fact about those norms, but about the system (or institution) they belong to, about the *law* (in the same sense, for instance, in which for a biologist is not an interesting fact about *me*, but about human beings, that my brain is bigger than that of, say, a cat or that I have exactly forty-six chromosomes). A legal norm like (6) is defeasible not because of some peculiarity of it, but because it is a *legal* rule and law is a regulatory institution (this was shown above by the fact that (1) was indefeasible). Given that law is a regulatory institution, legal norms (as any norm of any regulatory institution) are necessarily defeasible.

THE CIRCUMSTANCES OF DEFEASIBILITY

In this section I want to discuss the circumstances of defeasibility, that is the question of when and why it makes sense to say that a rule is defeasible. I hope to connect the discussion with the distinction between two models of institution offered above. Since the distinction will not be mentioned in the discussion of those circumstances, the latter, if correct, will give independent support to the former.

As was said above, it is an important fact that talking of defeasibility seems to be more plausible when legal rather than moral rules are concerned. In this section I will explore this point, with the hope of showing why this is the case. There are at least two moral philosophies in which the idea of rules being defeasible plays (or could play) an important role, and I consider them in turn. But before that, it would seem useful to pause to think whether it makes sense to speak of defeasible moral rules.

The case of the curious exception

An initial argument against this suggestion is provided, among others, by Paul Ramsey:

> The case of the curious exception is a case of a most elusive thing: by grasping for the features relevant to justifying it morally, one grasps nothing at all or else he grasps nothing exceptional. The so-called exception disappears in the very process of trying to find warrants for it. If there are relevant moral warrants for it, then the action can only be miscalled an "exception" . . .. It is an action falling within moral principles by whatever ultimate norm, not an action located beyond or outside principles. The effort to locate a *justifiable* exception can only have the effect of utterly destroying its exceptional character. The deed is found to be morally doable, it is repeatable, it is one of a *kind*. How rare or frequent is of no consequence to the moral verdicts we render. The same justifying features, the same verdict, the same general judgment falls upon the alleged exception, if it is justified; and so that act falls within our deepened or broadened moral principles (1969: 78).

"One grasps nothing at all or else he grasps nothing exceptional": if in the particular circumstances an exception has to be made to the rule, that only shows that the original formulation of the rule was too rough: "the action violated a former principle, no doubt; but it did not violate a better principle. Instead it may have been an instance of that principle more correctly apprehended and understood" (*ibid.*, 77). The grasping of the exception is not the grasping of an exception, but the realisation of the inadequacies of the moral rule the subject believed in. Alternatively, it might be the case that, after due consideration, the rule as it was all along has to be applied to the particular case: in this case "nothing at all" is grasped and the rule is applied to the case as it would have been to any other case.

From Ramsey's point of view, Miller's test for the existence of exceptions to moral rules does not make sense: it cannot ever be the case that "the rule applies but we are justified in not following it": that the rule applies *means* that we cannot ever be justified in not following it; that we are justified in not following it *means* that the rule as we knew it was defective, and a "deepened or broadened" version of it would show how it does not apply to the case:

> The fact is that if one attaches an exception-making criterion at any point along a line of reasoning from the more general to the more specific principles, all the moral insight that went before on the scale is immediately suspended. If one adds to the verdict: "never tell a lie or steal except to save life . . ." the exception-generating criterion: ". . . unless not-to-lie-or-steal-in-order-to-save-life would accomplish greater good on the whole", this promptly undercuts one's grounds for saying that "not-to-lie-or-to-steal-in-order-to-save-life" would be wrong or one's ground for saying that to-lie-or-to-steal-in-order-to-save-life would be right (1969: 86).

Therefore there cannot be exceptions to moral rules: the need for an exception can only arise because of a badly formulated moral rule, that is, a rule that is not a correct moral rule. Conversely, what we know as moral rules are not really rules, but rules of thumb. An action is correct not because it follows from what we take to be a valid moral rule, but precisely the other way around: that the rule is a valid rule is shown by the fact that it agrees with our intuitions about what is right to do in the circumstances. Rules here are "summary" rules in Rawls's terms (this does not mean that every application of the rule is arbitrary: *cf.* 139 n. 9 below).[1]

Can a moral philosophy circumvent this problem and claim a function for defeasible rules in moral reasoning other than as a rules of thumb? This is what I want to explore now. First we look at rule-utilitarianism and then at discourse ethics.

Act-utilitarianism and Rule-utilitarianism

As is known, this distinction was introduced by J O Urmson as a defence of J S Mill's utilitarianism. Urmson argued, against what he saw as "the received opinion", that Mill did *not* hold the ultimate test for the rightness or wrongness of an action to be "whether the course of action does or does not tend to promote the ultimate end" (Urmson, 1953: 130). Mill's view, indeed, was quite different (I quote only the section that is relevant for the rule-/act-utilitarianism distinction):

> A. A particular action is justified as being right by showing that it is in accord with some moral rule. It is shown to be wrong by showing that it transgresses some moral rule.
>
> B. A moral rule is shown to be correct by showing that the recognition of that rule promotes the ultimate end (Urmson, 1953: 130–1).

That is to say, the principle of utility is not to be used to evaluate the correctness or otherwise of particular courses of action; rather, it justifies some rules. A course of action is justified or otherwise when it is required or forbidden by a moral rule so justified.

Are these moral rules defeasible? Do they allow for exceptions? We have to be careful here, because we already saw that in this regard to talk of "exceptions" *simpliciter* might be misleading. A distinction was introduced above between "implicit" and "explicit" exceptions, and the criterion for distinguishing one from the other was whether or not the rule's formulation incorporates an exception. But moral rules have no canonical formulation, because in moral reasoning no practical authority is involved (at least not typically):[2]

[1] "What we take to be a valid moral rule": the point is an epistemic (about our knowledge of moral rules) rather than an ontological one (about whether or not there are such things as moral rules). The argument is silent as regards the ontological question.

[2] That is, utilitarianism does not recognise moral authority to anybody (though someone can have theoretical authority on the likely outcomes of an action), but other moral traditions might. This points to the fact that the claim that moral authorities do not exist is a moral rather than a conceptual claim.

hence the fact that an exception is needed for the case at hand immediately and directly obliterates any normative importance the rule had, because it shows the rule to be faulty. We are back to Ramsey's "case of the curious exception".

This is a crucial problem for rule-utilitarianism. To see it we can consider an example like Kant's: *A* knows where *B* is. C asks *A* where *B* is, in order (he duly informs *A*) to go there and murder her. Does *A* have a moral obligation to tell C the truth? (Kant, 1797).

Let us assume that the principle of utility justifies the rule "thou shalt not lie" (this means "recognition of this rule promotes general happiness"). What is *A* to do in the example? If she uses the rule to decide which course of action is the correct one, then she has to tell the truth. But the contribution to the general happiness that her telling the truth in this case will produce is (let us assume) minor, particularly when compared with the evil she will cause to be visited upon *B*.[3] If this assumption holds, it seems that a utilitarian would have to lie. But if she is to use the principle of utility, and not the rule, to decide how to act, then she is not a rule-utilitarian. If *A* is a rule-utilitarian it seems she will have the moral duty to tell the truth, thus bringing about (under our assumption) more suffering than happiness. In other words, it seems that *A* can be *either* a rule-utilitarian *or* a utilitarian, but not both *rule* and *utilitarian* (*see* Singer, 1963: 210, who says of Paley's distinction between "general" and "particular" consequences: "when properly defined, the distinction is a useful one. The system resulting, however, is no longer utilitarian").

But let us continue to assume that *A* is a true utilitarian. Her only way out seems to be for her to regard the rule as a rule of thumb. This solution, however, causes rule-utilitarianism to collapse into act-utilitarianism: it will never be the case that one has to do anything that is against the principle of utility, all things considered. The rules do not have any normative force of their own, they merely reproduce that of the principle of utility: in any case of conflict between the two, the rules cannot win (see the discussion about the Roman concept of *regula* in Chapter 6). So why should we bother with the rules in the first place? Is it not perverse to do so?

This is precisely J C C Smart's criticism of rule-utilitarianism (he calls it "restricted utilitarianism"):

> Suppose that there is a rule *R* and that in 99% of cases the best possible results are obtained by acting in accordance with *R*. Then clearly *R* is a useful rule of thumb; if we have not time or are not impartial enough to assess the consequences of an action it is an extremely good bet that the thing to do is to act in accordance with *R*. But is it not monstrous to suppose that if we *have* worked out the consequences and

[3] Here *A* would have to weigh the moral significance of the evils he will cause to be visited upon *B*, on the one hand, against the utility (if any) her telling the truth will produce *plus* the utility of the fact that her telling the truth in such a case is likely to reinforce a truth-telling society and so on. The assumption is, then, that taking into account *all* relevant considerations, lying to C would produce more utility than telling the truth. Surely this is not conceptually impossible.

> if we have perfect faith in the impartiality of our calculations, and if we *know* that in this instance to break *R* will have better results than to keep it, we should nevertheless obey the rule? Is it not to erect *R* into a sort of idol if we keep it when breaking it will prevent, say some avoidable misery? (Smart, 1956: 176).

Thus, rule-utilitarianism is argued to be incoherent: it either requires the agent to do what he knows is not (all things considered) to the greatest benefit (i.e. to do what is immoral) or it collapses into act-utilitarianism.[4]

Discourse Ethics

The second moral philosophy in which the idea of rules being defeasible plays an important role (the list does not purport to be exhaustive) is discourse ethics, in the form of a distinction between application and justification. In discourse ethics, moral norms (i.e. valid moral norms) are justified if they fulfil the condition (U),

> that all concerned can accept the consequences and the side effects its *universal* observance can be anticipated to have for the satisfaction of *everyone's* interests (and that these consequences are preferred to those of known alternative possibilities for regulation) (Habermas, 1983: 71).

Let us assume that the norm "thou shalt not lie" fulfils this condition (U). Does this mean that *A* has to tell the truth? Not necessarily, because (U) might also ground the validity of a different norm that in this case is to be preferred to the one forbidding lying. If, as it seems likely, this further norm can satisfy (U), then "the validity of the norm forbidding lying would have to be nullified or qualified by the restriction . . . that, in the case of the innocent person, priority has to be given to saving his life" (Günther, 1993b: 33). This would, however, imply that for every norm requiring justification all the situations to which it could conceivably be applied would have to be considered. This leads Klaus Günther, whose *The Sense of Appropriateness* we shall be following rather closely in the following paragraphs, to propose a "strong" version of (U), which I will label (U_S):

> (U_S) A norm is valid and in every case appropriate if the consequences and side effects arising for the interests of each individual as a result of this norm's general observance in every particular situation can be accepted by everyone (1993b: 33).

[4] Since this is not a book about utilitarianism, I am not interested in determining whether this is a final objection or not. It might well be the case that rule-utilitarians can offer an answer to Smart's objection. Indeed, Rawls's distinction between "practice-" and "summary-" rules could well be used to that effect. But this would be immaterial for the argument here. What is important for my argument is that if rule-utilitarianism is not to collapse into act-utilitarianism, Smart's point has to be answered. It would have to be an argument (I would claim) to the effect either that rules would not be defeasible or that the validity of rules can be ascertained using a criterion other than the one used to establish the existence of an exception. As we shall see, this latter claim is the central point of this section.

(U_S) comprises two different ideas: impartiality in what Günther calls the "universal–reciprocal" sense (among all those individuals to be affected by the consequences and side effects of the norm) and appropriateness (to every possible particular situation). Because of this, (U_S) is not workable: to justify a norm under it we would need to know the consequences and side effects of the application of any candidate in every particular case to which it could conceivably be applied. And "it is obviously the case that we never have such a knowledge at our disposal" (*ibid.*, 34).

Günther's solution for this problem is to introduce a new, "weaker" version of (U), (U_W) that, instead of comprising impartiality and appropriateness as (U_S) does, makes reference to the former only:

> (U_W) A norm is valid if the consequences and side effects arising for the interests of each individual as a result of this norm's general observance under unchanged circumstances can be accepted by everyone (1993b: 35).

Now, the justification of a norm does not say anything concerning the appropriateness of its application to any circumstances other than those actually considered. The necessity of knowing in advance all the possible situations to which it could conceivably be applied is removed, and (U) is made workable. But this comes at a price: under (U_S), to know that a norm was valid (justified) was to know that it was appropriate for every situation to which it could be applied. Under (U_W), the application of a valid norm to some of the situations covered by it is not necessarily appropriate, and it might well be defeated. This allows Günther to solve Kant's problem: the norm "thou shalt not lie" is a valid norm, i.e., one that can be justified according to (U_W), but its application to the particular situation of *A*, *B* and *C* is inappropriate.

To judge the appropriateness of the application of a valid norm to a particular unforeseen situation, a principle that incorporates the idea of appropriateness is needed: "we thus need yet another principle [in addition to (U_W)] which obligates us to examine *in every situation* whether the requirement of the rule, namely, that it be followed in every situation to which it is applicable, is *legitimate* too" (Günther, 1993: 37). This new principle, however, is not part of (U_W): the validity of a norm can be ascertained without considering all the features of every situation to which the norm could be applied. But reciprocally, (U_W) is not part of the application principle: the validity of a justified norm can be taken for granted at the level of application and that has as a consequence that in application discourses the participants need not consider all the aspects of *every* situation potentially covered by the rule. All that has to be done is to consider the particular situation in question (e.g. the situation of *A*, *B* and *C* only, and not all situations to which the norm "thou shalt not lie" could possibly be applied), "and for this situation only" (*ibid.*).

In this way, discourse ethics can distinguish between two kinds of discourse: in *justification* discourses, "what is relevant . . . is only the norm itself, independent of its application in a particular situation" (Günther, 1993b: 37):

is it for example, in the interest of everybody that everybody is under a moral duty not to lie? No reference to any particular instance of norm-application is in order here. This is taken up in *application* discourses, where "what is relevant . . . is the particular situation, independent of whether a general observance is also in the interest of everybody . . .. The subject matter is not the validity of a norm for each individual and his interests, but its appropriateness in relation to all the features of the situation" (1993b: 38).

This distinction between justification and application allows discourse ethics to distinguish between the *moral* and the *ethical* point of view. A justified norm is universally valid, that is to say, is valid for every possible context. Habermas believes that in this way he can defend "an outrageously strong claim in the present context of philosophical discussion: namely, that there is a universal core of moral intuition in all times and all societies" (1996c: 201). This core "stems from the conditions of symmetry and reciprocal recognition which are unavoidable presuppositions of communicative action" (*ibid.*). These conditions constitute the moral point of view, which is strong enough to ground the validity of moral norms, but their validity *only*:

> Deontic, cognitive and universal moral theories in the Kantian tradition are theories of justice, which must leave the question of the good life unanswered. They are typically restricted to the question of the *justification* of norms and actions. They have no answer to the question of how justified norms can be *applied* to specific situations and how moral insights can be *realised* (Habermas, 1985: 167–8).

This further question, i.e. whether or not a justified norm is appropriate to a given case, cannot be answered from the moral point of view, which is too thin to warrant such a judgement. Ethical considerations can defeat the application of a valid norm:

> Would the English, on first entering India and encountering the ritual of burning widows, have been entitled to stop it? Hindus would have said that this institution—the burial rite—belonged to the their whole form of life. In that case, I would argue that the English should have abstained, on the one condition that this life-form was really self-maintaining (Habermas, 1996c: 204).

Can discourse ethics with its distinction between application and justification avoid Ramsey's objection? Consider Albrecht Wellmer's critique:

> As far as the grounding of moral norms is concerned . . . the norms we are talking about here can only be "prima facie" norms (such as "thou shalt not lie"). But if that is the case, then the problems of application largely coincide with the problems of exceptional situations or situations of conflict (which means much the same as morally complex situations) . . .. [W]e might say that the problem we are dealing with in the process of moral grounding *is* a problem of application; what is being "applied" is the moral principle itself . . .. [W]e were looking there at principles like "human dignity is inviolable" or "every person has an equal right to the free development of his or her personality" . . . and asking what they *mean* in connection with behaviour towards women or homosexuals. In contrast to Habermas, then, I am of

> the opinion that in the case of morality, the problem of grounding has the character of a problem of application; what moral discourse is concerned with is the "application" of the moral point of view, whether to concrete social problems areas or to the situations in which individuals act (Wellmer, 1991: 205).

What follows from a norm complying with (U)? Two answers are in principle possible, according to Wellmer: it either follows that a norm is just or that it is right to act according to it in concrete situations. (U) seems to link these two questions, but this is its weakness: "(U) succeeds in binding justice to morality only at the price of assimilating moral problems to legal ones" (Wellmer, 1991: 148).

We have seem that according to Günther (and Habermas) *it does not* follow from a norm being valid under (U) (under (U_W) for Günther) that it is right to act according to it in a concrete situation (to claim otherwise would lead to absurd results, like *A*'s having to tell C where *B* is). But if this is the case, what does it mean to say that a norm is just (which is the remaining possibility)? Why should we care about the justice of a norm if the fact that we have agreed to it does not by itself imply that we should *act* according to it? It seems that (U) is implausible in either reading: if it is a guide to action in concrete situations it is absurd, if it is not it is irrelevant. And Wellmer's critique of the Habermasian (U) can equally be levelled, I suppose Wellmer would claim, against Günther's (U_W).

Or could it? Günther's answer to Wellmer's objection is to notice that "the distinction between rules and modes of action does not however appear that plausible if one considers that norms can be *reasons* for action" : the data that constitute the concrete situation draw their justifying force not from themselves, "but only from their connection to the prescribed action in the form of a warrant or norm (W) worded in non-singular terms" (Günther, 1993b: 52).[5] Without justified moral norms, "the data and the situation features can draw their justifying force, as reasons for or against an intended action, really only from themselves". The answer to the question "what should I do" would thus become a matter of Aristotelian judgement rather than discourse (Günther, 1993b: 53).

Thus, norms can work as reasons for action, as "warrants" (in Toulmin's sense) for the justifying force of the data and situation features of a concrete case. In doing so, moral norms, Günther claims, belong to and define a form of life, thus shaping the way individuals see the moral universe:

> norms belong to the form of life in whose context we interpret an application situation. When we choose an appropriate mode of action in a situation, this occurs in the light of norms which claim universal validity in the universal-reciprocal and applicative sense (Günther, 1993b: 57).

[5] Günther is here using the scheme of moral argumentation as conceived by Stephen Toulmin (1958: 97).

Precisely because justified norms can claim universal validity, they can be criticised "on a universalist level, namely, independently of our contingent for of life" at the level of justification.

I am not sure about Günther's success against Wellmer in this regard, but fortunately we need not enter into that debate any further. The reason for my discussion of discourse ethics here lies not in the intrinsic interest of discourse ethics, but in the light it throws on what I called before the circumstances of defeasibility. It is now time to advance the main conclusion of this section. For norms and exceptions to exist without one of them eating up the other, two conditions must obtain: *first*, there must be a difference in the criteria used to justify the validity of a rule and those used to judge the existence of an exception to it. If the criterion to ascertain the validity of a norm is encompassed by that needed to decide the existence of an exception, then when learning about the latter we grasp a better version of the former. When this is so, to discuss the existence of an exception (which in discourse ethics is done at the level of the application discourse) would be the same as discussing the precise content of a norm (which in the same vocabulary is done at the level of the justification discourse), and there would be no distinction between the two forms of discourse.

The second condition looks at the *functions* ascribed to the defeasible moral rules. If rules are defeasible, then knowing that they exist and what their content is will not tell us what to do, since our moral duty to act in a particular way will arise only in the light of the full information available when the concrete case appears and the application discourse is actually carried through. If, therefore, the only function performed by the moral rules is guidance of behaviour (by way of imposing duties and granting rights), then the general rules are uninteresting insofar as they remain general. For a moral theory to make sense of the notion of defeasible moral norms, then, a function has to be ascribed to moral norms which is not reducible to action-guidance.

This is indeed the problem of rule-utilitarianism, as identified above: what function do the rules fulfil, besides that of pointing out the course of action most likely to maximise utility? If the answer to this question is "none", as Smart assumed, then all the normative force of the rules would derive from the principle of utility, and utility-based considerations would have to defeat their application to concrete cases for all those cases in which the principle of utility and the rules do not recommend the same action. Rules can be nothing but rules of thumb, and he who looks for an exception will find "nothing exceptional", but at most a better formulation of the rule.

I believe Wellmer's argument can be understood in the same way: Wellmer's crucial point, indeed, is his claim that "what moral discourse is concerned with is the "application" of the moral point of view" (1991: 206). In other words, he assumes that moral discourse aims at deciding how to act in concrete cases. If this is indeed correct, it would appear as though Günther's distinction

> turn[s] general practical discourse into a superfluous arrangement or something just for fun: Why should we think about reasons first, when the decision about what we really are obliged to do depends on the concrete case? (Günther, 1993a: 149).

Günther's reply must show that deciding what to do in concrete cases is not the only point of moral deliberation. Indeed, that in justification discourses is not even the primary point. His answer, as we have seen, points to the constitutive functions that justified moral norms perform in relation to our moral practices and identity:

> Moral reasons, which are used for justification in concrete cases, shape the mutual relations between each of us as individual and as members of a moral community. They represent the characteristic traits of our intersubjectivity, i.e. the general expectations according to which we want to treat each other and how we want to be treated. For example, we don't want to be treated as someone who could be betrayed for any reason (Günther, 1993a: 143).

If Günther is right, justified moral norms are something more than rules of thumb; they are not simply provisionally adequate maxims, the validity of which will only be decided once they are put to the test of application to a concrete case. Notice the structure of the argument: in the first place, Günther needs to show that the principles that control application are different from those that control justification (this he does by the breaking up of (U_S) into (U_W) and a principle of appropriateness). Additionally, he has to assign some value or function to the fact of a norm being justified, a value or function that is independent of the norm's guidance of behaviour in concrete cases. Failure to meet *this* requirement is the problem with rule-utilitarianism, and the reason why rule-utilitarian rules can (according to Smart's argument) only be rules of thumb.

Whether or not Günther is successful in defending the distinction between application and justification discourse is something that need not concern us here. All that we need to notice is how Wellmer's point is that (to put it in my words) in ethics the circumstances of defeasibility are not present: everything that is morally relevant, he claims, should be taken up at the level of application; whatever the principles guiding the justification discourse might be, they have to be addressed at the level of application together with issues of appropriateness: "the problem we are dealing with in the process of moral grounding *is* a problem of application; what is being "applied" is the moral principle itself" (Wellmer, 1991: 205).

At the outset of this section I said I hoped to connect this discussion on the circumstances of defeasibility with the distinction offered in Chapter 1 between autonomous and regulatory institutions. The connection should be clear now. It is not a coincidence that rules in regulatory institutions are defeasible while they need not be in autonomous institutions. The explanation is precisely the existence of different criteria to judge rules from exceptions in the former only, but not (necessarily) in the latter. For consider, under what circumstances would we say that there is an exception to the rule that no football player can touch the ball with his hands? The answer is, the exception exists if, and only if, FIFA has passed a rule with that propositional content, like the one that authorises the goalkeeper to do so inside his penalty box. *But this is the same condition any rule has to pass to become a rule of the game.* Hence, in this context the rule eats up the exception, and the rule is indefeasible (if one looks for an exception, "one grasps nothing at all"). This is the opposite problem to that of rule-utilitarianism, where we saw that the exception eats up the rule ("he grasps nothing exceptional"). The explanation for this is that games are practices inside which there is no space for two or more independent criteria ("independent" because a game can allow for a set of criteria of validity insofar as they are built into one structure: FIFA, the FA, etc.). There is just one criterion to establish the existence, content and applicability of a rule, and because of this rules of games are indefeasible.

In regulatory institutions the rules exist because they have been created according to the institution's institutive rules, but this is not all that there is to it. The regulatory direction of the institution creates an independent criterion according to which the existence or non-existence of exceptions can be judged. Any explanation of defeasibility has to show how different criteria are used to ascertain the validity of a rule from those used to ascertain the existence of an exception to it (we saw that for Hart, e.g., those criteria were "the need for certain rules . . . and the need to leave open, for later settlement by an informed, official choice, issues which can only be properly appreciated and settled when they arise in a concrete case"(1994: 130)). If there is only one criterion, no norm can be defeasible: the exception collapses into the rule, or the rule collapses into the exception, "one grasps nothing at all or nothing exceptional".

We saw the importance of this plurality of criteria in the New Testament:

> Alas for you, scribes and Pharisees, hypocrites! You pay tithes of mint and dill and cumin; but you have overlooked the weightier demands of the law—justice, mercy and good faith. It is these that you should have practised, without neglecting the others" (Matt. 23: 23).

This is why the rule that forbids working on the Sabbath can be defeated on the basis of "justice and mercy and good faith". Only because the weightier matters of the law should not be overlooked, the exception does not collapse into the rule; only because paying tithes of mint and dill and cumin should not be neglected, the rule does not collapse into the exception.

NORMALITY AND DEFEASIBILITY

The same point could be expressed in a rather different language. We have seen that the idea of defeasibility is linked to that of *normality*, in the sense in which this idea appears in the *Digest*:

> Jul D.1.3.10 *Neque leges neque senatus consulta ita scribi possunt, ut omnes casus qui quandoque inciderint comprehendantur, sed suficit ea quae plerunque accidunt contineri* (Neither statutes nor senatus consulta can be written in such a way that all cases which might at any time occur are covered; it is, however, sufficient that the things which very often happen are embraced) (*cf.* also D. 1.3.3–6)

In other words, rules have to be applied in an exclusionary manner if the case is "normal", but other considerations come into play if the case is abnormal:

> Exceptions occur whenever a situation arises in which the particular events in issue bring into operation some legal principle or value of sufficient importance to override the presumptive sufficiency of the conditions stated expressly as conditions for the vesting of the right . . .. The general statement of the right is adequate if it stipulates what is necessary and sufficient for establishing the right in the common run of cases, subject to any express exceptions or provisos for regularly occurring and readily foreseeable (or doctrinally well-documented or case-law established) defeating factors. But the operation of background principles can be seen as raising the possibility of rather open-ended exceptions in cases of an exceptional or unusual sort (MacCormick, 1995: 103–4).

The idea of normality, following MacCormick, allows us to account for the formality of rules: under normal circumstances the rule is followed if the agent acts as the rule requires her to act, i.e. if she does what the rule says she has to do without considering the substantive merits of the case. When the case is out of the ordinary, on the other hand, the rule is not necessarily applicable: an implicit exception might exist.

Now the problem naturally is, how can the agent know whether a particular case is "normal"? If rules can be applied without evaluative considerations, then the classification of the case as normal has to be free of those considerations as well (because no application of the rule is possible before it has been established that the case is normal).

The last section's argument was that for rules to be defeasible two different criteria must be used: one to identify a rule and its content, another to judge its appropriateness. The idea of normality is grounded on this duality. Normal cases are those in which both criteria overlap: a rule the existence of which is justified by the first criterion does not produce, when its application to a particular case is judged according to the second, an inappropriate result. The case is therefore one in which the rule can "simply" be applied.[6]

When the issue is looked at from this perspective, it is obvious that *the rule* cannot tell the agent which cases are normal. In autonomous institutions, we saw that the autonomy of the institution implies that there is only one criterion according to which the correctness of an applicative decision is judged.

[6] NB. It might well be the case that because we are brought up in a society and come to know its practices (or even, as communitarians claim, those practices partly define our self-identity), in many cases we need not explicitly engage in deliberation to "simply" know whether or not the two criteria overlap. But this epistemic point, important as it might be, has no important consequence for an ontology of law.

This is crucially different in regulatory institutions, where the appropriateness of an applicative decision is to be measured according to the beneficial or harmful consequences that acknowledging different levels of formality to the rule in question will produce in the regulatory goals of the institution. Thus, it is an interesting fact about the *practice*, not about the *rules* of games that rules are indefeasible. Likewise, it is a fundamental question about legal *practice*, not about legal *rules*, whether and how legal rules are defeasible.

This chapter does not contain an account of the considerations according to which legal cases are judged to be normal or abnormal, rules defeated or not. Some thoughts on this issue will be entertained in the final chapter. What I have argued is that these considerations are not to be found in the rule the application of which is at issue. I now want to consider some of H L A Hart's early claims on the subject.

HART ON DEFEASIBILITY

Hart's first publication on legal theory was "The Ascription of Responsibility and Rights" (1948). In it, Hart claimed that legal concepts were "irreducibly defeasible":

> There is another characteristic of legal concepts . . . which makes the word "unless" as indispensable as the word "etcetera" in any explanation or definition of them. ... [T]he accusations or claims upon which law courts adjudicate can be usually challenged or opposed in two ways. First, by a denial of the facts upon which they are based . . . and secondly by something quite different, namely, a plea that although all the circumstances on which a claim could succeed are present, yet in the particular case, the claim or accusation should not succeed because other circumstances are present which bring the case under consideration under some recognised head of exception, the effect of which is either to defeat the claim or accusation altogether, or to "reduce" it, so that only a weaker claim can be sustained (1948: 147–8).

It should be noticed that this can bear two quite different interpretations (though there is no ambiguity if the whole section of Hart's article is taken into account): legal concepts are defeasible, says Hart, because they could be defeated by a defence based on circumstances that "bring the case under consideration under some *recognised* head of exemption". If this statement is taken to mean that the exceptions have to be previously recognised, then Hart is after all not talking of defeasibility nor about anything interesting or important: he is merely saying that a rule does not apply when it does not apply (*see* above at 123ff).

As we saw (above at 125) Hart seems to have confused this point in *The Concept of Law*, when he simply argued that "a rule that ends with 'unless ...' is still a rule" (1994: 139). If this is the meaning of the remark in "The Ascription of Responsibility and Rights", then it clearly does not support Hart's conclusions in it about the irreductibility of legal language: in this case, it could be possible to give necessary and sufficient conditions for the application of any legal concept, if we bother to list all the "recognised" exceptions to which it is subject.

But the article is clear enough for us to think that this was not Hart's intention when writing that passage. Hart goes to great lengths to show why such a strategy is bound to fail; therefore it does not seem unreasonable to think that the problem he was dealing with was not that of the possibility of explicit exceptions, but the different one of defeasibility of legal concepts (i.e. *implicit* exceptions to rules).

And it is precisely this point, I believe, that calls for further refinement. Hart's thesis in "The Ascription of Responsibility and Rights" was that legal *concepts* were irreducibly defeasible. But it is unclear why the fact that a new defence against the claim that there is, e.g. a contract between *A* and *B* means that the *concept* of a contract is defeasible: "the statement that there is no contract between *A* and *B* is an application of the term "contract", albeit a negative one" (Baker, 1977: 34).

In my opinion, the situation is clarified when we realise that what is defeasible is *a rule*, not *a concept*. Only because the rule was not applied could we say that the application of the contract was defeated in the case at hand. There are (legal) rules which define what a contract is. A "new defence" is precisely a defence against the application of (some of) these rules. In making the defence, counsel will use the concept to say that this case is not an instantiation of it.

As is known, however, in 1968 Hart disowned the claims made in "The Ascription of Responsibility and Rights", because "the main criticisms of it made in recent years are justified" (Hart, 1968b: v). One of the articles given as the source of such criticism contains, regarding Hart's claim that the concept of human action is itself defeasible, an objection that could be read along these lines:

> The rejection of Hart's second thesis [i.e. that "the concept of a human action is what Hart calls a 'defeasible' one"] does not mean that the essence of his valuable insight needs be abandoned; on the contrary, it can and it must be retained. It can be retained by maintaining that it is the concept of being deserving of censure or punishment which is really the defeasible one, not that of a human action. That is to say, if a person performs some untoward action, then he deserves to be censured or punished for having done it, unless he has a satisfactory defence. If he has such a defence, the claim that he is censurable for doing what he did is reduced or perhaps even altogether destroyed (Pitcher, 1960: 235).

Note that "being deserving of censure or punishment" is a consequence of the application of rules (or other normative standards). Here again, it is not the *concept* which is defeasible, but the *rules* according to which the judgement is made. The same goes indeed for Pitcher's remark: it is not the *concept* of being deserving of punishment, but *being deserving of punishment* that is defeasible.[7]

[7] *Cf.* MacCormick, 1995 for a similar view: "it is not after all the *concept* that is defeasible, but some formulated statement of conditions for instantiating the concept in given cases, or some

I do not know whether Hart included this particular point when he disowned his article as a whole. In *The Concept of Law*, however, what is subject to "exceptions incapable of exhaustive statement" (1994: 139) is a *rule*, not a *concept*, as is clear from the following paragraph (referring to the example of a person who promised to visit a friend only to realise, when the day came, that the promise could be kept only if neglecting someone dangerously ill):

> The fact that this is accepted as an adequate reason for not keeping the promise surely does not mean that there is no rule requiring promises to be kept, only a certain regularity in keeping them. It does not follow from the fact that such rules have exceptions incapable of exhaustive statement, that in every situation we are left to our discretion and are never bound up to keep a promise (*ibid.*).[8]

I do not think this can be denied, but *it does follow* that we should apply the rule and keep the promise *only after* we have checked the reasons that could defeat the rule in the particular case, and arrived at the conclusion that the situation at hand is normal enough for the rule to be applied.[9] This point is not a sceptical one about the impossibility of having rules once they are acknowledged to be defeasible, but the obvious one that a defeasible rule cannot be applied without deciding in the case that it was not defeated. Nor am I arguing that in each instance of rule-application the agent will be aware of her checking of all the potentially defeating circumstances. It is obviously true that she will not. But a conceptualisation of rule-following that does not leave conceptual space for this question is, because of this very reason, bound to be defective when applied to defeasible rules.

One way in which the argument of the previous chapters could be resisted is by pointing out to legal practice: it is not true to claim, it is sometimes argued, that the law can never be "simply" and "straightforwardly" applied. Lawyers, judges, politicians and others are all able (with more or less accuracy) to recognise instances in which the law is clear from those in which it is not, even

assertion, ascription or claim based on a certain understanding of those conditions" (102). MacCormick argues that it is the *claim* not the concept that is defeasible, and I think that the claim is defeasible because the *rule* upon which it is based is defeasible. Notice that in the last sentence of the quoted statement Pitcher seems to agree with this: it is "the *claim* that he is censurable" that is defeated, not the *concept* of being censurable.

[8] The fact that the sentence quoted above (i.e. "a rule that ends with 'unless . . .' is still a rule") immediately follows this statement makes the former even more intriguing: the point is *precisely* that, as I said before, the rule *does not have* an exception, i.e. it does not end with "unless ...".

[9] I am not claiming that no application of a defeasible rule can ever be conclusively justified. Answering this (mistaken) criticism of the possibility of having exceptions to (moral) rules, Miller said that "If the rule is recognised, if its application to the case in point is unquestioned, and if after careful examination no mitigating circumstances have been revealed—then the judgement has been justified. It is not probably justified; it *is* justified. In such a case, to cite the rule is to give a conclusive reason (Miller, 1956: 270). My claim is merely that before justifiably applying a defeasible rule (to any case!) we have to know that there is not, in the case, a reason not to apply the rule, even when the case at hand fulfils the (explicit) operative facts of a rule.

if they disagree on which cases are in between. We only need to consider the huge number of cases that never reach the courts to see that this argument needs to be addressed.

And addressed it will be. We begin by noticing that this is not necessarily an objection to the argument defended here. For all we know, it *could* be that all those cases are clear, not because no "fresh" judgement is needed to apply the rules in them, but because people do make a fresh judgement and they all come up with the same conclusion. Under this description, though those cases would still be clear in the sense that they would not reach the courts, etc., they would not be "clear" in the sense that they would still require a fresh moral judgement to be made.

Now, I do believe this answer is sound and true, but I do not want to pursue it here because I want to make a stronger claim (or perhaps I want to pursue what amounts to the same argument in the following way): I want to say that there are values or normative beliefs (I will leave this vague until the final chapter) that underlie legal practices, in such a way that without an understanding of them there is no way in which we can know what the law is for any particular case (unless, of course, we are told so by a person whom we have reason to believe knows what she is talking about). The problem is, those values/normative beliefs are not specifically legal, they are part and parcel of a wider social world we are brought up in; they are part of the *Volksgeist*. It is therefore difficult to step out of them and try to look at our legal system *as if* we did not know them. My claim is, however, that if we could do that we would see that we could not know what the law is for any particular case.

This is to be the next chapter's argument. I shall consider some legal problems taken from a setting far removed from our own, so removed that we are not inclined to think the people who lived in it shared our values/normative beliefs. My example will be Roman law, and the claim will be that it is difficult to know what the (Roman) law was for any particular case, except when we are told so by a Roman jurist.

6

A Roman Puzzle

En esas remotas páginas está escrito que los animales se dividen en *a*) pertenecientes al Emperador, *b*) embalsamados, *c*) amaestrados, *d*) lechones, *e*) sirenas, *f*) fabulosos, g) perros sueltos, *h*) incluidos en esta clasificación, *I*) que se agitan como locos, *j*) innumerables, *k*) dibujados con un pincel finísimo de pelo de camello, *l*) etcétera, *m*) que acaban de romper el jarrón, *n*) que de lejos parecen moscas.

J L Borges, *El Idioma Analítico de John Wilkins* (1941)*

This chapter attempts to offer an example of the way in which understanding the meaning of some legal system's *norms* (using this word in its most general sense, as referring to any standard) cannot be sufficient to apply them, that is, to know what the legal solution is for *any* particular case. I hope that this example will show how artificial is the idea that the meaning of a rule determines its application. But the discussion of the idea of *regula juris*, to be undertaken in the second section of this chapter, is interesting for broader reasons. The distinction between understanding a rule as *being* the law and *describing* it is highly relevant, I believe, to understanding legal science (only if rules are descriptions of the law they might "get it wrong" and call for correction).[1] The discussion to follow is not, then, just a discussion of an amusing fact about a system of law that ceased to be valid centuries ago.

When one thinks of the importance of Roman law for the evolution of the Western Legal tradition, more often than not one's interest is focused upon Roman legal material. To some extent this is only natural, since Roman institutions have been "transplanted", to use Alan Watson's metaphor, to most Western legal systems and beyond. Still today, centuries later, there is a strikingly clear continuity between the content of the rules of the German BGB or the French *Code Civil* regarding, say, *emptio venditio* and the relevant rules of Roman law. Though this point should not be overstated (of course there are important differences between the two), it should also be uncontroversial: that

* "On those remote pages it is written that animals are divided into *a)* those that belong to the emperor, *b)* embalmed ones, *c)* those that are trained, *d)* suckling pigs, *e)* mermaids, *f)* fabulous ones, *g)* stray dogs, *h)* those that are included in this classification, *i)* those that tremble as if they were mad, *j)* innumerable ones, *k)* those drawn with a very fine camel's-hair brush, *l)* others, *m)* those that have just broken a flower vase, *n)* those that resemble flies from a distance".

[1] Rules "get it wrong" in cases like those discussed by Planiol (above, at 119 n.5), or in cases like *Bolling* v. *Sharp* (347 US 497 (1954)), where the American constitution's restriction of the equal protection clause to states ("no *state* shall deny...") was eventually disregarded.

is one of the main reasons why most European law students have to study Roman law as part of their syllabus (*see* Zimmermann, 1995).

In an important article published in 1974, Tony Honoré invites us to shift our focus, and to look not at the rules, nor the concepts, of Roman law:

> A scholar interested in Roman law is sometimes asked to say in what the contribution of Roman law to our modern legal culture consists. When I am asked this I think first of the *rules* of Roman law which, through the various sorts of "reception" have found a niche in modern European legal systems. Then I turn to the *concepts*, like ownership, which have become embedded in our thinking and in our social ways. But perhaps one should attach equal or greater importance to a third area of influence, namely, the *method of reasoning* which modern legal cultures have inherited from Roman law (Honoré, 1974: 84).

This might seem to be a bold claim indeed. After all, everybody knows the importance of the *rules* and the *concepts* of Roman law. Why was the Roman method of *legal reasoning* so peculiarly important? After analysing the kind of arguments the Romans used, Honoré concludes that they can be reduced to two: "open arguments [i.e. principles] and appeals to rules of law" (1974: 93). This is hardly surprising. After all, *every* argument is either an open argument or an appeal to a rule of law. But this is not the important point. What is important, according to Honoré, is that the Romans developed a "canon of unacceptable arguments" (*Ibid.* at 91).[2]

The idea that there are certain arguments that in the context of legal justification, of legal discourse,[3] are out of place is linked to the idea of formality, in the sense given to that term by Patrick Atiyah (1984). It is not necessarily the case that unacceptable arguments are completely irrelevant for a correct solution of the case (i.e. correct, all things considered), but they are nevertheless unacceptable as arguments for a *legal* decision. Honoré tells us that there were, broadly speaking, two kinds of arguments that the Romans, in opposition to the Greeks, did not accept in legal argumentation. The first were, to adapt his terms, "system-biased" arguments, that is, arguments whose force depended upon "idiosyncratic features of religious, moral, philosophical or political thought systems" (Honoré, 1974: 93). The second were *ad hominem* arguments. The point I want to focus upon is that from this viewpoint the constraints that limit legal discourse are not *rules*, but arguments. If we were to adopt Honoré's viewpoint we would see the law not as a collection of (more or less general) solutions for cases, but as one of *acceptable arguments.* Though Honoré himself seems to have thought otherwise, the canon of legal argument is not one more rule alongside the rules concerning, say, the validity

[2] For a similar view, see Frier (1985: 15): "The doctrine of "autonomous law", which appear for the first time in Cicero's *pro Caecina*, was to remain the guiding ideology of the legal profession for some two millennia, through all vicissitudes of social and economic circumstances".

[3] I will use "legal argumentation", "legal justification" and "legal discourse" as related concepts: legal justification is what legal argumentation is about, and legal discourse is legal argumentation considered as a social practice.

of a will (like the *regula catoniana*), but something that fulfils the role of justifying the application of the norms of the system (Honoré in fact appears to believe that the canon is a rule of recognition. *See* 1974: 73).

ROMAN COMMON SENSE

In Chapter 1, I have argued for a distinction between what I call "autonomous" and "regulatory" institutions. The claim was that what distinguished autonomous from regulatory institutions was the fact that only the existence of the latter was explained and justified by the need to regulate a particular sphere of social life. The former was characterised as an institution the existence of which is to be explained and justified because it allows people to engage in an activity that did not exist before. Therefore, though autonomous institutions do regulate a sphere of social life, they regulate it only to constitute their object, not because the regulation of that sphere is seen to have any independent value (independent, that is, from the fact of the institution being constituted).

An important consequence of an institution being autonomous is that the application of its rules does not call for justification. If the particular requirements of the *stipulatio* were challenged, the only correct answer would have been "this is simply what you have to do". The same happens in games, as Wittgenstein showed (1958: § 66). This does not mean that the content of the rules could not be evaluated. What it does mean is that whatever the result of that evaluation might be, it has no impact on the application of the rules. Some of the formalities of the *stipulatio* might have been extremely unhelpful, even damaging, when looked at from a sociological or economic point of view (as indeed they were: *see* Watson, 1985b). But this is immaterial to the decision whether or not a particular *stipulatio* was valid. After all, if the law is not seen as a regulatory institution—i.e. if its existence is not explained by, nor seen as having anything to do with, its regulatory relation with some sphere of social activity—why should the (less than perfect) regulation it necessarily implies be an objection to its application?

A peculiarity of Roman legal development is that, although the Romans abandoned this formalistic conception of law at quite an early stage, the old ideas about the law survived for centuries. What they did was not only to adopt a regulatory conception of the law: a whole new, parallel system evolved, a system that existed beside, not instead of, the old and formalistic *ius civile*:

> When classical jurisprudence began its work it found, alongside the *ius civile*, the *ius honorarium* already in a state of strong development: the *ius civile* strict and rigid in its basis though certainly modernized in some details by later legislation and by borrowings from magistral law; the *ius honorarium* progressive and subject to constant further development (Kunkel, 1973: 82).

The formalism characteristic of the *ius civile* was in striking contrast with the flexible *ius honorarium*. While the *ius civile* kept its formalism throughout the centuries of Roman legal development, the *ius honorarium*, under the authority of the Praetor's edicts, was moulded and refined until it reached high levels of legal sophistication (notice, incidentally, that the praetors did not have authority to make new law: what they could do was to declare, once a year, how they were going to *apply* the *existing* law. Maybe this can account for the parallel existence of the two systems over time; maybe the fact that the praetor was not seen as *changing* the law but simply accommodating its application, may explain both the fact of the survival of the old *ius civile and* the extraordinary level of flexibility and progressive development of the *ius honorarium*).[4]

The English Common Law is generally thought of as a good analogy to the Roman legal system (*see* Stein, 1992).[5] The analogy should not be overstated, and we are at risk of doing just that if we think of the existence of the *ius civile* and the *ius honorarium* as meaning the existence of two different and separated sets of rules (in Rome there was only one system of "courts"). The difference was in the kind of arguments that were acceptable in disputes covered by one or the other. Good faith, for example, was a good argument to rely upon in a case concerning sale, but not in a case concerning the interpretation or enforcement of a *stipulatio*.

This is not to say that the parallel existence of both systems was completely irrelevant, nor that the *ius honorarium* was infinitely flexible, and here we come across an intriguing feature of Roman law. Romans are known not to have been interested in theorising about the law. They did not, for instance, have a *theory* of obligations. It is true that in Justinian's *Institutes* we do find a systematisation of the sources of obligations that could be said to be the starting point of a general theory of obligations (Inst. 3.13.2), but it is nonetheless also true that it reflects the particular reason the *Institutes* were written for (as a textbook for students) rather than the general approach of Roman jurists (*see* Honoré, 1991: 506–7 for a different view). When Roman jurists bothered to hold general views about, for example, the sources of obligations, they did so in a highly unsystematic fashion, merely listing different sources: "*Obligamur aut re aut verbis aut simul utroque aut consensu aut lege aut iure honorario aut necessitate aut ex peccato*" (Mod. D. 44.7.52.*pr* "we are bound either *re*, or verbally, or by both of these at the same time, or by consent, or by statute, or by praetorian law, or by necessity, or by wrongdoing"). This seems to be as systematic a classification of the sources of obligations as Jorge L Borges' classification of animals.

[4] For example, some of the problems created by the rigid nature of the *stipulatio* were solved by the granting of remedies for extortion and fraud, in the form of *exceptiones*. Notice that "the point of an *exceptio* is precisely that the defendant is not denying the validity of the plaintiff's case. He is merely claiming that there is another fact that ought to be taken into account. In other words, extortion or fraud did not invalidate a *stipulatio*" (Watson, 1985a: 26). The *Praetor* did not modify the *ius civile* when he decided to grant an *exceptio*. *See* also (Watson, 1981: 189).

[5] I am grateful to Professor Reinhard Zimmermann for this reference.

This cavalier attitude with the theory of private law was related to the fact that they did not try to find general rules to cover classes of cases, but correct legal solutions for particular situations. As has been claimed,

> the great strength of the Roman mind lay not in theoretical construction but in the technically accurate mastering of actual individual cases. In this sphere the classical jurists remained unsurpassed. With sublime sureness of touch they applied the methods of logical reasoning, the technique of the procedural formulas, and the complicated rules and conventions which resulted from the existence side by side of legal institutions old and new, civil and magistral, elastic and strictly formalistic (Kunkel, 1973: 111).

They had, most of the time, a very practically-oriented method. Legal technicalities were not, most of the time, an obstacle to their obtaining the solution they deemed convenient. Their approach to the solution of concrete cases was, most of the time, predominantly practical: legal doctrines were, most of the time, used when they could serve some practical ends and after that they were dropped if that was necessary (*cf.* Schulz, 1936: 41).

Two examples might be of use here. The first concerns *servitutes* (servitudes). They were thought of as a burden land carries for the benefit of neighbouring land. Originally, the obligation for the burdened land had to be passive, i.e. the owner of the burdened land was under a duty *not* to do something (not to interfere with someone's right of way, right to drive beasts, right of light, and so on). Servitudes could not impose a positive obligation on the owner of the servient land.[6] This, however, was soon perceived as unsatisfactory, and a new kind of servitude, *oneris ferendi,* was recognised,

> with reference to a servitude imposed for the purpose of providing support, an action is available to us, to compel the servient owner to maintain the support and repair his buildings in the way provided for when the servitude was created (Ulp. D. 8.5.6.2).

Ulpian then presents the objection that this runs against the nature of servitudes, *servitus in faciendo consistere non potest,* but he answers immediately, and without offering further argumentation:

> However, the view of Servius has prevailed, so that in this particular case, a man can claim the right to compel his opponent to repair a wall, so that it can support the load (*ibid.*).

The case of the servitude *oneris ferendi,* we are told, "is [an] instance of the readiness of Roman jurists to abandon principle when principle was inconvenient" (Watson, 1970: 55; on *oneris ferendi* in general *see* Watson, 1968:

[6] *See* Pomp. D. 8.1.15.1: "*Servitutium non ea natura est, ut aliquid facias quis, ueluti uiridia tollat aut amoeniorem prospectum praestet, aut in hoc ut in suo pingat, sed ut aliquid patiatur aut non faciat*" ("It is not in keeping with the nature of servitudes that the servant owner be required to do something, such as to remove trees to make a view more pleasant or, for the same reason, to paint something on his land. He can only be required to allow something to be done or to refrain from doing something").

191ff). Watson goes even further, and claims that the explanations offered by some authors for the existence of *oneris ferendi* are "unsatisfactory since they are all too subtle and over-sophisticated" (1968: 199). No special theory is needed to explain its existence, since

> there is . . . really no problem about the historical origins of this servitude. The utility of having such a right of support from a neighbour's wall is obvious. And it is equally obvious that such a right to be fully useful must be a real and not just a personal right. But in the Roman framework such a real right could only be a servitude or at least be like a servitude. In the circumstances, the recognition of a servitude of support was virtually inevitable—it would reflect nothing but discredit on the quality of the Roman jurists if no such right had been recognized (Watson, 1968: 199).

The second example concerns the *in iure cessio*, used to transfer ownership of certain things. Both parties would appear before a magistrate. The transferee would claim the thing as his, the transferor (i.e. the owner) would assent to this claim and the judge would declare the thing as being the property of the transferee (Gai. 1.2.24). This being, technically speaking, a judicial proceeding, the decision could only affect the parties to the action. "But here as elsewhere, legal logic, once it had served its turn, was less important to the Romans than convenience, and the magistrate's decision was treated as meaning that the transferee was in actual fact the true owner" (Watson, 1970: 52).[7]

This is what has earned Roman jurists justly deserved recognition.[8] It is, though, only half of the story. We must now turn to the other half.

LOCATIO CONDUCTIO AND THE PROTECTION OF THE LESSEE

The first example has to be *locatio conductio*, i.e. the contract of hire. If we are to follow Watson in this regard (1985a: 16), *locatio conductio* was the residual category for all bilateral contracts that were not sale and in which the obligation of one of the parties was in money. If no money was due, not one, but three contractual forms were used: mandate, deposit and loan for consumption (the last two were *real* contracts; mere agreement was not

[7] Another example, if it were needed, of this attitude is provided by the case of hire-purchase, which was dealt with as involving two transactions: *locatio conductio* (*rei*) and *emptio venditio*. The rights and duties of the parties were adjusted in a "most flexible and undogmatic manner" (Zimmermann, 1990: 531ff).

[8] *Cf.* Watson (1972: 26): "I have tried to show by means of a few examples that, at least sometimes, the Roman jurists were more concerned to reach a sensible practical result than to follow the dictates of a rigorous logic, that they were not ivory-tower philosophers but sensible men dealing with contemporary problems of living. Though it may be felt that this diminishes the claims of Roman law to be a system of universal unchanging validity, it must make us accept the Roman jurists as individual human beings. And we must give credit to their sophistication". *See* also Stein (1966): "It is perfectly true that the Roman jurists were empirical rather than systematic in their approach to legal problems. They were less interested in certainty and predictability than in ensuring just decisions which accorded with their idea of the nature of things" (at 102).

enough to bring them about: the actual delivery of the thing was also required. Hence they were also unilateral: to use a technically inaccurate language, they were born with one party's obligation already executed, therefore only the other had an obligation under the contract. *Mandatum* was also unilateral, though for other reasons). Thus *locatio conductio* was, along with *emptio venditio*, one of the main contracts in Roman law. Now, if we focus mainly on *locatio conductio (rei)*, we find that

> the legal position of the lessee was . . . very precarious. The lessor could, during the life of the contract and in contravention of the same, deprive him of the use of the thing leased, his only remedy being the *actio conducti*. The classical jurists simply state the legal rule: the lessee is not the possessor of the thing, and therefore cannot insist on its enjoyment in the face of prohibition by the lessor (Schulz, 1936: 24)

The fact that the lessee was not a possessor had important consequences; not only could he not insist on enjoyment of the thing in the face of prohibition by the lessor, but he also could not use the *actiones in rem* nor the possessory interdicts in order to protect *his* use of the property against third parties:

> If, for instance, the lessee lost the factual power [over the thing] through an unlawful act committed by a third party, only the lessor had the interdict (provided he was possessor; in sub-letting the principal lessor still had the interdict); the lessee could only hold the lessor liable under the contract, but not directly the third party (Kaser, 1965: 86).

The owner could also evict the lessee at any moment, even if the parties had agreed upon a specific term of tenancy (*cf.* Zimmermann, 1990: 378). In all those cases the lessee had no protection against the lessor except his *actio conducti*.

The fact that the lessee was not possessor is intriguing, given that Roman law granted possession to many other holders of things: "why is the lessee not possessor while the pledgee, the tenant at will (*precario*) and the sequester are possessors? This question is not put at all, nor are a dozen others" (Schulz, 1936: 24).

At the same time, living conditions in Rome were rather bad, and the availability of houses a constant problem. We are commonly tempted, Zimmermann warns, to judge living conditions in Rome according to what we know about "leisurely country towns like Pompeii or Herculaneum" (1990: 345). Only the well-off could afford to live on their own, while the rest had to live in rented *insulae*, and they usually had to sub-let "every room in their cenaculum which they could possibly spare" (*cf.* Zimmermann, 1990: 346).

In this context, it seems strange that the position of the lessee was so weak. Zimmermann explains this by reference to the fact that

> jurists created the Roman lease law with only one segment of the market in mind: it was meant, primarily, to resolve the problems arising from upper-class housing. It

> was not designed to oppress or to relieve the lot of the poor: they simply did not feature. Roman law was actional law and where there was no litigation, no law could be developed (1990: 348).

This explanation seems plausible indeed, but it alone cannot explain the whole issue. First, part of the cause of the position of the lessee was that he was not recognised as having possession, while Romans were ready to grant possession in other situations. Second, stability in tenure is not only (though arguably mainly) a need of the worse-off. A buyer might be as interested in the thing not having hidden defects (regarding which the Romans were ready to grant the buyer an action against the seller) as a rich lessee in having *some* stability of tenure (concerning which they were not).

Summing up, then,

> Roman lawyers dealt with the particulars of lease of residential space in very much the same manner as they dealt with any other problem brought before them. They appear to have been insensitive to the social dimensions of this type of contract, and certainly they did not make any special effort to relieve the lot of tenants (Zimmermann, 1990: 348).

If this is true, then the sense in which the Romans were so concerned about the finding of appropriate solutions for particular cases has to be qualified. They were not "practical" in the sense we would use that term today. They were indeed "insensitive to the social dimensions of their opinions". Their attention to particular cases was driven by their concern to find the correct solution, granted, but that was measured from *a strictly legal point of view*. Only when those "social dimensions" could somehow be classified as legal could they enter the debate and thus affect their decision. Intriguingly enough, we would nowadays call this attitude "formalist" in its most pejorative sense.

PERMUTATIO AND *EMPTIO VENDITIO*

The second example I want to use, the case of *permutatio* (barter), shows this fact even more clearly. For the Romans there was a significant difference between *emptio venditio* and *permutatio*. The former is "one of the most remarkable achievements of Roman jurisprudence" (Zimmermann, 1990: 230). It was a purely consensual contract; it could thus be contracted by parties not present together, through messengers, or even by correspondence (D. 18.1.2); the actions emanating from it (*actio empti* and *actio venditi*) were *bonae fidei*. Among the claims that could be secured with the *actio venditi* we find the "price for which the object was sold"; also "after the day of delivery, interest on the price" (Ulp. D. 19.1.13.20), and any expenditures on the object of sale made by the seller (Ulp. D. 19.1.13.22, *see* generally Zimmermann, 1990: 277ff). The vendor, on the other hand, had to grant the purchaser *habere licere* (peaceful possession). He was not under the obligation of making the purchaser owner. What if the vendor was not the owner? In that case the purchaser could not acquire ownership: *nemo plus iuris ad alium transferre potet, quam ipse habet* (Ulp. D. 50.17.54), though he would acquire *possessio*. If his *habere licere* was not interfered with, therefore, he would acquire ownership by *usucapio* in what would seem to us a rather short term (two years for landed property, one year otherwise); if it was, he could naturally not acquire by *usucapio*, but then the vendor was liable for eviction, and this was also covered by the *actio empti*.

The Roman law of sale had, thus, a refined structure in which no serious defects can easily be spotted. By the time of the classical lawyers, it was not only defensible from a policy point of view, but it also accorded with the modern sense of justice and fairness (*see* the references mentioned by Zimmermann, 1990: 280). This is, in all likelihood, what was responsible for the extraordinary impact that the Roman law of sale was to have on the Western legal tradition: "even where modern legislators have chosen not to follow the example of Roman law, the latter provides the background against which to evaluate such a decision and to appreciate its implications" (Zimmermann, 1990: 230).

Permutatio, on the other hand, is substantively the same as *emptio venditio*. Both of them are exchanges, but while in *emptio venditio* one of the things exchanged is money, in *permutatio* this is not the case. The question, then, presents itself: are the *actiones* provided for *emptio venditio* available to the parties to a contract of barter? The Sabinians claimed that they were, indeed, based upon a historical argument:

> All buying and selling has its origin in exchange or barter. For there was once a time when no such thing as money existed and no such terms as "merchandise" and "price" were known; rather did every man barter what was useless to him for that which was useful, according to the exigencies of his current needs; for it often happens that what one man has in plenty another lacks. But since it did not always and easily happen that when you had something which I wanted, I, for my part, had something that you were willing to accept, a material was selected which, being given a stable value by the state, avoided the problem of barter by providing a constant medium of exchange (Paul. D. 18.1.1.pr).

This, along with a quotation from *The Iliad*,[9] was the Sabinians' argument to consider barter a form of sale. The Proculians' answer (which according to Paul was the "sounder one", D. 18.1.1.1) was that

> one thing is to sell, another to buy; one person again is vendor and the other, purchaser; and, in the same way, the price is one thing, the object of sale, another; but in barter, one cannot discern which party is vendor and which, purchaser (Paul, D. 18.1.1.1, *in fine*).

[9] "From the rest Achaean soldiers bought their rations,
some with bronze and some with gleaming iron,
some with hives, some with whole live cattle,
some with slaves, and they made a handsome feast" (*Iliad* 7, 472 [545–9]).

This latter view did prevail in the end, and the consequence was that "*permutatio* remained within the "no man's land" of unenforceable *pacta*" (Zimmermann, 1990: 532). The interesting point to notice, however, is that the whole issue was dealt with without considering its practical consequences.[10]

Could it be that it had none? This seems difficult to believe (Watson, 1985a: 23f): in Roman law a *nudum pactum* was not enforceable unless it could be made to fit one of the categories of consensual contracts (*emptio venditio, locatio conductio*); even when (later) the rise of the *actiones praescriptis verbis* made it possible for the parties to a contract of barter to avail themselves of an *actio* modelled upon the *actio empti*, barter was not a consensual contract, and an *actio praescriptis verbis* would be granted only to the party that had already performed his share: *ex nudo pacto non oritur actio*. This would mean that the parties had to be face-to-face to conclude the contract, i.e. that one of the main advantages of the *emptio venditio* against the stipulatio could not operate. Further, and considering that money was a late invention in Rome (dating back only to *c*.275 BC), it could easily be argued that the very same reasons that caused the development of the *emptio venditio* would have been reasons for applying its solutions to *permutatio*.[11]

REGULA IURIS

In these and other cases, what is intriguing is not only that the Romans reached legal conclusions so at odds with "the ordinary problems of living", but also that they did not seem to have thought that the law was problematic. They did not use the kind of arguments that we would expect to hear from practical-and-reluctant-to-theorise jurists; they did not suggest changes in the law; they did not consider the economic, social or, in general, wider consequences of their opinions as these sorts of arguments were, it seems, ruled out by the Roman canon of legal argument. Policy considerations were not arguments that a Roman jurist would use in grounding his position. In this regard the Roman legal discourse is strikingly uniform:

> The politico-economic conditions underlying the establishment of a legal rule are nowhere described or even mentioned. No economic considerations enter into the law. The economic meaning of a legal institution, the normal economic functions it

[10] *See* Schulz (1936: 98f): "Why may a servitude not consist in *faciendo*? Why is the lessee not possessor? . . . Why is barter (*permutatio*) not a consensual contract? Why does the rule *semel heres semper heres* exist? And so on and so forth. None of these questions, to which one might add dozens of others, were so much as asked, let alone discussed and answered by the jurists" (98–9). The fact that *oneris ferendi* was a servitude, though it consisted in *faciendo*, makes the whole thing more intriguing: why were Roman jurists willing to derogate from their principles on some occasions, and on some occasions *only*?

[11] On the rise of the *actiones praescriptis verbis see* Zimmermann (1990: 532ff). On the consequences of the *permutatio* being *nudum pactum*, *cf*. Watson (1968: 23f).

> is destined to fulfil, the economic reasons for its introduction—all these are set aside on principle as non-juristic (Schulz, 1936: 24).

The peculiar point, as I hope will be by now evident, is that the two features of Roman legal reasoning we have been considering seem perfectly opposite. We would naturally expect a theoretically-minded jurist to assign great value to theoretical considerations, as we would expect a practically-minded jurist to dismiss theoretical arguments and go instead for the practical consequences a given ruling is likely to have. But in the case of the Roman jurist, we find a very curious mixture: on the one hand, they did not have much interest in theory, they were only concerned with the solution of particular cases. On the other, they were not able to adequately solve some particular cases only because of their (underlying) theories. They did not say they preferred one legal interpretation to another because of practical, down-to-earth reasons. In some cases, however, practical considerations caused them to derogate from their concepts (witness *oneris ferendi*), while in others the concepts proved more powerful (*permutatio*). This different attitude to similar problems is not discussed, not even noticed, by any Roman jurist (as Schulz said: "these questions are not put at all, nor are a dozen others"). *Pace* Watson, sometimes they do seem to have been "ivory tower" jurists, though at other times they indeed behaved like "sensible men dealing with contemporary problems of living" (but the fact that practical problems were approached in this widely different range of ways was itself not appreciated). They seem to have been rather schizophrenic in this regard.

In other words, Roman legal reasoning was formal, but not consistently formal. Sometimes they paid attention to those problems of living, but sometimes they were completely oblivious to them. One could say, though, that this is precisely what one would expect to find if the law is a system of (badly designed) exclusionary rules. This section examines the explanatory power of this hypothesis. I will be rejecting it, because of the very simple reason that, as a matter of historical fact, Romans did not see the law as a system of rules.

We start with the Roman concept of "rule" (*regula*), the definition of which opens the important last title of the *Digest, de diversis regulis iuris antiqui* ("of various rules of ancient law"):

> *Regula est, quae rem quae est breuiter enarrat. non ex regula ius sumatur, sed ex iure quod est regula fiat. per regulam igitur breuis rerum narratio traditur, et, ut ait Sabinus, quasi causae coniectio est, quae simul cum in aliquo uitiata est, perdit officium suum* (Paul D. 50.17.1: "A rule is something which briefly describes how a thing is. The law may not derive from a rule, but a rule must arise from the law as it is. By means of a rule, therefore, a brief description of things is handed down and, as Sabinus says, is, as it were, the element of a case, which loses its force as soon as it becomes in any way defective").

This seems to be as far as it could be from the idea of an exclusionary reason. *Causae coniectio* (translated here rather cryptically as "the element of a case") was a technical term of procedure (G. IV. 15. *cf.* Stein, 1966: 69). Before presenting their case in detail to the judge in the second stage of the *legis actio* procedure, the parties had to give the court a brief summary outline. If this summary (*causa coniectio*) was satisfactory, the judge could reach a decision without further ado. If, on any point, the *causa coniectio* was not, the whole exercise was useless, since the court "then had to proceed to the next stage of the action at which the matter was submitted *in extenso*" (Stein, 1966: 69). Likewise if the application of a *regula* to a particular case was not completely satisfactory, "it has lost its point [and] there is nothing for it but to go through the whole field step by step" (*ibid.*).

Stein claims that there were two conflicting views as to the correct understanding of a *regula*: according to the first, Sabinian view, we have already seen that a rule was a brief description of the subject-matter and did not have a normative force of its own. According to the second, which Stein ascribes to Celsus, a leader of the Proculians, "a *regula*, despite the existence of exceptions, is not just a neutral statement of facts; it is normative. Unless an exception can be justified, it applies to all the cases which fall under its principle" (Stein, 1966: 71). His main argument for the existence of these two views is Celsus's claim, after stating the *regula Catoniana*, that "*quae definitio in quibusdam falsa est*" (D. 34.7.1.*pr in fine*: "in some cases, this statement of the rule is misleading"). Stein recognises that "at first sight this seems to be another way of putting Sabinus's view that if a *regula* is wrong in anything, it is vitiated", but goes on to argue that

> there is a difference of emphasis between saying that any exception vitiates a rule, which thereby loses its *officium*, as does Sabinus, and stating the rule, but adding that in certain cases it is false, i.e. does not correspond to the facts, as does Celsus (1966: 71).

The distinction is not entirely clear, however, since Sabinus's claim has to be understood as a case of the rule losing its force (*officium*) for the case, not generally: if the solution offered by the rule to the case is "in any way defective", then the rule becomes completely useless for the solution of the case. Celsus's dictum amounts to very much the same: in certain cases the rule is false (notice that Celsus claims that in some cases the rule is *false—falsa est*. Not invalid or inappropriate, but *false*. This seems to cohere with the Sabinian view that a *regula* is a description of the law. It seems to assume that the law can be known through other means, and the function of the rule is to save the decision-maker the time this examination of other means would take—we shall come back to this shortly). This idea of the rule being *false* is, I believe, to be understood as its being a false description of the law. Under this interpretation, therefore, no significant difference appears between the views of Celsus and Sabinus. The tension that Stein finds is one that reflects, in his view, the grammatical controversy between analogists and anomalists (*ibid.*). We need not get into this problem, since even if Stein is correct, a *regula* would not have exclusionary force: it would be, as the *tertium comparationis* in any analogical reasoning, the starting point, not the end, of the discourse (on analogy, *see* Brewer, 1996). The force of the rule is given by its being a correct description of the law, and if, for whatever reason, the description turns out to be false, the rule has no force whatsoever: *In his, quae contra rationem iuris constituta sunt, non possumus sequi regulam iuris* (Jul. D. 1.3.15: "we cannot follow a rule of law in instances where there has been a decision against the *ratio iuris*"). How accurately the rule describes the facts is something that cannot, naturally, be settled by the rule itself. It follows that all substantive considerations can be raised to challenge the accuracy with which the *regula* briefly deals with its subject-matter: rules are not *the* law, but *descriptions* of it. We are, in fact, explicitly warned against granting a *regula* exclusionary force: "*Omnis definitio in iure civili periculosa est: parum est enim, ut non subuerti posset*" (D. 50.17.202: "Every definition in civil law is dangerous; for it is rare for the possibility not to exist of its being overthrown").[12]

Plautus and Sabinus, writing in the first century AD, were familiar with the concept of *regula*.[13] But it was not until the second century AD that the term became common. By that time momentous changes in the structure and sources of Roman law and Roman administration were under way, and to those changes we have to turn our sights to follow the development of the concept (Stein, 1966: 74; *see* generally Wolff, 1951: 109).

The changes that should concern us here are related to the political structure of the Roman state. The traditional Roman structure of sources of law was undergoing important modifications: Hadrian (117–139 AD) had the praetorian and aedilian *edicta* cast in perpetual form by Julian in *c*.130 AD, after which those magistrates lost their power to issue further *edicta*. Furthermore, the power of popular assemblies to enact *leges* was gradually taken over by the Senate. But the most important innovation, for our purposes, was that the Emperor came to be the principal source of law: by virtue of his *imperium* he had the power to issue *edicta*; he had judicial powers and hence opportunities to issue judicial judgements (*decreta*); and he was each time more frequently asked for advice which he gave as *rescripta*.[14]

The increasing legal workload undertaken by the imperial office made the bureaucratisation of the Roman state necessary. Hadrian reorganised his

[12] "*Definitio* is synonymous with *regula*" (Schulz, 1936: 40n). Stein's translation for the second phrase is "for they give the impression that they have a general application and cover all the cases, when in fact they do not" (1966: 70).

[13] According to Stein the archetype of *regula* was the *regula Catoniana*, D. 34.7.1.*pr*, dating back to the second century BC (Stein, 1966: 66).

[14] *See* generally, Stein (1966: 74f). From the fact of the Emperor being the main source of law it does not necessarily follow that he was seen as *creating* the law; this issue is (rather briefly) taken up below. For the time being, suffice it to say that since the times of Hadrian the imperial civil service had to process a growing demand for legal advice. We leave open, for the time being, the question of whether this growing demand was to be explained by the fact of the Emperor having power to create new law.

advisory *consilium* and appointed the heads of the two schools, the Proculians Neratius and Celsus and the Sabinian Julius, as members of it. At the same time, a subordinate class of civil servants with knowledge of law was required, and thus a legal career in the imperial civil service was made possible for the first time.[15] While these officials had no interest in the law for its own sake, as many classical jurists seem to have had, they needed to tackle a growing demand for imperial pronouncements on law (*decreta*, *edicta* and *rescripta*; collectively called imperial constitutions).

This is the context in which the concept of *regula iuris* became common in Roman legal parlance. The concept was not unknown before, as D. 50.17.1, quoting Sabinus, shows, but it was in the late classical period that *Libri Regularum* started to appear. The first book of rules (called *Regulae*) was due to Neratius, leader of the Proculians and member of Hadrian's *consilium*. Two features of this kind of legal literature are worth stressing: first, the rules are offered as dogmatic and precise statements of the law, without the usual support of authorities or further arguments. Secondly, this kind of literature is small compared with the huge bulk of the classical commentaries. Both of these facts support Stein's interpretation of the rise of this type of legal literature as a consequence of the increasing bureaucratisation of the Roman administration. As we have seen, one of the consequences of this process had been the creation of an imperial civil service integrated by subordinate officials who were not jurists but had some legal training, and who were, in Stein's view, the main addressees of the *regulae*:

> Clearly the *Regulae* were written for people who knew some law but who were not interested in arguments and reasons, i.e. people who required working rules of thumb to guide them in the routine cases with which they had to deal. I suggest that the typical reader whom the authors of *Regulae* had in mind was a subordinate official in the bureaux *ab epistulis* and *a libellis* (1966: 80–81)

The statements of law had to be short and dogmatic, for this was precisely their point: to allow the official to answer questions and give advice without having to study the whole subject-matter (hence the analogy in D. 50.17.1.*pr*, mentioned above, between *regula* and *causa coniectio*).[16] The *regulae* were not formal reasons for decision, but working rules of thumb: rules to be followed when no particular feature of the case suggested that a straightforward application would not be appropriate, and to be abandoned as soon as

[15] "After Hadrian's reforms, it was possible for a young man to spend his whole career in the legal bureaucracy. When his training was completed he might become *advocatus fisci* or secretary of one of the chiefs of bureaux. One of these bureaux, *ab epistulis*, handled the voluminous exchange of letters between the Emperor and the drafting of appropriate rescripts. Another bureau, *a libellis*, dealt with petitions of private individuals. The majority of these would involve legal issues, and the head of his bureau was therefore a jurist" (Stein, 1966: 78).

[16] *Ibid.* at 80–1. As Honoré has said, referring to "the average executor's manual": "such works are written on the assumption that executors do not need to understand the law but only to apply certain rules by rote" (1974: 103). *Regulae* do not have a normative force of their own; they are legal rules of thumb.

such a feature was discovered. In this light, though a *regula* is clearly a reason for action, it is not a reason to exclude any consideration whatsoever: all the relevant substantive reasons apply, and the point of the *regula* is that, given the nature of the case, the right balance of reasons would usually be the one reflected in the rule.[17] There is nothing in the rule, however, that warrants the official not to consider any reason that could modify this prima-facie conclusion. We can now see that the concept of a *regula*, as contained in D. 50.17.1.*pr* (attributed to Paul, who was a member of Hadrian's consilium: *cf.* Stein, 1966: 82) makes perfect sense: an official could rely on a *regula*, because it was a faithful (and brief) description of its subject-matter. But if for some reason the *regula* turned out to be a false description, then it could (it would have to) be set aside altogether. This explains Javolenus's warning (in D. 50.17.202, quoted above at 153) as well as the late-classical jurists' concern with the *fraus legi facta* (*cf.* D. 1.3.29 and D. 1.3.30).

Let me pause briefly on the subject of *fraus legi facta*, defined by Paul in the following manner:

> D. 1.3.29 (Paul, *libri singulari ad legem Cinciam*). *Contra legem facit, qui id facit quod lex prohibet, in fraudem uero, qui saluis uerbis legis sententiam eius circumuenit* ("it is a contravention of the law if someone does what the law forbids, but fraudulently, in that he sticks to the words of the law but evades its sense").

And Ulpian repeats practically the same in D. 1.3.30. It is not a coincidence that Ulpian and Paul, both of them late-classical jurists and authors of *libri regulae*, were concerned with *agere in fraudem legis*. Indeed, given their concept of *regula*, the tendency to think of the rule as *being* the law instead of merely *describing* it was something that had to be resisted. Zimmermann points out that the idea of *fraus legi facta* was alien for pre-classical jurisprudence, characterised as it was by "a strictly formalistic approach" (Zimmermann, 1990: 703).

To conclude, the legal materials were not considered by Roman jurists to be exclusionary reasons. Yet their legal reasoning was formal to a remarkable extent; only certain arguments were used. Political, economic or social consequences of their decisions were not something they would take into account to modify their opinions. Some of the solutions offered by the law of the Romans were remarkably reasonable: as we have seen, there is an argument to be made, in the case of the *emptio venditio*, to the effect that the solutions afforded by Roman law to cases falling under the heading of the law of sale were both adequate and reasonable (*cf.* above at 142ff). But they failed to adopt this broader perspective for many legal situations, with the consequence that those reasonable solutions they already knew were not to be applied to substantively similar situations. Interestingly enough, they even failed to see

[17] This is not to say that, since the official would have to consider all the substantive reasons before arriving at his or her decision, the *regulae* as *regulae* were useless. The bureaucrats might have *other* reasons not to consider (some) substantive reasons: think, for example, of the need to solve a large number of cases in a limited amount of time.

the problems that this attitude was bringing about. There is no suggestion that the fact that the rules of *emptio venditio* were not applicable to *permutatio* was something negative; there is no complaint about the hardship that the lessee's weak position in a *locatio conductio* (*rei*) could create; there is no suggestion, more interestingly, to the effect that the law could be changed, and this is the attitude of jurists which are famous for being inclined to look for appropriate solutions for particular cases rather than formulating grand theories and overarching concepts, of jurists that "must be given credit" for their "sophistication" in the "handling of individual cases"!

The fact that some rules concerning *locatio conductio*, *permutatio* and many others seem so incomprehensible to us is to be explained by the further fact that we do not know that much about the Roman ways of thinking about the law. They clearly had a very strict canon of legal argument that excluded most references to extralegal effects of legal decisions, but we are not in a position fully to *understand* that canon: we can only attempt to reconstruct it from the material contained in the *Corpus Iuris Civilis* and other Roman sources. The *Corpus Iuris Civilis* is not a *Code* in the modern sense of the word: it is, mainly, a collection of opinions about what the law requires in particular cases under consideration (*see* Stein, 1966: 87; *see* also Friedrich, 1956: 2f). Alasdair MacIntyre's tale about Western philosophy in *After Virtue* is literally true in the case of Roman law: "what we possess . . . are the fragments of a conceptual scheme, parts which now lack those contexts from which their significance derived" (1985: 2).

On the other hand, it is precisely because of the *Corpus Iuris Civilis* not being a codification in the modern sense that we can reconstruct part of the Roman attitude and thus hope to have a reasonably accurate understanding of the system of Roman law. Imagine that we have only the *regulae* of, say, *emptio venditio*: would we be in a position to know whether these rules were to be applied to *permutatio*? This shows that understanding the meaning of some legal material is not enough to apply it: to do the latter it is necessary not only to know the meaning, but also how formally that "meaning" should be applied; in other words, which substantive considerations are excluded.

We can see that a theory which explains the emergence of *oneris ferendi* is, *contra* Watson, crucially important not only to know what the Roman law of servitudes was, but also and more importantly, to understand Roman law itself. We need a theory that explains why the Roman jurists sometimes derogated from their principles as a matter of course and why that appears not to have even occurred to them in other cases. Such a theory needs to be (as we shall see shortly) not only a historical explanation of the emergence of *oneris ferendi* and the denial of the status of possessor to the lessee in the *locatio conductio* (*rei*). It must be a theory about the way in which the Romans thought about the law. It must teach us when and why they would have been willing to derogate had they had the opportunity to do so. It must teach us what did they see when they were looking at the law. Lacking this theory, we fail to understand the mixture of dogmatism and practicality the Roman jurists display, and failing to understand this mixture we cannot say when, according to Roman law, one had to be dogmatic and when practical.

To know how to apply Roman law we need, in other words, to understand which reasons would be accepted by a Roman jurist as showing the substantive similarity of two different situations. They distinguished between a tenant at will and a lessee, between barter and sale, but not between *oneris ferendi* and older forms of servitudes. If we apply our modern criteria to these cases problems will emerge, arbitrary distinctions will appear here and there. But we cannot apply *Roman* law (as opposed to our interpretation of the Roman legal material) without understanding the rationale behind the ways in which Romans classified particulars in the world.[18]

One could use history to explain these different attitudes, could, for instance, try to discover the historical *causes* of the weak position of the lessee. Alan Watson, for example, suggests that the development of the different contractual forms that constitute what we could anachronistically call the "Roman law of contract" was a piecemeal development of particular forms from the most ancient and abstract contract, the *stipulatio*. Every major contract the Romans knew is, in Watson's view, a derogation from the strict requirements of the *stipulatio* (except *societas*, which need not concern us here).

This is clearly not the place (and I am more clearly not the person) to discuss the historical accuracy of Watson's hypotheses. What is important, though, is that what we needed to know is not only what the historical *causes* of the evolution of each contract were, but also the *reasons* for them.[19] In order to learn the way the Romans thought about the law, it is not enough for us to learn that the Roman contracts evolved from *stipulatio*. We need to know the *reasons* behind that development. Why did *mutuum* (loan) break loose from the ritualism of the *stipulatio*, while it did not evolve in such a way as to be flexible enough to include commercial lending? Why did the Romans never develop a written contract, one that would be similar to the *stipulatio* in that it was defined by its form, not its function, but that could have solved many of the problems and shortcomings of the *stipulatio*, while at the same time they were willing and able to derogate from the *stipulatio* in so many other cases? The Romans did know about written contracts, common in Athens and commented on by Gaius (G. 3.134). Why did they not derogate from the *stipulatio* in this respect, as they did regarding *mutuum*, *depositum* and the like? Why did a consensual contract of barter (*permutatio*) not develop alongside *emptio venditio*? "Why did they apply, in some branches of

[18] I am not claiming that we know nothing about Roman law and that everything written on that subject is just "our interpretation of Roman legal material". As argued before, we can reconstruct the Roman image of law from their opinions concerning particular cases, and this reconstruction can be more or less successful. The point is merely about what needs to be reconstructed for that enterprise to be successful.

[19] On reasons and causes, *see* Ewald (1995: 1924ff).

the law at least, those strict, formalistic principles though they were fully aware of the possibility of unjust results?" (Daube, 1944: 75). Questions of this Schulzian type could, as Schulz himself claimed, be multiplied tenfold. Watson's might be a good explanation of the origins of those particular contracts that *did* develop; it does not, however, explain the selectivity of Roman legal development, i.e. why only *some* (and sometimes in some respects only) contracts evolved towards a more flexible and reasonable application, while others kept the rigidities they were born with. A sound historical explanation will not do without some hypothesis about Roman legal thinking.

Consider, for example, Stein's explanation for the fact that the age of legal capacity (set at 14) was not raised, though it could have been reasonable to do it, offered by him to illustrate "the cautious Roman approach to legal reform":

> The Romans were *reluctant to contemplate* such a change, which might have had all manner of unforeseen consequences. They *preferred* to leave it to the praetors in the exercise of their discretion, to reverse the effects of transactions where it appeared that advantage had been taken of the youth's inexperience (1999: 11f, emphasis added).

This seems to imply that there was at the time some form of legislative debate in which the option of changing the law and raising the age of legal capacity was entertained. The suggestion seems to be that in that debate the possibility of producing "all manner of unforeseen consequences" led the Romans to take the *decision* not to change the law, giving instead discretion to the praetor.

An explanation of this sort could in principle be imagined for the weak position of the lessee, or for the status of *permutatio* vis-à-vis that of *emptio venditio*. Maybe what we need in these cases is simply more historical information; maybe we have not been able to realise the problems the recognition of possession to the lessee could create, or those that would be produced by a consensual contract of *permutatio*.

The problem is, we are not offered such reasons. Neither are we offered the reasons Stein finds concerning the raising of the age of legal capacity. As we have seen, all we get is a statement of the solution, without any traces of the political discussion that Stein's argument assumes went on before. Stein's explanation is anachronistic in the sense that it makes sense for *us*, but it does not make sense from the Roman point of view.[20]

[20] A similar observation can be made concerning Bernard Jackson's argument in his "Literal meaning: semantics and narrative in Biblical law and modern jurisprudence" (Paper read at the 1999 meeting of the International Association for the Semiotics of Law, Arrabida, 17–20 June 1999). Jackson's claim is that some features of ancient law are to be explained by the need to find legal solutions that could, so to speak, be self-enforcing, i.e. that did not call for a strong state to step in and enforce the law. Again, this might explain the *causes* of ancient law's rigid formalism, but it does not show the *reasons* for it. It is unlikely that there was, at that time, a meeting of Roman politicians discussing whether or not to introduce some flexibility in the rigid formalism of, say, the *stipulatio*, in which the "formalists" prevailed because of the weakness of the Roman state (I am, of course, not implying that Jackson claims this, but trying to explain why a historical or economic or political explanation of the *causes* of the evolution of some particular legal institution does not amount to an identification of the *reasons* for it).

"Because men tend to do what they think they are doing" (Pound, 1958: 6), historical explanations are useful tools in the reconstruction of Roman legal thinking: when they are true, they are a constraint upon, as well as a guide to, the right hypotheses about legal thinking. If they cannot shed light on this, historical explanations will be little more than mere anecdotes.

Watson acknowledges the role of legal thinking in legal evolution. Indeed, he argues that "law develops by lawyers thinking about the normative facts, whether in the abstract or in relation to hypothetical or actual societal facts" (Watson, 1985a: 33). Lawyers' thought is in turn shaped by legal tradition. Hence "legal development is determined by their [i.e. lawyers'] culture; and social, economic, and political factors impinge on legal development only through their consciousness" (Watson, 1985a: 118). But Watson does not see that, as we have seen, knowledge of this "thinking" is relevant not only to explain legal evolution, but also to know what follows for particular cases from the existence of a general rule.[21]

Maybe this is something that we simply cannot know, if only because our knowledge of the Roman mind is restricted to our sources. The Romans did attach, for example, much importance to the fact that the obligation under a contract was to hand over a sum of money: Roman contracts are either unilateral or one of the main obligations is expressed in money. Why was money so important? The answer is that we do not know, and without knowing that (and some related issues) it is very difficult to understand the Roman system of contracts.

At this point the reader might get impatient: we *do* know, understand and argue about the Roman law of contract. Books are published and lectures given continually on the topic. Could not this very fact be cited as a decisive objection to the argument presented here? In the face of our ignorance about the Roman understanding of the law (as opposed of what we know about the Roman legal materials) we *can* know what the law was concerning, for example, sale or hire or deposit or agency. In fact, the impact Roman law has had in the development of Western legal systems could hardly be exaggerated. It thus seem that there is no need to know anything but the rules of a system of law in order to be able to make sense of it.

To answer this objection one can distinguish two levels of understanding, two senses in which we can be said to have understood a legal rule (Ewald, 1995: 2101ff). We can understand the rule's meaning, and in this weak sense of "understanding" all we need is to master the relevant language. As Ewald puts it, "*this* level of comprehension is available to any literate adult, ancient or modern" (*ibid.* at 2101). But we can understand the *meaning* of a legal rule without knowing how to apply it to any particular case.

[21] These are the "two souls" that dwell in Watson's writing, according to William Ewald: one who emphasises the relative autonomy of law from social forces and the importance of legal culture, while the other claims that the law can be reduced to black-letter rules (Ewald, 1995: 491).

"Knowing how to apply it" represents the second level of understanding. As Hegel said (*see* above, at 60) there is an obvious sense in which someone who has only memorised that 2+2=4, 2+3=5, 2+4=6, and so on, has not understood the rule of addition, however many operations "and so on" stands for. The "weak" understanding of Roman law is just like that: *how can we know which situations not described in the* Digest *would have been treated by Roman jurists with the flexibility they displayed concerning* oneris ferendi, *and which ones would have been treated with the rigid formalism they showed concerning* locatio conductio *or* permutatio?

This is this chapter's crucial point: we do not know how formal the application of the norms of Roman law was; we do not know which sort of substantive considerations were irrelevant (i.e. pre-empted), etc. If we manage to achieve an understanding of Roman law that allows us to have at least working hypotheses about the application of Roman rules to cases not mentioned in the *Digest*, we could be said to be on our way to have understanding Roman law in a stronger and more significant sense. To attain this level of understanding, however, knowledge of Latin will not be sufficient: we will have to try to think, to see the world, as a Roman. This need is not evident when we are dealing with modern legal systems (at least Western legal systems), because "the modern law student can take [it] for granted. [It] ha[s] become part of the atmosphere, a part of the surrounding culture, a part of the Volksgeist, and indeed a part of the language itself" (Ewald, 1995: 2102f).

7

Legal Reasoning and Legal Theory Revisited

> It is no uncommon thing to find thus in quite great minds two distinct and even incompatible conceptions mingling together under cover of the inevitable looseness of language; absorbed as they are in formulating new ideas, such minds have not the time to make a critical examination of what they have discovered.
>
> SIMONE WEIL, *Oppression and Liberty* (1955)

When H L A Hart wrote *The Concept of Law*, legal reasoning as such was not in the philosophical agenda. Consequently, he later acknowledged that in that book he had "said far too little about the topic of . . . legal reasoning" (1994: 259). We have already seen, however, that the problem was, in a sense, not that Hart said too little, but that he said too much about legal reasoning. Indeed, I hope to have shown that in *The Concept of Law* one can find, hidden behind the open texture thesis, two explanations of legal reasoning. What was needed, in consequence, was a "companion" to *The Concept of Law*, an examination of the way in which a powerful explanation of the nature of law such as Hart's could further the understanding not only of what the law is, but also of how the law works, or, better, how people work with the law: a theory of the application of the law (i.e. legal reasoning). We are now told that Neil MacCormick's *Legal Reasoning and Legal Theory* purported to be such a companion (MacCormick, 1994: xiv).

A Hartian explanation of legal reasoning has to be seen to flow from, or at the very least to be consistent with, the central claims Hart made in the "mother" theory. I hope it is not very controversial to say that one of the central tenets of Hart's theory of law was that at a conceptual level law is independent from morality, that is, what the law ought to be is not the same as what the law is.[1] These two questions are, in Hart's view, not only

[1] There is some discussion as to the precise content of what is sometimes called "the separability thesis" (*see*, among others, Füßer, 1996; Coleman, 1996). This has to be kept in mind, since my argument would not affect some versions of the thesis. Consider Shiner's (admittedly "crude") version: "the existence of law is one thing and its merit or demerit another" (Shiner, 1992). I do believe (along with most positivists, natural lawyers and realists of different denominations) that in this sense the thesis is true. I think, however, that I can bypass this debate because in any plausible reading that thesis must mean, for legal positivists, that from the fact that the law ought to be different it does not follow that it is different.

different, but conceptually different: it is possible to establish what the law is without inquiry into what the law ought to be; no conclusion about what the law is follows from arguments about what the law ought to be. At the same time, Hart saw that any theoretical explanation of the nature of law must explain why and how it is possible for competent lawyers, judges and lay persons to disagree not only about what the law ought (morally) to be, but also (and much more importantly in this context) about what the law actually is. Now, the explanation of the latter kind of disagreement cannot be grounded upon the existence of disagreement about what the law ought to be, since if that were the case, the law as it is would not be conceptually different from the law as it ought to be (that is, it cannot be the case that we disagree about what the law is *because* we disagree about what the law ought to be, if these two questions are conceptually different). Hence we got Hart's *open texture* thesis.

The importance of this thesis is that it performed the role of supplying a morally neutral explanation of legal disagreement, thus allowing us to explain disagreement about what the law is in a way that was not parasitical on disagreement about what the law ought to be. This was, therefore, the explanation (at least the *kind* of explanation) required by Hart's theoretical commitments, if his theory was to have any consistency. But Hart noticed (*see* above, at 89ff) that the idea of open texture, important as it might be, did not explain the whole of the fact of legal disagreement when looked at from a legal-reasoning perspective, i.e. clarification of the meaning of words is not always the kind of information that would be useful to lawyers, judges and lay persons when they are discussing what the law is in concrete cases. Hart realised that in many of these cases what was discussed was not whether a particular *x* was an instance of a general X, but rather whether or not a particular (otherwise clear and unambiguous) rule was, in a legal sense, meant to be applied to the facts that configured some concrete case. Hence he offered, in the same pages of *The Concept of Law*, a second explanation of the fact of legal disagreement, one based on the claim that there is a built-in tension in law between (what I called) predictability and appropriateness.

Now, it is in my view a crucial point that the implications of this second explanation for a theory of law are at odds with the central claim of Hart's book identified above. In the first explanation, what made a case hard was a "value-free" feature, i.e. the open texture of the relevant words. This is why Hart was free to say that in clear cases the application of rules does not require the decision-maker to exercise a "fresh judgement" (1994: 135). From the universe of cases courts will have to solve from now on, some of them are (or will eventually be) marked by the fact that they belong to the penumbra of meaning of the relevant words; the identification of those cases as hard will not imply, therefore, that evaluative ideas about what the law ought to be will be smuggled in at the moment of ascertaining what the law is. When the "mark" of open texture is discovered the court will have reached the outer limits of the law: it can then discuss about what the law will be after the court's decision, in the light of what the law should be, only because there is no law on the matter. Notice that nothing guarantees that this will be uncontroversial. There can be disagreement on whether skateboards and push-chairs are "core" or "penumbra" instances of the word "vehicle". That is to say, I think Raz is correct when he says (1985: 218) that it is false "that all factual matters are non-controversial" and that "all moral propositions are controversial". What is important here is not that according to the open texture thesis the application of the law is non-controversial, but that any *legal* disagreement will not be *moral* but *factual* (or verbal, or conceptual) disagreement: are push-chairs and skateboards, *as a matter of fact*, vehicles?

The second explanation (legal disagreement as the consequence of the tension between predictability and appropriateness) does not work so nicely, though it represents more faithfully the reality of legal reasoning. In it, the "mark" that singles a case out as hard is an evaluative feature: the case is (will be) marked as hard if predictability's requirements are overridden by those of appropriateness, i.e. if the solution offered by the rule is inappropriate enough for the demand of predictability to be defeated in the case. Notice that, in this view, to "discover" the "mark" that would allow us to classify a case as clear or hard is to exercise a "fresh judgement", as it is to answer the question of how pressing the inappropriateness of a norm ought to be for the demand for predictability to be overridden, the answer to which will depend on the relative importance those values are taken to have. From this standpoint the question of what the law is cannot be differentiated from that of what the law ought to be. In other words, *for the court* the question "*is* this pram a vehicle?" is linked to the question "*ought* this pram to be considered a vehicle?" (consider the common judicial way of posing this kind of problems: "should skateboards be considered as vehicles *for the purpose of this law*?").[2]

If this is correct, there is no way in which we can say that there is a *logical* distinction between these two questions. To see why, it seems useful to divide Hart's view on hard cases into two parts: one that contains a test about what makes a hard case hard, and another that explains what is going on once a case is recognised as such. We have seen that two answers can be found in *The Concept of Law* for the first problem. The answer to the second problem is that in hard cases there is no settled law, hence the courts have to exercise discretion. Now, I have argued that the first, non-moral test for the first problem (the *open texture* thesis understood as a thesis about language rather than about the law) has to be rejected, and something along the lines of the tension between predictability and appropriateness must be accepted instead. If we then retain the original second part (the claim that in hard cases courts have discretion) the

[2] The fact that Hart himself sometimes (e.g.; 1967: 106) phrased the question in these terms (as one of ascertaining whether a particular x is an instance of a general X for the purpose of a given law) shows that he failed to notice that he was offering two explanations. If his open texture thesis (understood as a thesis about language) is true, then there are core instances that are recognisable as such, regardless of the purpose of any law: *see* Schauer (1991: 212ff).

incompatibility between what we would then have and the *core* of Hart's philosophy of law (as identified above) is evident: In this modified version, Hart's view on hard cases would be: (i) a case is hard when the application of the (prima-facie) law is deemed objectionable (i.e. when the prima-facie solution is such that the demand for appropriateness is stronger than the demand for certainty); (ii) when a case is hard, the law is unsettled, and the courts have discretion. In short, when the application of an otherwise clear legal rule to a case that belongs, so to speak, to its *core* of meaning produces an objectionable result, *it is the law* that there is no law on the subject. What the law *is* for the case depends upon what the law (i.e. the balance between predictability and appropriateness) *ought* to be for the case. When the (prima-facie) law *ought to be* different, it *is* different. *Lex iniusta non est lex*!

Now, is this "ought" a moral "ought"? It might appear that the answer is obviously yes: the point is, why is predictability important, and why should we care about appropriateness? As Raz has claimed, those values cannot but be moral, since "there is no other justification for the use of an autonomous body of considerations by the courts" (1993: 318). But we should be careful here. Hart is indeed careful not to talk of these values as moral values, at least in *The Concept of Law*. And in "Positivism and the separation of law and morals" he is explicit in denying that this is a moral ought: "we should remember that the baffled poisoner may say, "I ought to have given her a second dose"" (1958: 70). Hart also points out that "under the Nazi regime men were sentenced by courts for criticism of the regime. Here the choice of sentence might be guided exclusively by consideration of what was needed to maintain the state's tyranny effectively" (*ibid.*).

So Hart believed that the solution to the conflict between appropriateness and predictability can be based upon purely instrumental, non-moral considerations. But the obvious question is, what are these considerations instrumental for? In the poisoner's case, they are instrumental in achieving a goal previously and independently given, i.e. to kill the woman. In Nazi Germany, they "might" have been instrumental to the independently given goal of maintaining the state's repressive apparatus.

That the goal is *previously given* means, obviously, that there cannot be an instrumental "ought" before the goal has been specified. Therefore, when the application of the law is at issue, that goal cannot be something like "to follow the law", since the court is trying to establish what the law is for the case (it would be equivalent to saying that the goal for the poisoner is to administer the poison, a goal that is useless as a guidance for the problem of *how much* poison "ought" to be administered). The important point is, how can the court establish what the goal is?

Notice that the answer is not to be found in another rule of the system, because of the same reason Hart argued that "canons of interpretation" could not succeed in eliminating uncertainty (1994: 126): because those rules would also be subject to the problem.

Still, is this a moral "ought"? I hope we can see now that we do not need a positive answer to this question (positive though I think the correct answer is) in order to know that simply by allowing the distinction between clear and hard cases to be constituted by the solution to the competition between certainty and predictability, Hart has given up a positivistic theory of law. Hart's answer to the rule-sceptic was to claim that the application of rules to a majority of cases does not call for "fresh judgement", with the obvious implication that the decision-maker did not have discretion to solve those ("core") cases. But this is an answer that works only if the first version of the open texture thesis is accepted, since only this version does not make the characterisation of a case as clear or hard dependent upon the very kind of judgement that is supposed to be absent from one kind of case. In the second version, however, since the distinction itself is based on such a judgement, Hart is left with no answer to the rule-sceptic. However controversial or uncontroversial the decision to characterise a case as "clear" or "hard" might be, it is a fresh judgement for the making of which the court has discretion.[3]

This is an important point, so let me proceed step by step: we begin by noticing that in order to determine whether a case is clear or hard one has to determine *first* whether the particular case under consideration is one of those to which the rule applies. According to the *first* version of the open texture thesis, this is a matter of grammar, and the question, "does the rule apply?" is internal to language (remember Marmor's claim, quoted above, that "the relation between a rule and its application is a grammatical one, that is, internal to language"). This explanation works well in the sense that it draws a distinction between clear and hard cases which is the *kind* of distinction required by Hart's theory of law, but it does not work in the sense that the problems that come up in legal reasoning are *not*, most of the time, problems of semantic classification. As a description of legal practice, therefore, the first version of the open texture thesis has to be abandoned.

The second step involves noticing that Hart himself perceived that this was the case and offered a second version of that thesis, one in which the answer to the question of whether a rule applies is *not* internal to language. Here, a rule applies when its application to the particular case under consideration is appropriate (or at least not inappropriate enough for the demand for certainty to be outweighed). Here what the law is for the case cannot be known until the competition between predictability and appropriateness is decided, hence

[3] We could go further into this point, though, for the argument presented in this chapter that is quite unnecessary. Hart's claim that the "ought" in question might be an instrumental "ought", instrumental in achieving some (independently given) goal seems to leave him rather close to Dworkin: since what the goal is and how best to achieve it will determine how the balance between predictability and appropriateness has to be solved in the particular case, what the law is for this case will depend on the identification of that goal, and the chosen goal will have an impact upon the content of the rules (remember that we cannot know whether the case is clear or hard until we have solved this tension). This seems a different way of saying that the law is an interpretive concept (*see* Dworkin, 1986: 46ff).

the law cannot be applied without a fresh moral judgment. A necessary connection between law and morality has been found.

Third step: we are confronted with the objection that though here a sourceless evaluative judgment is called for, it is not a *moral* judgment. The conclusion arrived at in step two was unwarranted, because the values of predictability and appropriateness, as they appear in the problem of application, are not *moral* values.

I have three answers to this objection. The weakest is to claim that it is not an objection at all. I have shown that, according to Hart's own views, legal rules cannot be applied without the decision-maker having to come up with a fresh judgment. So it is for Hartians to choose: either they allow the connection between law and morality at the point of application (in the manner indicated in the second step above) or they must embrace full rule-scepticism, because Hart's answer to the rule-sceptic was that there are very many cases in which the decision-maker is *not* required to make a fresh judgment.

My second answer is fairly weak. I do not have to argue for the moral nature of the "fresh judgment" involved in the solution to the tension between certainty and appropriateness; having shown that it is called for in all cases of (legal) rule-application, the *onus* is shifted to the objector, so that it is not enough for her to point out that that judgment *could* be non-moral: she has to offer an argument why it *is* non-moral.

The third and strongest answer, of course, would be to go all the way and argue that it is indeed a moral judgment. As I said before, I think this last claim is true, but it is important to see that I do not need to argue its truth for the argument against Hart to succeed. On this assumption I shall proceed.

To decide whether or not that judgment is a moral judgment one has to ascertain first the meaning of "moral". In some cases it will be fairly easy to establish the truth of my claim. Consider this understanding of "moral": "I will use "moral" to encompass all matters of value" (Raz, 1994: 88 n6; *see also* the passage quoted below, at 189 n. 19). On Raz's understanding, then, there is no doubt that the judgment decision-makers have to make in all cases is *moral*, and a clear connection would have been established between law and morality.

But maybe it makes sense to distinguish moral and non-moral evaluative judgments. Among non-moral evaluative judgments we could find instrumental judgments, instrumental, that is, for ends that are not in themselves moral (like poisoning a person). Here we come full circle to Hart's position, which has recently been defended by Matthew Kramer (in the context of a discussion of whether Fuller's eight precepts of the "inner morality of law" are moral requirements at all):

> When Hart characterized the Fullerian principles as merely principles of "efficiency for a purpose", the purpose to which he referred was the very purpose that Fuller himself imputed to law . . .. Hart was not positing any goal outside the overall process of law-creation and law-administration; he was accepting Fuller's

> contention that the end of law consists in functioning as a system of rules . . .. Apropos of that general end . . . Fuller and his eight precepts did in fact lay down conditions of efficacy, in that most deviations from those precepts impair the realization of law's dominion (Kramer, 1999: 51).

I do not want to express an opinion on whether Kramer's claim is correct regarding Fuller's eight principles. The main reason it was quoted here was to see whether it could flesh out the objection against the consequences of my second reading of Hart's open texture thesis. Recall that the strong version of my argument was, since a rule, according to the law, is not to be applied when it would produce too inappropriate a result in the particular case, it follows that no rule can ever be applied without the decision-maker answering the question of whether the application of this rule to this case is too inappropriate. Since the decision on the competition between certainty and appropriateness is a moral decision, it follows that law and morality are necessarily connected at the level of application. Recall further that the objection against this argument focused upon this *not* being a moral decision, and this is where Kramer's argument could be of use. Can this decision receive the same, instrumental reading as Fuller's eight principles?

The answer has to be negative. What gives Kramer's argument concerning Fuller's inner morality of law initial plausibility is that he can easily show that comprehensive failure to comply with any of them "would be incompatible with the very *existence* of legal norms rather than merely with their *effectiveness*" (1999: 52). But the problem of application is different. There is nothing conceptually or theoretically (as opposed to substantively) absurd in a system in which the problem of application was not recognised as a problem. We have seen that a good argument can be made (Schauer), and historically *has been made* (Montesquieu), to the effect that the application of general rules to particular cases has to be mechanical.[4] Concerning the competition between certainty and appropriateness, it is simply not true to say that failure to recognise that competition as legally relevant would "be incompatible with the very *existence* of legal norms rather than merely with their *effectiveness*". On the contrary, it might make the law *more* certain and its application cheaper and simpler. I conclude that Kramer's instrumental reading of Fuller, however plausible it might be concerning Fuller's inner morality of law, could not defend Hart against Hart: the decision of how best to serve the moral values of appropriateness and certainty can only be a moral decision.

The tension between legal theory and legal reasoning is explained, at least in part, by a difference in perspective between the two: when building a legal theory, what is at the centre of attention is a set of questions like "what is the

[4] I am here referring to Schauer's *normative* argument (contained in the long quotation above, at 115); Schauer goes on to say that since that position has something to be "said for" the fact that legal rules are defeasible is to be explained as a consequence of a contingent decision to reject that argument. It is this latter claim of Schauer's that was subjected to criticism above.

law?" "when are we entitled to say that a legal system is valid (exists)?" "how can we know whether a particular rule is part of this or that (or of any at all) legal system?" (*see* Raz, 1980: 1f, for a useful typology of the questions a legal theory must answer to be "complete"). At this level it is hard to deny the difference between the law that is and the law that ought to be. The mere fact that many people can sensibly think the law of their land to be unjust, that is, different from what it ideally ought to be, shows that there is such a distinction.

But when the focus of the enquiry is shifted to legal reasoning, this clear difference is upset. It is still possible to apply a law that is different from the law that ought to be, and often judges decide one thing while at the same time they think that a different decision ought to have been made but for the content of the applicable law.[5] But we have seen that in order to apply the law, the judge has to decide how best to balance the values of predictability and appropriateness in the instant case. The obvious fact that judges sometimes have the legal duty to decide a case in a manner they think is not (morally) the best shows that the law does indeed pre-empt some substantive issues that would otherwise be prompted by the case. But the equally obvious fact that a law does not exclude *all* the substantive considerations (e.g. the consideration that the man who shed blood in the streets of Bologna was a barber, and that he was shaving a customer), even when it *prima facie* appears to do so (because, as we have seen, the Bolognese statute said that the words had to be taken literally, without interpretation) shows that there is more to ascertaining what the law is than getting the meaning right. And it is somewhat ironic that Hart himself gave such an accurate description of what this something else is, that is, the solution of a tension between the values of predictability of judicial decisions and their appropriateness to the particular case at hand. To repeat, what the law *is* for the case cannot be known before deciding how the competition between predictability and appropriateness *ought to be* resolved.

One could, I suppose, insist on the idea that this is not a problem, and to do so one would have to argue that an answer to the question "what is law"? does not have any consequences for an answer to that of "what is the law for this case?". If it could be shown that an answer to the first question does not imply an answer to the second, this chapter's argument would be mistaken. And indeed, it it has been claimed that "it has been a central presupposition [of analytical jurisprudence] that there is a clear distinction between the philosophical question, 'What is law?' and the lawyer's question, 'What is *the* law for this or that matter?'" (Marmor, 1995: v).

[5] Hence the italicised last phrase at the end of the first paragraph above at 164 was, in a way, a rhetorical excess. But it was only exaggerated, not plainly false: sometimes laws that produce unfair or unjust results when applied to a particular case are not laws for that case, and that suffices to put in question of the separability thesis, according to which from the fact that a legal solution is morally objectionable it does not follow that it is legally mistaken.

Now, there is an obvious sense in which these are two different questions, i.e. in the same way in which the question "What is cancer?" is different from the question "Does this person have cancer?". But this is not to say that an answer to the first question does not imply (at least part of) an answer to the second, in the same way in which the answer to the first of Marmor's questions implies (at least part of) an answer to the second (indeed, to say that x has consequences for y assumes the existence of a [more or less] "clear distinction" between x and y).

It is not clear to me whether Marmor was claiming that for analytic jurisprudence the two questions were different in the sense that an answer to one did not imply an answer to the second, or only that they were different, without any further claim. In the latter sense, he is surely right, but it would not be an objection to my main argument in this chapter; in the former, it would indeed be an objection, but (I would claim) it would not be true as regards "analytic jurisprudence," nor would it be correct in its own terms.

But the fact is, it is common for positivist authors to complain that they are being misunderstood when a particular description of legal reasoning is claimed to be a consequence of legal positivism. "Legal positivism", they say, "is a theory about law, not a theory about legal reasoning". Thus Matthew Kramer, for example, has criticised Michael Detmold (1984) for endorsing

> the notion that legal positivism calls for a slavish adherence to the letter of the norms in any particular legal system . . .. In fact, jurisprudential positivism does not prescribe any particular mode of adjudication; it certainly does not prescribe a blind fidelity to absurd or iniquitous requirements laid down by statutes or other sources of law (Kramer, 1999: 114).

A simple answer here would be that Kramer is cashing in on the ambiguity of normative words like "prescribe" "fidelity" "calls for", and the like. If we read these terms in their moral sense, then of course Kramer is correct: legal positivism does not morally prescribe anything. But positivism does "prescribe blind fidelity to absurd or iniquitous requirements" in the sense that it declares those requirements to be law, and in so doing recognises those requirements as legally binding on judges in the sense that they give content to their legal obligations. The fact that fining the businessman or punishing the barber is grossly unfair or otherwise absurd, does not make any difference, according to "jurisprudential" positivism: that the law *ought* (morally) to be different (i.e. that it ought to contain an exception for the businessman or for the barber) does not *make* it different. Granted, the judge's legal obligation to do something that is absurd or iniquitous might have a very limited, or even no moral weight, but according to positivism the requirement can be legal and notwithstanding also absurd and iniquitous. When it comes to legal reasoning, what is *legal* about it is that it aims at establishing what is the *law* for the case, hence if we are reasoning legally we have to take those iniquitous requirements as (legally) binding.

Recall the cases discussed by Planiol (119, n. 5 above): in all of these cases it was obvious to Planiol that since the law *ought* to be different it *was* indeed different. This is the move that positivism cannot allow, and this is the reason why it has to describe Planiol's arguments as advocating law reform. And insofar as we want to apply the law, rather than our own personal convictions about what the law should be, "jurisprudential" positivism indeed "calls for" our rejection of Planiol's attempts at law-reform until they are properly sanctioned by the legislator.

Indeed, Kramer seems to concede this, when shortly after the quoted passage he claims that

> A necessary conjunction between morality and law-in-its-application would be a devastating blow for jurisprudential positivism, even if no such conjunction could be established between morality and law-as-a-scheme-of-norms (*ibid.*, 119).

Hence, legal positivism is committed to a theory of legal reasoning that negates the "necessary conjunction" between morality and "law-in-its-application". Generally speaking, the point could be formulated thus: legal reasoning is about which applied legal statements follow from some pure legal statements when some facts are true. A theory of law specifies what counts as pure legal statements, hence a theory of law determines, up to a point, legal reasoning ("up to a point", because a theory of law might be compatible with more than one account of the fact-finding process). In this chapter we shall see that if this link between legal reasoning and legal theory is severed, the consequence is rule-scepticism of the most radical kind; if it is mantained, then "jurisprudential positivism" indeed calls "for a slavish adherence to the letter of the norms".

Raz has also argued that legal theory and legal reasoning are very different things. He sees that "by American law, American judges have to decide cases according to American law" (1998a: 280), and generally, that a judge's "duty (under the system in whose courts they sit) is to judge in accordance with the rules of that system" (*ibid.*, 281). A theory of law has to indicate what counts as American law or, indeed, as "following" a rule of law.

But, Raz continues, judges have applied legal rules long before any theoretical account of law was available. In other words, legal philosophy "merely explains the concept [of law] that exists independently of it" (*ibid.*, 281). Hence, a theory of law is not *required* by any agent to be able to understand and apply the law. Would this not imply that a theory of law has no consequences for a theory of legal reasoning?

Not that fast, though. The fact that I can boil water presupposes the truth of a theory that allows for water to be boiled (here "presupposes" can be understood to mean "is evidence for"). My possibility of boiling water is not brought about by any theory, and I need not manage any theory to be able to boil water. But my boiling of water would falsify a theory that was committed to the "unboilability" of water. This point is conceded by Raz when he claims that "if some theory of law yields the result that American law is not law, it is a misguided theory of law" (*ibid.*, 280). When judges reach a particular legal decision, they assume the truth of a theory of law that would (at least) allow for that decision (here "assume" cannot, of course, be replaced by "offer proof of"; it could instead be replaced by "commit themselves to").[6]

But, Raz could argue, there is no reason for the judge actually to make any theoretical assumptions, and this should readily be granted. The important point is not about what needs to be inside the judge's head when she is rendering judgment, it is, rather, about the presuppositions of her action. And it is a presupposition of her action of passing judgment that a theory of law allows for that decision to be correct. If the judge becomes convinced of a theory that would not allow for her judgment, she can decide either to change her substantive opinion on the case or to declare the theory mistaken, but cannot hold both without inconsistency. And the other way around, the fact that normative language is used, for example, assumes that some theoretical explanation of the normativity of law is correct. This does not mean that every judge will have to have this assumption on his or her head when deciding cases. As a matter of hard fact, a judge could continue to use normative language even after accepting a theory that does not allow for the normativity of law (how she could avoid the charge of inconsistency, however, I fail to see). But it does mean that a true theory would have to offer an explanation either of the normativity of law or of the mistake participants to the legal practice commit every time they use normative language.

The bottom line here is this: the interesting relation is not the relation practice-theory (i.e. should the practice follow the theory?), but the relation theory-practice (should the theory follow the practice?). I believe that theories like a theory of law are attempts to describe and understand practices like legal practice, and from this follows my argument about the connection between a theory of law and a theory of legal reasoning: if it can be shown that legal practice functions in ways that contradict the theory then, unless it can be shown that participants are mistaken (a difficult though not impossible task, since we are talking of social practices), the theory is mistaken. I remain agnostic on the issue of whether a participant to the practice should change the ways in which she participates because she has been convinced by a theory that what she has been doing is impossible.

[6] It is difficult to understand Raz's claim that judges "need not make any specific assumptions about the content of the rest of the law or of the way to establish it when they believe that it makes no difference to the case before them" (1998a: 279). He seems to be claiming that judges need not make any assumptions when they assume that they need not make any assumptions: how else are we to understand the judges' "believing that the (rest of the) law does not make any difference to the case before them"? This *is* an assumption about the content of the law.

DEDUCTIVE REASONING AND LEGAL ARGUMENTATION

The challenge for a unified Hartian(-like) theory of law *and* legal reasoning is, then, to harmonise these two perspectives, that of legal reasoning and that of legal theory. Now I want to consider in some detail what is probably the most sophisticated attempt to meet this challenge, i.e. Neil MacCormick's *Legal Reasoning and Legal Theory*.

That MacCormick's is an attempt to meet this challenge is clear from the new foreword of the paperback edition, where he says that "the analytical positivist approach to legal theory espoused by Hart is open to challenge, and has been challenged, for an alleged inability to give a satisfactory account of legal reasoning, especially reasoning-in-adjudication. This book took up that challenge" (MacCormick, 1994: xiv). In particular, I take his argumentation concerning the role of deductive reasoning in law as constituting the best available analysis of clear cases in the tradition of legal positivism.

This is the reason why, before considering MacCormick's argument, it is necessary to address the issue of syllogistic (or deductive) reasoning in Hart's theory of law. Hart himself sometimes showed little sympathy for the idea that legal decisions can be reached in a deductive manner: he argued that "logic is silent on how to classify particulars" (1958: 67). Commenting upon this and related passages from Hart's work, Marmor claims that nothing could be further from Hart's mind than the idea of the application of a rule to a clear case being a matter of logic. Defending Hart, Marmor has claimed that "it is easily discernible that whatever it is that connects a rule to its application cannot consist of logic or analyticity" and he then argues,

> as Hart put it, "logic is silent on how to classify particulars" but it is precisely this classification to which his distinction between core and penumbra pertains. In other words, we must keep separate what might be called "rule-rule" and "rule-world" relations; logic and analyticity pertain only to the former, not to the later kind of relation (1994: 128).

And he concludes by saying that "neither Hart nor any other legal positivist must subscribe to the view that the application of legal rules is a matter of logical inference" (*ibid.*).

Marmor is right when he claims that the distinction between core and penumbra is not a matter of logic, but let us ask the question "why is the core/penumbra important for Hart?" And the answer is: because, *in addition* to the existence of a core and penumbra of meaning for most (all) concepts, Hart claimed (in the first interpretation of the open-texture thesis) that a state of affairs constitutes a clear *legal* case when in some of its descriptions it is encompassed by the *core* meaning of some applicable rule, and hard otherwise. It is with this further claim that a space for logic and deductive reasoning appears:

> we have to decide whether to call this that we see a "man" . . .. But once we have made the decision, what we do is to assert it as true that this before us is a man . . .. And it is this assertion of the minor premiss as true, together with the assertion of the major as true, that logically requires the truth of the conclusion (MacCormick, 1992: 218).

Or, to put it in Marmor's terms, *once* the relation rule–world has been settled, once the particulars of the case have been recognised to be in the core of meaning of the relevant words, then all that is left is to perform a syllogism.[7] This is so because when the relation "rule–world" has been established then a relation between rule–rule has to be established, i.e. a relation between a general rule (like "it shall be a misdemeanour, punishable by fine of £5, to sleep in any railway station") and a particular one ("the defendant should pay £5"). Logic does not answer the question of whether a Cadillac is a vehicle; this is something that follows from the very meaning of "vehicle", in such a way that not to see this is to show plain ignorance of English. But *once* that question is answered, logic (in the positivist view) must be able to answer the question of whether that Cadillac is to be allowed in the park.[8]

A Theory of Legal Argumentation or a Theory of Legal Reasoning?

Neil MacCormick began his *Legal Reasoning and Legal Theory* with a forceful argument for the importance of syllogistic reasoning in law, that is, for the idea that *modus ponens* alone can render, in some cases, fully justified legal decisions. With this claim he faced the challenge of those who would like to deny this:

> If this denial [of the possibility of legal reasoning being deductive] is intended in the strictest sense, implying that legal reasoning is never, or cannot ever be, solely deductive in form, then the denial is manifestly and demonstrably false. It is sometimes possible to show conclusively that a given decision is legally justified by means of a purely deductive argument (1994: 19).

[7] There is a significant difference in the way in which logical language is used by logicians and lawyers: for the latter "syllogism", "deduction" and "logic" are, broadly speaking, synonyms, while for the latter they are quite different (however related) things. *See* Kneale and Kneale (1962).

[8] To see that Marmor's claim that Hart does not "subscribe to the view that the application of legal rules is a matter of logical inference" (1994: 128) is simply false, all that is needed is to read the passages in which Hart talked about *hard* cases, in order to see what is their implication for *clear* cases: "human invention and natural processes continually throw up such ["penumbral"] variants on the familiar ["*core*"], and if we are to say that *these ranges of facts* do or do not fall under existing rules, then the classifier must make a decision *which is not dictated to him* . . ." (Hart, 1958: 63, implying that the decision is indeed dictated to the classifier regarding "core" ranges of facts); "If a penumbra of uncertainty must surround all legal rules, then their application to specific cases *in the penumbral area* cannot be a matter of logical deduction, and so deductive reasoning . .. . cannot serve as a model for what judges, or indeed anyone, should do in bringing particular cases under general rules. *In this area* men cannot live by deduction alone" (*ibid.*, at 64, implying that the application of legal rules to cases in the "core" area can be a matter of logical deduction. All the emphases in these quotations are mine).

The importance of this claim should by now be evident. If it can be shown that in *some* cases at least legal reasoning *can* be *solely* and *strictly* deductive in form, then all that will remain to be done is to specify (as MacCormick tries to do in Chapter 3 of his book) the presuppositions and limits of deductive reasoning. Once we know these presuppositions and limits, we would be free to say that those cases in which some of those presuppositions fail (or those cases that are beyond such limits) are *hard cases*, where there is no difficulty at all in accepting that the question of what the law is (or better, will be) for the case can be linked to that of what the law ought to be for it. This is the reason why MacCormick's argument, if successful, could be used to defend a theory of law like Hart's.

Before examining MacCormick's argument in some detail it would pay, I believe, to pause for a while on what precisely it is that MacCormick is claiming when he says that the *Daniels* decision was justified in a deductive manner.

This is important because MacCormick's thesis is open to an interpretation that would render it harmles against the anti-Hartian challenge *Legal Reasoning and Legal Theory* was supposed to answer. Indeed, we shall see that MacCormick himself sometimes seems to understand his argument in this way.

For a start, consider Robert Alexy's theory of legal interpretation as set out in his *A Theory of Legal Argumentation* (1989). In it, he begins by distinguishing what he calls "internal" from "external" justification:

> Legal discourses are concerned with the justification of a special case of normative statements, namely those which express legal judgements. Two aspects of justification can be distinguished: *internal justification* and *external justification*. Internal justification is concerned with the question of whether an opinion follows logically from the premisses adduced as justifying it; The correctness of the premisses is the subject-matter of the external justification (Alexy, 1989: 221).

For Alexy, the problem of internal justification *is* that of deductive reasoning: "problems associated with internal justification have been widely discussed under the heading 'legal syllogism'" (*ibid.*, 220). Now, the important point here is that no decision is fully justified if it has not been externally *and* internally justified. For the external justification, non-deductive reasoning is typically needed. Once the premisses have been (externally) justified (using whatever criteria is used to justify premisses: consequential reasoning, purposive interpretation, authority reasons, etc.), then it is possible to say that the decision is fully justified if it follows in a formally valid manner from those (externally) justified premisses.[9]

[9] For example, in Hart's case of the electrically propelled toy car and the "no vehicles in the park" rule, the premise "a toy car is a vehicle" would have to be justified according to the requirements of external justification. But once that question is settled, all that is left is to *deduce* from the statement (thus justified) "this toy car is a vehicle" and the rule "no vehicles in the park", the conclusion that this toy car is not allowed into the park.

Notice that for Alexy (unlike MacCormick) the requirement of the justification being deductive has nothing at all to do with the fact of the case in which it occurs being clear or hard. The difference will usually lie in the fact that the (external) justification of the premisses will normally be more controversial in hard cases than in clear ones; but however controversial the external justification of the premisses, once they have been justified, the internal justification takes over in the same way for one case or the other. Thus, in the context of a theory of legal argumentation, aimed at establishing "how fully to justify a legal judgement" (Alexy, 1989: 2), deductive reasoning is to be used in every case.[10]

We can now see how MacCormick's thesis can be rendered irrelevant as an answer to the challenge to *The Concept of Law*, i.e. by taking it to mean simply that a form of deductive reasoning is somehow important for legal reasoning. In any case syllogistic reasoning can play a part. To see this imagine the mother of all hard cases, then settle (according to your moral or legal intuitions) the controversial aspects of it and on you go! You are now ready to solve the case with "syllogistic reasoning playing a role".

These are the reasons why I believe this is not a correct interpretation of MacCormick's claim. But if this interpretation is incorrect, then how are we to understand MacCormick's argument? To answer this question we can recall Joseph Raz's distinction between what he calls the "narrow" and the "wide" versions of the sources thesis (1985: 214–15). The wide sources thesis "claims that the truth or falsity of [pure and applied] legal statements depends on social facts which can be established without resort to moral argument" (*ibid.*, 214). In these cases, all that is needed to solve the case is to find the applicable rule(s), and establish the relevant facts, while the narrow sources thesis is silent concerning applied legal statements. I believe that MacCormick's claim, as his analysis of *Daniels* makes clear, is precisely that sometimes the justification of a legal decision can be purely and wholly deductive in form, and it can be presented as a syllogism which features as major premisses only legal rules (and as minor premisses only statements of fact): "all of the major premisses involved in the argument [in *Daniels*], not all of which were expressly stated, are rules of law for which contemporary authority can be cited" (MacCormick, 1994: 29) or, as he claims just a couple of pages below,

> It will be observed that in the above analysis of the argument each stage in the argument is a valid hypothetical argument the premisses of which are *either* statements of propositions of law which at the material time were true for legal

[10] I will talk about (a theory of) *legal argumentation* to refer to (a theory that specifies) the ways in which judicial decisions are fully and satisfactorily justified, and (a theory of) *legal reasoning* to refer to (a theory that explains) how applied legal statements are derived from pure legal statements. The distinction between a theory of legal reasoning and a theory of legal argumentation collapses under a theory like Dworkin's, insofar as he makes legal reasoning dependent upon legal argumentation. In a theory like Hart's (giving the open texture thesis the first interpretation) they can be distinguished: Hart's theory of legal reasoning would be his distinction between *core* and penumbra and his acceptance of (10), while his theory of legal argumentation would be an analysis of deductive reasoning (for clear cases) and a theory of discretion (for hard cases).

purposes, *or* findings of fact which are also for legal purposes taken to be true, or intermediate conclusions derived from such premisses (*ibid.*, 32; emphasis added).

Thus MacCormick's argument is not one about what makes a legal justification a good and complete one, as Alexy's was, but about the existence of some cases that can be solved in a deductive manner using as premisses only statements of propositions of law and findings of fact.

Actually, later in the book MacCormick seems to acknowledge that in the first sense (judicial syllogism as internal justification) "moments" of deductive reasoning exist even in hard cases, which are characterised by the fact that "deduction comes in only after the interesting part of the argument, settling a ruling in law, has been carried out" (*ibid.*, 197).

In Alexy's terms, the internal justification starts off only after the external justification has taken place, since only after the external justification (what MacCormick at 197 calls "settling a ruling in law") the major premisses to be used by the internal justification will be found. MacCormick's claim in Chapter 2 of *Legal Reasoning and Legal Theory*, then, amounts to saying that in some cases no external justification is needed beyond that provided by what he calls "the fundamental judicial commandment": "thou shalt not controvert established and binding rules of law" (1994: 195). These are the cases that in jurisprudential jargon are called "clear" cases, the cases that Hart distinguished on the basis that in them, rules can be applied without courts being required to make what he called "a fresh judgment" (Hart, 1994: 135): I take "without the need for fresh judgement" to mean here "without premisses needing external justification (beyond MacCormick's judicial commandment)".

This might seem an instance of labouring the obvious, and indeed I think it is. My only justification for it is that MacCormick himself sometimes equivocates between presenting his thesis as one about legal argumentation (deduction has a role to play in legal justification) and as one about legal reasoning (some cases can be decided following a strictly syllogistic line of reasoning). I will come back to this point later in this chapter (at 182f below), and we shall see that it is important to clarify this ambiguity.[11]

[11] In the meantime, a single example will show, I hope, that this is not an instance of labouring the obvious. MacCormick's quotation above (at 173), where he was talking about how "we have to decide whether to call this that we see a 'man' (etc.)" might be one in which transformed his important thesis (about legal reasoning) into a thesis about legal argumentation. To appreciate this we have to look at the passages I omitted from the quote before. To the case of (we have to decide whether to call this that we see an instance of) a "man" that I have already quoted, he adds the case of (we have to decide whether to call this that we see an instance of) "failing to take reasonable care towards a neighbour", and then he goes on to say that "from a logical point of view, the point is that once this difficulties [in the interpretation of "reasonable care"] are resolved in a given case and you decide that this person is one that on this occasion did fail to take reasonable care, you are logically banned from asserting the failure, asserting the principle, and denying that there was . . . breach [of contract]" (MacCormick, 1992: 219). This is evidently not an argument to show that in some cases legal reasoning can be "solely" deductive in form, but to show that "moments" of deductive reasoning can appear in judicial decisions (to show, we might say, that *once* the truth of the premisses has been (externally) justified, then the internal justification is sufficient fully to justify a judicial decision).

Daniels v. *Tarbard*

We are now ready to examine MacCormick's example of a case in which a purely syllogistic justification of the decision is possible. His example was *Daniels and Daniels* v. *R. White & Sons and Tarbard* (1938 4 All ER 258). Though MacCormick has made this case famous, it seems appropriate to give a brief description of its facts: Mr Daniels bought a bottle of lemonade (R White's lemonade) in the defendant's (i.e. Mrs Tarbard's) pub. He took the bottle home, where he and Mrs Daniels drank from it. As a consequence, they both became ill, because (as was proven later) the lemonade was heavily contaminated with carbolic acid. Mr and Mrs Daniels sued the owner of the pub and the lemonade's manufacturer. While the latter was absolved from liability, the former was held liable and ordered to pay damages to the (first) plaintiff. MacCormick's claim is that the court's decision follows in a deductive manner from these facts plus the legal rules as they were in 1938.

As a matter of fact (of logic, rather), however, MacCormick could not have shown that the court's reasoning in *Daniels* was strictly deductive without using the relationship of material implication, "$\supset$". "$\supset$" is used instead of "if *in any case* . . . then . . ." (1994: 29).[12] But legal rules do not rule for *all* cases, even if their language may induce one to think they do. They do not rule "in all cases, if . . . then . . .", but "if in normal cases . . . then . . .". This point should not be particularly controversial against MacCormick, who has recently put forward the thesis that legal rules rule for "normal" cases, establishing what is to be "presumptively" the case (1995). Furthermore, MacCormick explicitly rejects in Chapter 3 of his book the move made by some authors of explaining defeasibility on the basis of moral disagreement about the issue of whether or not the law ought to (moral "ought") be applied. He thinks that in those kinds of cases what is at issue is not whether there are moral reasons to break the law, but what the law actually is:

> [A] positivistic description of the system as it operates *cannot* answer a particular kind of question which may be raised *internally* to a legal system: the question as it might be raised for a judge in a hard case: "Why ought *we* to treat every decision in accordance with a rule valid by our criteria of validity as being sufficiently justified? and that is a question which can be, and from time to time is, raised . . .. For my part

[12] This follows on from n. 7. MacCormick probably does not mean material implication in its technical sense. In symbolic logic, ($p \supset q$) "is true if "not-p or q" is true. But "not-p or q" is true in any one of the following cases: (1) p is true and q is true; (2) p is false and q is true; (3) p is false and q is false [S]o long as p is false, no matter what q is, "p implies q" is true; and so long as q is true, no matter what p is, "q is implied by p" is true" (Cohen and Nagel, 1934: 127). This is because "*material implication* is the name we give to the fact that one of a pair of propositions happens to be false or else the other happens to be true" (*ibid.* at 128). But MacCormick wants to say, I believe, that ($p \supset q$) means something else, to wit, that *because* of p then q. MacCormick mentions this problem, and claims that "nothing turns on that" (MacCormick, 1994: 28n). I take him to be offering a stipulation of the meaning of "$\supset$", so that it means "if in any case p, then (because of p) q".

> *I should be reluctant to treat such questions as being non legal simply because of a definitional fiat* . . .. To treat such arguments as ideological-but-not-legal (which is what Kelsen and, in effect, Hart do) on *a priori* grounds seems to me unsatisfactory (MacCormick, 1994: 63; the fourth emphasis is mine).

To put it in the words used above, if rules are understood as referring to *normal* cases, then they simply cannot be applied without having previously established that the case is *normal.* It is still possible to say (with Kelsen and Hart) that as a matter of law all cases are normal (or, what amounts to the same thing, that legal rules are, according to the law, to be applied to *all*, instead of *normal*, cases), but this implies a definitional fiat that begs the question: the *fiat* of saying that according to the law legal rules are to be applied to all cases (or that according to the law all cases are normal), however absurd the result might turn out to be. Only after this *fiat* will the decision not to apply the law because of these absurd outcomes become an "ideological-but-not-legal" one. MacCormick is reluctant to endorse this solution, and hence he is committed to claim that, as a matter of law (and not as a matter of ideology or morals), legal rules apply to normal cases (this is, of course, a thesis MacCormick has explicitly endorsed: *see* MacCormick, 1995).

But if MacCormick accepts that laws are to be understood as referring to *normal*, instead of *all*, cases, then it is difficult to see how he can claim that the decision in *Daniels* was *strictly* and *solely* deductive. Lewis J held Mrs Tarbard liable "with some regret, because it is rather hard on Mrs Tarbard, who is a perfectly innocent person in the matter" (*cit.* in MacCormick, 1994: 21). He thought the application of the law to be inappropriate for the case. It is easy to see why: Lewis J assumed that in a civil liability case it is normally the position that if the defendant is "a perfectly innocent person in the matter", judgment should not be passed against him or her. In other words, the "innocence" of the defendant is usually a relevant substantive consideration when he or she is sued for compensation. Because in the court's understanding the rules excluded this consideration, their application to this particular case produced some inappropriateness: they demanded judgment to be passed against a "perfectly innocent person". But this inappropriateness was not, in Lewis J's view, important enough for the need for predictability to be waived.[13] In other words, he took the rules as being formal enough to trump the inappropriateness of finding against a "perfectly innocent" party, this consideration not being strong enough to make the case "abnormal". This "fresh judgement" was, for Kelsen and Hart (as MacCormick says) not required by the law: it was "ideological-but-not-legal". But MacCormick sensibly rejects this position as based upon a definitional *fiat* that effectively begs the question. Hence, for MacCormick this "fresh judgement" is *legal*, i.e.

[13] It must be borne in mind that I have legislated the meaning of "predictability", in such a way that it encompasses all the values that stand for a formalistic application of a legal rule. Predictability in its non-stipulated sense is normally the most important of them (hence the stipulation), but it need not be the only one.

what *the law is* for the case cannot be known before it is made. Therefore MacCormick's syllogism will not be formally valid unless it is stated as a premiss. This can clearly be seen when attention is paid to MacCormick's translation of the court's decision into logical notation:

(xvi) If a seller has broken a condition of a contract which he was required to fulfil, the buyer is entitled to recover damages from him equivalent to the loss directly and naturally resulting to him from the seller's breach of the condition;
(xv) In the instant case, the seller has broken a condition of the contract which she was required to fulfil;
(xvii) ∴ In the instant case, the buyer is entitled to recover damages from her equivalent to the loss directly and naturally resulting to him from the seller's breach of the condition (MacCormick, 1994: 31–2).[14]

This is translated as (the left column is MacCormick's, while the right contains my translation of MacCormick's logical notation half-back to English, according to his stipulations in *ibid.* 23 and 28f, which for ease of exposition I will use thereafter):

(xvi)	$y \supset z$	(xvi)	In any case, if *y* then *z*;
(xv)	*y*	(xv)	In the instant case, *y*;
(xvii)	$\therefore z$	(xvii)	Therefore in the instant case *z*.

MacCormick is clearly correct in claiming that (xvii) follows from (xvi) and (xv). But the point is that (xvi) is not a correct description of the law as it was at the time, and we have already seen that elsewhere in the book (and in other writings, most notably MacCormick, 1995) MacCormick agrees with this. If we correct (xvi) by introducing the idea of "normal cases", we would get

(xvi') In normal cases, if *y*, then *z*;
(xv) In the instant case, *y*;
(xvii) Therefore in the instant case, *z*.

And this is not a valid deductive argument: to be one it needs a further premiss:

(xviii') The instant case is a normal case.

MacCormick's preferred option (that legal rules establish what is "presumptively" to be the case) makes this problem even more noticeable. For consider:

(xvi") If *y*, then presumptively *z*;

[14] MacCormick's complete syllogism is considerably longer (*cf.* 1994: 30ff). The objection I am presenting now could, however, be directed against any of its parts, therefore it is enough for me to quote a section of the reasoning. It is also worth noticing that though MacCormick now believes that a judicial syllogism like *Daniels'* should be represented using predicate rather than propositional logic, I have retained his original representation of it (*see* MacCormick, 1994: xv; MacCormick's change of mind was prompted by White, 1979).

(xv) In the instant case, *y*;
(xvii) Therefore in the instant case, z.

Again, (xvii) does not follow. What does follow is

(xvii") Therefore in the instant case, presumptively *z*.

But (xvii") does not, of course, justify a legal decision (Detmold, 1984: 22–6). It does not tell anybody what the law is for the instant case: it only states what the law "presumptively" is, unless, of course, we add a further premiss:

(xviii") In the instant case, the presumption has not been defeated.

What MacCormick calls "the pragmatics of law" (1994: xiii; 1995) would not be of much use here. "A rule that ends with 'unless...' is still a rule", of course, but it cannot be applied unless the exceptional circumstance is not present. The rule might be such that the "default" position is that the exception does not exist, but even in this case the justification would, from a logical point of view, be incomplete (i.e. invalid) if this circumstance is not asserted. For consider,

(xvi"') In any case, if *y*, then *z*, unless the court is satisfied of *w*;
(xv) In the instant case, *y*;
(xvii) Therefore in the instant case, *z*.

Again, (xvii) fails to follow. For the argument to be formally valid, a premiss such as the following is needed:

(xviii"') *w* has not been proven (or "the court has not been satisfied of *w*").

Following Hart, we have already seen that "*w*" here stands for a fresh judgment to the effect that the inappropriateness of the application of the rule to the particular case is important enough for the demand for predictability to be waived. As a premiss, therefore, (xviii) (and its variants) is neither a rule of law nor a statement of fact, but an evaluative judgment: "in this case the result offered by the rule is not inappropriate, or at least not to a significant extent". In other words, even in as clear a case as *Daniels* and even assuming that the court has the obligation to apply the law, no decision can be reached in a syllogistic manner using only rules of law and statements of fact as premisses. The fact that the absence of *w* need not be argued, important as it is from a pragmatic point of view (no external justification is needed to regard it as absent), is immaterial from a logical point of view.[15]

[15] *Cf.* MacCormick (1994: 29), where MacCormick rightly points out that to the premisses stated by Lewis J a further one should be added, one "which is so trivially obvious that its omission from the express statements of Lewis J is scarcely surprising—namely that the transaction described in (i) above was intended by each of the parties to be a purchase by Mr. D. From Mrs. T. and a sale by her to him". Maybe the premiss that states the normality of the instant case (or that the presumption in favour of the solution offered by the rule according to its meaning is not defeated in the instant case) is equally trivially obvious in many cases, but as MacCormick recognises the fact

In short, the only way in which MacCormick's claim could succeed is assuming the definitional fiat he (rightly, in my view) rejects in Chapter 3.

Now, it could be argued that I have missed the point, that the fact that the rule should be applied to the particular case at hand is one of the presuppositions (and it thus constitutes a limit) of deductive justification. In *Legal Reasoning and Legal Theory*, MacCormick says that one of the presuppositions of legal reasoning is that "every judge has in virtue of his office a duty to apply each and every one of those rules which are "rules of law" whenever it is relevant and applicable to any case brought before him" (1994: 54). Hence, the counter-objection would continue, if it is doubted whether the rule should be applied to *this* particular case, then we are going beyond one of the limits of deductive reasoning, while MacCormick's thesis was meant for those cases in which those presuppositions are satisfied. But this cannot be an answer to my objection to MacCormick's claim, since I am assuming that the court has to apply the law; what I am contesting is that in finding what the law is for the case, the court will necessarily have to assume that the case is "normal" if rules like those in *Daniels* are to be applied as they were in that case. This, again, could be used to defend MacCormick's position only if one were to claim that the rule applies to *all* cases as a matter of law, however justified (from an "ideological-but-not-legal point of view) the court might be in not applying it to the particular case. Only given that assumption could MacCormick say that the process of finding a solution is (or can in some cases be) deductive: given the relevant rules as they were in 1938, and the facts of *Daniels* as they were proven in court, the conclusion could be reached in a deductive manner. By the same token, however, he would have to say that given Pufendorf's report of the Bolognese law (and the facts as he told them), we could reach the conclusion that the barber had to be punished in the same deductive manner. What we would add in the latter case would be an "ideological-but-not-legal" argument to the effect that punishing the barber is too absurd for the court to do it. MacCormick's argument cannot succeed without this *a priori* distinction between the legal and the ideological, a distinction that he himself thinks is unjustified.

Since I have argued against this distinction in Chapter 4 (and especially since MacCormick himself rejects it), there is no need to repeat those arguments here. What interests me now is to point out the incompatibility of MacCormick's legal theory with his account of legal reasoning.[16] We know

that a premiss is "trivially obvious" does not mean that it is not required for the formal validity of the inference, though it might very well mean that the court is justified in not stating it.

[16] I am referring here to MacCormick's legal theory as it can be found in *Legal Reasoning and Legal Theory*. His position is nowadays different: "[I] no longer accept nearly as much of his [i.e. Hart's] theses about law as I did in 1978" (1994: xv). My own comments about *Legal Reasoning and Legal Theory* are not to be seen as a criticism of MacCormick's legal theory, since (I would claim) his later work can accommodate most of the claims made here, but about the tension between the perspectives of legal theory and legal reasoning, a tension that permeates his argument as originally presented. In my view, the fact that he does "no longer accept as much of Hart's theory" goes a long way to explain why he can now accommodate most of the claims made here.

that *Legal Reasoning and Legal Theory* was meant to be a Hartian explanation of legal reasoning. Hence, it had to claim that *some* cases were clear in a Hartian sense, that is, their outcome could be determined according to the rules alone (that is the gist of Hart's criticism of rule-scepticism). If those cases are completely determined by the rules, it must be possible to reconstruct the justification of a solution to them according to the deductive model. That is to say, if it is the case that "the life of the law consists to a very large extent in the guidance both of officials and private individuals by determinate rules which, unlike the applications of variable standards, do *not* require from them a fresh judgement from case to case" (Hart, 1994: 135) then in those cases the court's decision can be represented in a syllogistic way, in which the only presupposition needed (along with statements of fact and of legal rules) is that the law ought to be applied, in which no premiss containing a "fresh judgement" is needed for the formal validity of the inference. This is the significance of MacCormick's argument in Chapter 2 of *Legal Reasoning and Legal Theory* as an analysis of clear cases according to Hart. But in the following chapters, in which he undertook to build up a theory of legal reasoning, he was driven to positions which are incompatible with the claims of the (legal) theory.

Thus, when discussing the issue of clear and hard cases, he starts by noticing that "in truth there is no clear dividing line between clear cases and hard cases" (MacCormick, 1994: 197). There is a spectrum of cases, ranging from the hardest to the clearest, and across that spectrum "it could never be judged more than vaguely at what point" interpretative doubts could become significant enough for the court to have discretion. Now, instead of offering (like Hart with his open texture thesis in its first interpretation) a value-free test to distinguish a clear from a hard case, he finds the explanation of this uncertainty at the divide between clear/hard cases to be in "differences in the dominant style of different periods in the history of legal systems" (1994: 198). Later on we are told that "when we talk of differences between judicial styles . . . what we are talking about is or includes the degree of readiness which a judge manifests correctly to declare that presumption [i.e. the presumption that "obvious meaning should be preferred"] to be overridden" (1994: 207).

In this view, how pressing the absurdity of the result produced by the application of the rule to the particular case should be for the judge to permit the presumption in favour of the obvious meaning of the words to be overridden is not something the rule can settle; it is a problem generated by the conflicting demands of predictability and appropriateness. A case cannot be decided before considering whether it will be treated as a "normal" case (and given—and excluding—this decision a deductive justification could be reconstructed) or as one in which substantive considerations show that the case is abnormal, that is, is one in which the presumption must be overridden.

To emphasise, if what makes a case clear rather than hard (and vice-versa) is a judgment about the correct balance between two values (i.e. a fresh judgment), then at least some hard cases *are* hard because they *ought to be* so.

The only reason, I submit, why MacCormick thinks he can claim *both* that the decision in clear cases can be justified in a syllogistic manner (using as premisses only statements of fact and of legal rules) *and* that rules apply only to normal cases (or that they establish only what is to be "presumptively" the case) is that he (as we already saw) equivocates between the two different claims identified above concerning what we could call the "deductive element" in legal reasoning.

MacCormick's argument was originally presented against those who held the thesis that "legal reasoning is [n]ever *strictly* deductive" (1994: 19). We were told that if this denial "is intended in the strictest sense, implying that legal reasoning is never, or cannot ever be, *solely* deductive in form, then the denial is manifestly and demonstrably false. It is sometimes possible to show *conclusively* that a given decision is legally justified by means of a *purely deductive argument*" (1994: 19). Later in the book, however, Chapter 2 was supposed to have been directed against "those who deny that deductive logic is *relevant* to the justification of legal decisions" (1994: 45), and in the new foreword to the 1994 paperback edition the argument has definitely changed: now it is presented against "recurrent denials by learned persons that the law *allows scope* for deductive reasoning, or even logic at all" (1994: ix). In the same piece MacCormick seems to reject his own claim that "it is sometimes possible to show conclusively that a given decision is legally justified by means of a purely deductive argument" when he now claims that "deductive reasoning from rules *cannot* be a self-sufficient, self-supporting, mode of legal justification. It is *always* encapsulated in a web of anterior and ulterior reasoning from principles and values . . ." (1994: xiii; all emphases added).

In my opinion, the quotations from the new foreword reflect MacCormick's present view of the "centrality of deductive reasoning for legal reasoning" and they have to be understood in the light of Alexy's distinction between external and internal justification. So understood, the claim refers to the possibility of translating a given decision in syllogistic terms as being usually the clearest and safest way to check whether or not the decision was fully justified, whether or not all of the issues requiring external justification were settled according to the requirements of the external justification).

But in this sense Chapter 2 does not answer the challenge to legal positivism it was designed to answer. If it is to provide an answer, it has to be taken as meaning that sometimes it is possible for legal decisions to be fully justified through a syllogistic chain of reasoning that uses only statements of fact and of legal rules (including definitions and the like) as premisses. Only in this sense would the thesis imply, if correct, the rejection of the argument presented up to now. Only in this sense it could help Hart to show that in some cases no fresh judgment is needed for courts and officials to apply the rules. But for this argument to work, an *a priori* distinction has to be made between the legal and the ideological. Since MacCormick is unwilling to make this *ad hoc* distinction, the argument fails to prove that sometimes legal decisions can be "purely" and "solely" deductive in form.

The reasons for considering MacCormick's argument in some detail were, as stated above, not only concerned with the intrinsic value of it; it also helps us illustrate an important tension between legal reasoning and legal theory. Depending upon the perspective adopted as a starting point one can reach, following natural and plausible steps, incompatible conclusions. When MacCormick adopted the perspective of legal theory, that is, the perspective of an enterprise directed to understanding what law is, when a legal system exists and the like, he was driven to the Hartian view that sometimes rules are there, so to speak, and can sometimes be "straightforwardly" applied.

When he adopted the perspective of legal reasoning, that is to say, one that tries to understand how the law is applied (to my knowledge, his book is still one of the few, not to say the only one, self-avowedly positivist work in which the discussion of decisions given in *actual cases* plays a crucial methodological role) he could not live up to that: the conclusions for legal reasoning that would follow from the "legal theory" thesis are just too implausible, too *ad hoc*.

I want to claim that this is not a problem of MacCormick's alone. We have seen how this problem emerges in Chapter 7 of *The Concept of Law*. It also appears in one way or another in the work of many of the most sophisticated authors writing today on legal theory. In the final two sections of this chapter, we shall be looking at this issue as it appears in the work of Frederick Schauer and Joseph Raz.

RULES AS ENTRENCHED GENERALISATIONS

Schauer's main thesis throughout *Playing by the Rules* is that rules are "entrenched generalisations". Generalisations, that is to say, because a rule singles out some states of affairs (i.e. those that match the rule's operative facts) on the basis that the purpose of the rule (what Schauer calls the "underlying justification" of the rule) will be served if the rule's consequence is triggered when they occur. The generalisation is *entrenched*, and the standard a rule, according to Schauer, if it "control[s] the decision even in those cases in which that generalization failed to serve its underlying justification" (Schauer, 1991: 49). If we ask why does he think that rules are entrenched generalisations, we are told at the outset that it is precisely this entrenchment that characterises a rule: rules "furnish reasons for action simply by virtue of their existence *qua* rules, and thus generate normative pressure even in those cases in which the justifications (rationales) underlying the rules indicate the contrary result" (1991: 5). Thus, rules cannot be rules without being "necessarily *sticky*, resisting current efforts to mould them to the needs of the instant" (1991: 82).

Hence, the watermark of a rule-based decision-making process is that it can be sub-optimal, since if the standards to be applied are *rules* they must have some normative force that is not exhausted by their underlying justification. Some cases therefore are to be solved by application of the rule even if they would not be so solved were we to follow the rule's underlying justification rather than the rule itself.

How do rules achieve this sub-optimality? They do so, Schauer tells us (*ibid.*, at 100), by preventing the decision-maker from considering the full range of otherwise relevant considerations. It follows from this that if the decision-maker can, when she thinks the application of the rule to the case to produce absurd or otherwise unfair results, allow into the decision-making process considerations the rule was supposed to pre-empt no sub-optimality is possible, and the standard would turn out not to be a rule, after all. If an implicit exception to rule *r* is introduced every time the decision-maker comes across a case covered by *r* but not by its substantive justification, then the normative force of the rule would be exhausted by the reasons for it. No space for sub-optimality would be found and *r*, despite appearances, would not be a rule (*cf.* the discussion on rule-utilitarianism, above at 127ff).

This conceptualisation of rules seems to imply, or so Schauer seems to think (at least sometimes, as we shall see), a definite answer to the problem of defeasibility: he accepts Hart's argument that "a rule that ends with 'unless...' is still a rule" (*cf.* Schauer, 1991: 155), but he sees that without the distinction between implicit and explicit exceptions this answer misses the point. Thus, he argues,

> the issue is not whether rules may have exceptions and still be rules, for of course they may. It is whether rules may be subjected to exceptions added at the moment of application in light of the full range of otherwise applicable factors and still be rules, and the answer to that question is "no" (Schauer, 1991: 116).

Since to say that a rule is defeasible is to say that it can be defeated by the introduction of the kind of exceptions that Schauer has just ruled out, what Schauer is effectively saying is that there is something in the concept of "rule" that makes them indefeasible. This is, as we have seen, the necessary consequence of a conceptualisation of rules as exclusionary reasons: the problem of appropriateness does not present itself, for the considerations that would prompt it are excluded from the outset.

This is Schauer-the-philosopher-of-rules. Schauer-the-philosopher-of-practical-reasoning, though, has a rather different story to tell (I shall call them "strong" Schauer and "weak" Schauer, respectively).

Weak Schauer does not take long to introduce important qualifications to strong Schauer's conclusions. The important point for him is not (the strong claim) that rules cannot have exceptions introduced at the moment of application and still be rules, but rather (the much weaker claim) that they cannot be "continuously malleable":

> this resistance [i.e., of a rule to a recalcitrant experience[17]] need not be absolute. Still, if there is *no* resistance, then no instances will occur in which rule-generated results differ from justification-generated ones. For rule-based decision-making to be other than a different name for particularistic decision-making, the rules employed in the former must pre-exist any particular application of them, and must supply *some resistance* on that application (1991: 84n, emphasis added).

According to this last quotation, it seems clear that the answer to the question of "whether rules can have exceptions introduced at the moment of application in light of the full range of otherwise applicable factors and still be rules", that for strong Schauer was a resounding "no", has to be, for weak Schauer, a cautious "*yes*, but not concerning *every* recalcitrant experience".

Weak Schauer also sees, however, that a characterisation of rules as exclusionary reasons distorts the decision-maker's practical reasoning in many situations (*cf.* Schauer, 1991: 90f). This is his argument for rejecting Raz's claim that in cases of implicit exceptions the decision-maker can consider them only if they are beyond the *scope* of the rule, i.e., only if they were not excluded in the first place. Schauer's consideration of legal (or, in general, practical) reasoning according to rules leads him to accept that rules are not as entrenched as they appeared to be.

In a way, the core of the book is a running commentary on the way in which rules cannot be exclusionary, though they have to have *some* level of formality to be rules. Sometimes he seems to reject (10), i.e. the idea that the meaning of a rule determines its application, even though he explicitly collapses a rule with its formulation. He distinguishes applicability from validity, the latter being a necessary though not sufficient condition for applicability: "validity is of course not a sufficient condition for applicability, for many perfectly valid laws do not apply to me" (1991: 120n). He argues, following Hart, that what is left is the *internalisation* of the rule. An agent has internalised a rule when she "treats a rule's *existence* as relevant to the question of what to do" (*ibid.*, 121). Furthermore,

> internalizing a rule *qua* rule supposes that it is the rule's status as a rule that is internalized, rather than the rule's underlying justifications, and thus internalization of a rule is meaningful only if the reasons for action produced by the fact of internalization persists even when the agent *disagrees* with the content of the rule (Schauer, 1991: 122).

It is here that the question of whether (10) is true reappears: during my discussion of it I always assumed that the decision-maker had internalised

[17] Schauer calls "recalcitrant experience" the case of a particular that, though included in a generalisation, should not be included according to the generalisation's justification (1991: 39f). Thus, the justification for, e.g. the generalisation contained in the Bolognese statute was (let us assume) that those who shed blood in the streets usually do so in the course of violent behaviour. The purpose of the statute was to forbid violent behaviour in the streets. A "recalcitrant experience" is the barber's case, which is covered by the generalisation, though not by the generalisation's justification.

MacCormick's "fundamental judicial commandment": "thou shalt not controvert established and binding rules of law" (1994: 195). That was never used as an argument against (10); it was assumed all along that courts recognised valid law as binding and as giving rise to reasons for them to decide. The argument above was that *after* the agent has internalised the rules, there is something else that has to be settled before any application of the rule is possible. The question, then, is not "why should (or does) an agent take the existence of a rule as a reason for action?" (Schauer, 1991: 122) but rather "given that an agent recognises that the existence of the rule is a reason for action, how should she understand that reason?".

Schauer believes that grasping the meaning of an internalised rule is a sufficient condition for applying it. Therefore, when he is confronted with the issue of defeasibility (in most of the book) he has two answers: sometimes he argues that if a rule is a rule, exceptions to it cannot be introduced at the moment of application; sometimes he says that they can indeed, provided that that does not happen concerning every recalcitrant experience. Eventually, weak and strong Schauer try to reach a compromise to speak with one voice, so they claim that implicit exceptions can be introduced only in extreme cases, only when the application of the rule is "*egregiously* at odds" (1991: 205) with its underlying justification, when the reasons for not applying the rule are "*particularly* strong" (*Ibid.* at 204).

Now, why should that pressure be "*particularly* strong"? Why should the rule-based solution be "*egregiously*" inappropriate? Schauer's only answer for this is the need to preserve a distinction between a rule-based and a particularist decision-making procedure: if in every case in which the application of the rule is deemed to be inappropriate an exception can be introduced, then the rule provides no guidance. But notice that from this obvious fact it does not follow that the pressure has to be "particularly" strong; all that follows is, as Schauer himself recognises elsewhere in the book, that it has to have "*some* degree of resistance" (1991: 118, emphasis added). In other words, all that is needed is that the rule should control the decision in *some* cases in which the solution it provides is not the most appropriate. Even if the resistance of the rule is very weak, that does not mean that the rule offers no resistance. Even in such a case we are likely to find some cases in which the result indicated by the rule is inappropriate, though so slightly inappropriate that even a rule with very weak resistance would justify the decision-maker in disregarding that fact.

Schauer's demand that the inappropriateness of the rule for the particular case should be particularly strong is strange, since he distinguished, in his discussion of Raz's exclusionary reasons, "the idea of exclusion and the weight of the exclusionary force" (1991: 91). Once these two ideas are distinguished there is no warrant to claim that the inappropriateness has to be particularly strong: why cannot the "weight of the exclusionary force" of different rules be different? Though the internalisation of a rule consists in the internalisation of its status as a rule, the weight of the exclusionary force that is attached to it is determined by reasons other than the mere existence of the rule (in other words, how much exclusionary weight a given rule has is something that is said *about* the rule, not *by* the rule).

Notice how Schauer's distinction between "the idea of exclusion" and the "weight of the exclusionary force" undermines his critique of Fuller (discussed above, at 115ff), based as it was on the idea that the meaning of a rule determines its application, i.e., (10). The point here is that once the distinction between the idea of exclusion and the weight of exclusionary force is introduced, (10) must be abandoned. From the fact that there are *core* meanings of rules it does not follow that there are clear cases under the rule. Having accepted this distinction, a clear case is one in which *two* (not one) conditions are met: (i) the facts of the case clearly fit the relevant rule's operative facts, *and* (ii) the weight of the exclusionary force attached to the applicable rule is such that the substantive considerations that could lead the court to a solution other than the one offered by the rule are pre-empted.

To recapitulate: as with MacCormick's, Schauer's argument is subject to the tension between legal reasoning and legal theory that is the subject of this chapter. When he looks at the law (at the rules) from the point of view of a theorist trying to explain how it is the case that sometimes courts and officials do what they know is not the best thing to do strong Schauer is driven to endorse an exclusionary-like account of legal reasons. When he is trying to explain how courts and officials can be justified in so deciding, weak Schauer has to accept that rules are not exclusionary after all, that they can be overridden by the substantive considerations they were supposed to have pre-empted in the first place. The Schauers try to solve this problem by demanding that in this latter case the inappropriateness has to be "egregious" or "particularly strong", but we have seen that this is an *ad hoc* move without warrant.

LEGAL REASONING, RULES AND SOURCES

In Chapter 2 I argued that the sources thesis does not allow for a plausible understanding of the defeasibility of legal rules, but maybe my argument misses the point. Could it be that the sources thesis has no implications whatsoever for legal reasoning? I have also argued that a theory of law, in defining what counts as "law" and thus supplying the premisses from which reasoning, when *legal*, proceeds, implies a theory of legal reasoning, but that would not be agreed upon by authors such as Raz. Indeed, Raz believes that "commitment to the sources thesis does not commit one to formalism or to the autonomy of legal reasoning" (Raz, 1993: 317).[18]

[18] Raz here means by "formalism" the thesis that "the art of legislation, and more generally law-making, is that of moral reasoning. But legal reasoning is reasoning about the law as it is. As such it is free from any infection by moral reasoning. One can reason morally about legal reasoning but not in it, not as part of it" (1993: 314).

In 1985, however, Raz presented an argument that could easily lead one to believe that the sources thesis indeed implied some form of autonomy for legal reasoning. There Raz distinguished, as we have seen (above, at 68ff) between the wide and the narrow versions of the sources thesis. Recall that using Raz's language, we can say legal reasoning is reasoning about which applied legal statements are true (or valid) when some contingent facts are also true. Under the *narrow* interpretation, therefore, the sources thesis is silent concerning legal reasoning, since it is silent concerning applied legal statements. Since in 1993 we find him categorically saying that the sources thesis does not commit one to the autonomy of legal reasoning, we would be forced to understand that as an endorsement of the narrow, as opposed to the wide, interpretation of the sources thesis.

But we have also seen that for Raz the wide and the narrow versions of the sources thesis stand together, at least if moral facts are not contingent. So the narrow version, together with the claim that moral facts are not contingent, imply the wide version, and the wide version implies the autonomy of legal reasoning. Since Raz wants to say today that the sources thesis does not imply the autonomy of legal reasoning, it would seem as if he owes us an explanation of how moral facts are contingent.

I argued above (at 69) that if the authority of law is to be an argument for the sources thesis, it can only be for the *wide* version. Let me briefly restate my argument: if the law is to have authority-capacity, then it has to be possible for subjects to *act* according to it rather than according to their judgment as to the balance of reasons. It follows that the requirement cannot *only* be that subjects should be able to figure out what is the meaning of the general rules of law. It must also include that they have the *possibility* of knowing what they require from them in particular circumstances. In other words, they must be able to get applied legal statements without having to rely on their moral judgment. If they cannot do that, then the law cannot comply with the normal justification thesis and the authority cannot fulfil its mediating role.

But actually, the distinction between the narrow and the wide versions of the source thesis was not mentioned by Raz in 1993. Was Raz's "On the autonomy of legal reasoning" a rejection of it? We are not given an answer to this question.

Instead Raz offers two different reasons why legal reasoning is not autonomous from moral reasoning: the first has to do with the fact that, "if our sole concern is to work out what ought to be done in order to obey the intentions, purposes or goals of the law-makers, we will often find ourselves faced with conflicting directives" (Raz, 1993: 315). In this case, a choice is necessary, and the choice cannot be guided by source-based considerations. It follows that they have to be moral considerations.[19] But this in turn is not

[19] Raz claims that non-source-based considerations cannot but be moral considerations, "for there is no other justification for the use of an autonomous body of considerations by the courts" (Raz, 1993: 318). Therefore the question of the autonomy of legal reasoning can only be the question of its autonomy from moral reasoning.

compatible with the thrust of the authority-based argument for the sources thesis. Recall that the argument was that if the authoritative directives *claim* legitimate authority, it follows that they *can* have authority. If they can have authority, it follows that they must posses the non-moral conditions for having authority, one of which was that the subjects must be capable of establishing the directives' "existence and content in ways which do not depend on raising the vary same issues which the authority is there to settle" (Raz, 1985: 203). But now Raz seems to be claiming that when applying source-based material our "sole concern" is not to apply the directives thus recognised, but to decide "what ought to be done in order to obey the intentions, purposes, or goals of the law-makers". Raz seems to be claiming that our *sole concern* should be that of second-guessing the authority, going beyond the meaning of the directive to check whether or not that meaning is a correct reflection of the authority's "intentions, goals and purposes". But we should not second-guess the authority, if the sources thesis is true.[20]

Let me pause for a while on the meaning of the "should" that appeared in the last sentence. Since we are considering whether or not legal reasoning is autonomous from moral reasoning, it seems appropriate here to understand this "should" in its moral sense. The previous paragraph's last sentence, so understood, assumes that the authority is legitimate.

Needless to say, in many situations this will not be the case. Sometimes the authority will be a *de facto* authority and courts will have no reason at all to follow its directives. But this is immaterial to the discussion of the autonomy of legal reasoning, since, from Raz's point of view, the authority's legitimacy will be relevant only for establishing whether it fulfils the moral conditions of legitimate authority, and this is of course a moral question ("how, all things considered, should the courts decide the case?"), which is different from the legal question ("how, according to law, should cases be decided?"). The fact that courts sometimes have the moral duty to disregard authoritative directives does not demonstrate anything about legal reasoning, since that is a question about whether or not the law ought to be applied, while legal reasoning deals with the question of what the law is for the case (Raz, 1993: 312). If this is the only way in which moral reasoning and legal reasoning are connected, the latter could still be autonomous from the former.

But Raz wants to deny this, since he wants to claim that "legal reasoning is an instance of moral reasoning". Therefore he has to show why legal

[20] Raz could claim here that I missed the point, which is the fact that the law displays "plurality of conflicting values . . . due to the fact that [it] is a product of human activity" (Raz, 1993: 315n). But consider Fuller's case. Here it might well be the case that there is a "plurality of conflicting values" (select the pair of your choice: predictability against appropriateness, keeping railway stations clean against fairness, or whatever), but the fact is, the source-based material does offer a solution: fine the first man and acquit the second. The problem created by the "plurality of conflicting values" will only be seen by the court if it does precisely what it is *not* supposed to do, i.e. if it "raises the very same issues which the authority is there to settle" (*cf.* Raz, 1985: 203). No conflict is evident if the court follows the law as identified according to the sources thesis.

reasoning is moral reasoning, even when the question of whether or not the law ought (morally) to be applied is not taken into account. To do this he distinguishes between "reasoning about the law" and "reasoning according to law". The first "is governed by the sources thesis" (Raz, 1993: 316), hence if we restrict our view to it an autonomous form of legal reasoning will appear. But we should not leave aside the second aspect of legal reasoning, i.e. "reasoning according to law", and once we pay attention to it, Raz tells us, we shall realise that it is "quite commonly straightforward moral reasoning" (1993: 317). That reasoning according to law is different from reasoning about the law is shown by that fact that

> The law itself quite commonly directs the courts to apply extralegal considerations. Italian law may direct the courts to apply European community law, or international law, or Chinese law to a case . . .. In all these cases legal reasoning, understood to mean reasoning according to law, involves much more than merely establishing the law (Raz, 1993: 317).

This might be so, but that does not show that legal reasoning is a form of moral reasoning. The most it could show is that Italian legal reasoning is a form of European legal reasoning (not that this makes any sense). So let us consider whether legal references to morality rather than to Chinese law would fare better for Raz. Would the fact that a legal system may contain references to morality show that legal reasoning is a form of moral reasoning?

I hope the answer to this question is evident: insofar as particular rules make references to morality, then "reasoning according to law" is more than "reasoning about the law". But this argument is not enough to prove that "legal reasoning is an instance of moral reasoning" any more than the fact that sometimes engineers should consider aesthetic considerations makes engineering reasoning an instance of aesthetic reasoning.[21]

In brief, Raz does not want to draw the implications of his legal theory for legal reasoning. He tries to show that the sources thesis does not commit one to the thesis of the autonomy of legal reasoning, and to say that he has to make space for something to be left after the existence and content of the source-based material has been established. In the end, he can only offer the rather small space provided by the fact that sometimes the law instructs courts to apply extralegal considerations and he offers this as a ground for the grand thesis that legal reasoning *is* moral reasoning.

But maybe this space is not *that* small, because it might be that the law sometimes makes *implicit* references to morality. But to show this Raz would need an extra argument, since "implicit" references to Chinese law are not common at all in Italian law. And indeed, in his article, "On the nature of law" (Raz, 1996) Raz tried to offer an argument that could be understood

[21] Additionally, this argument of Raz's would have to face the same objections that were addressed against a similar argument of Schauer's (*see* above, at 115f), for it too makes theoretically irrelevant one of the most salient features of law in the last 20 centuries.

along these lines. In that piece he wanted to defend his version of legal positivism against the charge that it misrepresents legal reasoning. The "standard objection", to it, he says, when its implications for legal reasoning are drawn, is that

> would we not expect two clearly separate stages in legal reasoning: an interpretive-factual stage and a (purely) moral one? First one would establish what authoritatively laid down law says on the issue at hand, and then either it does not provide a determinate disposition of the issue, or if one wants to determine whether the way it disposes of the issue is morally acceptable, one would move to the second purely moral stage in the argument. In fact we do not find that legal reasoning divides in that way. Legal reasoning displays a continuity through all its stages (1996: 19).[22]

To show how this objection actually reinforces rather than refutes his views on the nature of law, Raz invites us to consider interpretation in the arts. A good interpretation of a play or of a piano sonata is, he tells us, an interpretation that combines *tradition* with *innovation* in the right way, and because of this reason there cannot be a general theory of interpretation: "innovation defies generalisation. A theory of originality, in the sense we are considering, is self-defeating" (Raz, 1996: 20). What the objection points to, says Raz, is that a theory of legal reasoning would be required to explain how best to combine "the two aspects of legal reasoning. On the one hand legal reasoning aims to establish the content of authoritative standards, on the other hand, it aims to supplement them, and often to modify them, in the light of moral considerations" (Raz, 1996: 19). But how this combination should be achieved is not something that any theory can answer, hence the fact that positivism cannot offer a such "self-defeating" theory does not show it to be a defective theory of law.

Let us go along with Raz's thesis that there cannot be a theory of interpretation because "tradition" and "originality" defy generalisation. *Before* he can use this argument to support the sources thesis, however, he has to show why "originality" is important in legal reasoning. Instead of explaining this, however, he shows how this is the case when what is being interpreted is a piano sonata or a play and then immediately (and rather surprisingly) he claims "*hence* its [i.e. interpretation's] importance in law" (1996: 20).[23] I do

[22] Raz incidentally airs some doubts as to what he sees as the tacit assumption of this objection: "I believe that this point is overstated, and that legal reasoning is not all of a kind" (at 19). The objection, however, does not need to assume that "legal reasoning is all of a kind". Indeed, I believe that insofar as he defends the wide sources thesis it is *Raz*, and not the objector, who would be committed to the doubtful thesis that legal reasoning is all of a kind (insofar as it is *legal*, of course. My claim is that the sources thesis does not leave any room in *legal* reasoning for *moral* reasoning).

[23] The whole paragraph says: "The same is true of interpretations of plays or of other literary works. A work can be understood and (in the case of a play) performed as a celebration of the natural world, or as a utopian reflection on social ideals. Or it can be seen as an exploration of the rift between generations or alternatively as a crisis of adolescence and immaturity. Here again, different, even contrasting interpretations, can be consistent with the original. Interpretation is the activity which combines reproduction and creativity. Hence its importance in law" (Raz, 1996: 20).

not want to express here an opinion on the subject of the similarities and differences between artistic and legal interpretation, but it cannot go unnoticed that, from *Raz's* point of view there should be a crucial difference: *law claims authority*. For Raz, we must remember, the fact that the law claims authority implies that it makes it illegal for courts to

> entertain moral argument about the desirability of regarding a certain fact (e.g. a previous enactment) as a reason for a certain action but will once the existence of the relevant fact has been established through morally-neutral argument hold it to be a reason which they are bound to apply (Raz, 1980: 214).[24]

And this in turn must mean, if anything, that courts are not supposed to "combine originality with tradition" when they are applying the law, that they are simply supposed to identify the existence and content of the directives and then apply them. In short, Raz's claim that legal reasoning has two dimensions can help him only if he begs the whole issue, which is precisely that the sources thesis does not allow for legal reasoning to display those two dimensions.

Indeed, why should legal reasoning be interpretive? Raz answers:

> The explanation lies in the authoritative nature of law: When trying to establish the legal status of an action, we need to ascertain whether any of the authoritatively binding rules and doctrines bear on it and if so how. That means establishing what has been done by the authorities, what decisions they have taken and what they mean" (1996: 19).

But, unless Raz wants to claim that ascertaining the meaning of an authoritative directive (or its existence as such) is impossible without considering the moral reasons it purports to adjudicate (in which case that authoritative directive would evidently lack "authority-capacity"), the *mere* fact that legal reasoning is about identifying the existence and ascertaining the content of authoritative directives does not imply that legal reasoning must have two aspects. If we remember the importance Raz placed on the non-moral conditions for authority-capacity (*see* Raz, 1985) I suppose we could be tempted to say that *precisely* because legal reasoning is about what authoritative directives there are and what they mean it cannot be moral reasoning.

Towards the end of the article we are reminded that

> the prominence of interpretive reasoning in legal reasoning results from the fact that in law the two aspects of legal reasoning, that is establishing the content of authoritatively endorsed legal standards and establishing the (other) moral considerations which bear on the issue, are inextricably interwoven (Raz, 1996: 22).

But were not these "other" considerations pre-empted by the authoritatively laid down directives? Had we not been told before (in *Practical Reason and*

[24] I assume here (as before, *see* above, at 110) that when Raz says that courts "will" or "will not" do something he is really speaking of what the law requires courts to do, rather than trying to predict what courts, as a matter of empirical fact, will do.

Norms) that from the legal point of view legal rules are standards "all of which the primary organs [i.e. courts] are bound to act on to the exclusion of *all* other conflicting reasons" (Raz, 1992: 143, emphasis added)?

If the sources thesis is correct, legal reasoning cannot display these two aspects, because legal rules would pre-empt all the considerations that would constitute the second aspect. It can, of course, be the case that once the content and existence of those directives has been established the different question of whether or not they ought (morally) to be applied can be entertained, but this could not be legal reasoning: it would be moral reasoning *simpliciter*. And here we go back to the objection Raz tried to answer. He thought that he could answer simply by pointing out that no theory can solve the problem of how best to combine tradition and innovation. But if I am correct, he has to explain why legal reasoning displays those two aspects to begin with.

Responding to an objection raised by Gerald Postema (1996), Raz has recently made another important concession to defend the sources thesis *and* to deny that it implies some form of "autonomy" for legal reasoning: he now "reject[s] any thesis of the autonomy of legal reasoning, at least if that includes anything more than reasoning to the conclusion that the content of the law is such-and-such . . .. [N]o such reasoning can by itself support *any judicial decision* in common-law countries" since there courts can resort to a number of "devices to ensure that the law as applied to the case is not unjust" (Raz,1998b at 4, emphasis added).

Here the wide version of the sources thesis seems to be clearly abandoned. No applied legal statement can ever be obtained, at least in common-law countries, without relying on moral argument. But this concession has another important consequence. According to Raz, "by the sources thesis courts have discretion when required to apply moral considerations" (1979a: 75).[25] Hence, what we are effectively being told here is that courts (at least in "common law countries") *always* have discretion. No judge (at least in common-law countries) will *ever* have a legal obligation to decide *any* case in one particular way. No legal rule will ever (at least in common-law countries) control any judicial decision, because judges will always have discretion to decide any case. Here we reach the same conclusion that we reached when discussing the issue of gaps in law: the sources thesis implies either strict formalism (in its wide version) or complete rule-scepticism (in its narrow version).

Indeed, in *The Morality of Freedom*, Raz did answer an objection that seems similar to the point under discussion here. The objection claimed that "in every case authoritative directives can be overridden or disregarded if they deviate much from the reasons they are meant to reflect". This could be one way of describing the position of common-law judges according to Raz. But in

[25] Or again "the point of the sources thesis is not that courts never rely on sourceless considerations, but rather that when doing so they are not relying on legally binding considerations but exercising their own discretion" (Raz, 1979b: 59).

The Morality of Freedom Raz saw that such a concession "defeats the pre-emption thesis since it requires every person in every case to consider the merits of the case before he can decide to accept an authoritative instruction", thus denying that authoritative directives "can serve the mediating role assigned to them above" (1986: 61). If the sources thesis is true, then either legal reasoning is completely autonomous or the law (at least in Commom Law countries) cannot have authority.

We have seen that knowledge of the norms of a particular legal system is not enough to know what the law is for actual cases. What *else* is needed? This is going to be the subject of the final chapter. As many authors have realised (I consider below the work of Patrick Atiyah and Robert Summers, Roscoe Pound, Bruce Ackerman and Mirjan Damaska), there is a connection between ideas about the law and the law itself. The task is to identify the sort of ideas that are relevant and the nature of that connection. In brief, the argument will be that ideas about the law (which in the next chapter will be called an "image of law") have the direct consequence of determining the sort of arguments that count as legal arguments; they shape what Honoré called the "canon of legal argument". To this we now turn.

8

The Powers of Application

> Rules should be sufficiently sensible and sufficiently straightforward so that anyone who so desires and is blessed with average powers of application may be able to understand, on the one hand the useful ends they serve, and on the other hand the actual necessities which have brought about their institution.
>
> SIMONE WEIL, *The Need for Roots* (1942–3)

THE FORMALITY OF LAW

An important feature of legal discourse is its formality, that is, the fact that legal decisions are restricted with regard to the considerations that are deemed to be relevant for their justification. Even in what Max Weber would call (1978: 654ff) a system of substantive rationality, we would expect that once a legal problem has been settled by an official, that decision would imply, among other things, that at the very least *some* of the considerations that the official took into account when he was deciding the case cannot be raised again at the moment of executing his decision.[1] If we keep in mind the fact that formality is not an all-or-nothing concept but admits of degrees, we will not fail to see that, however grand this claim might look, it actually is rather obvious.

How should this formality be explained? This is, in my view, the central question of a "unified" theory of law and legal reasoning. Some legal philosophers have argued that what explains the formality of legal discourse is some feature of the legal material. Laws are rules, rules are exclusionary reasons. They cannot but conclude, then, that the identification of the existence and content of those exclusionary reasons has to be possible without considering the excluded reasons. I have tried to show how this position leads either to rule-formalism or to rule-scepticism. In this chapter I will try to offer an alternative explanation for the formality of law, one that gives priority to legal *practice* rather than to legal *rules*, (this is why Mark Knopfler was right: lawyers come before the rules). The undeniable initial plausibility of the exclusionary-reasons account of legal rules and reasoning is given by this idea of the law's formality. If that account is rejected, an alternative explanation for this idea has to be offered.

[1] It could be claimed, indeed, that the more "substantive" a system is, the more formal the decision becomes once taken.

This alternative explanation, which will be explored in this chapter, looks at the social practice of legal discourse, at what that practice looks like for the participants to it. In this view, it is not a feature of legal material (i.e. laws) that explains the formality of law, but something *about* legal practice as a whole. Legal discourse becomes formal in the sense we are familiar with when the participants start seeing legal adjudication as being *about* something in particular.[2] This is what differentiates law from other social practices. Legal discourse can be about the discovery of magical rules that are part of the fabric of the world, or the fair solution of interpersonal conflicts, or the implementation of state policies and so on. This alternative explanation has two important advantages: *First*, it can explain differences between the law and other rule-based social practices: why hard cases are important in law but not in other institutional practices, like games. *Second*, it can also explain legal disagreement in a way that is crucially closed to the previous perspective: as disagreement about *how formal the law is*, that is, whether or not it is formal enough to exclude those peculiarities of the case that would otherwise give rise to reasons for deciding otherwise. This is a question that is not to be solved using any evaluative argument whatsoever, but only those that can be presented as legally relevant, that is, arguments that are related to the participants' understanding of the practice. This explanation is closed to the exclusionary-reasons perspective, since those arguments point to substantive considerations that would be excluded if laws were indeed exclusionary reasons. To explain the formality of law on the basis of laws being exclusionary reasons cannot but misrepresent the phenomenon of legal disagreement, since in hard cases disagreement is *precisely about what according to that perspective could not be an issue*: are the substantive reasons allegedly pre-empted by the applicable rules important enough to be *in*cluded?

How pervasive legal disagreement will be in a given legal practice is something that will depend upon that self-understanding: in ancient Roman and biblical law (as discussed in Chapter 1) Romans and Jews understood legal practice in such a way as to make legal disagreement almost completely non-existent. In nineteenth-century Britain or America, as we will see later, contract law was understood as being about fairness in exchange, but since fairness (at least fairness as a relevant legal consideration) was understood in highly formal terms, the application of contract law was markedly formalistic. Changes in this perception of what a fair exchange is have made contract law

[2] This might seem strange to any reader familiar with Ronald Dworkin's writings (especially Dworkin, 1986). He invites us to consider the practice of courtesy in an imaginary society. At first the participants took the rules for granted, but with time they develop what Dworkin calls "an interpretive attitude" (1986: 47) The fact that participants develop this interpretive attitude seems to imply that rules are applied in a less formal way. My remark that the law becomes formalised when participants develop such an attitude (to use the Dworkinian jargon) has to be understood in the light of my discussion of Honoré's claim that the Romans' most remarkable legal invention was the canon of legal argument. The introduction of the canon increases the formality of law, since the function of the canon is to exclude "non-legal" arguments. This was indeed the difference between Roman and Greek "legal" reasoning.

in the twentieth century far less formalistic than it was a hundred years ago, at least in modern Western legal systems (*see* Atiyah, 1984).

Recall (for the last time) Fuller's case. According to the exclusionary-reasons explanation of the formality of law, it should be understood as a case in which what the law requires is to fine the first man (though the court might be inclined to take the *moral* decision not to apply the law to the case). All the reasons that could be offered not to fine the man are among those that according to this perspective are, as *legal* reasons, excluded. On the alternative account to be offered in this chapter, the problem is created not by lawyers' and judges' disagreement as to what the morally best solution is, but by their disagreement about how formally the "no sleeping in the station" rule should be applied. Should it be applied as a perfect exclusionary reason, in such a way that even babies sleeping in push-chairs should be fined? Or should it instead be applied as a Roman *regula*, i.e. with a very low degree of formality, meaning that all of those, and only those, who by their behaviour in the station cause the nuisance the legislator tried to prevent with the rule, should be fined, regardless of their actually being asleep in the station or not, and their sleeping only be taken as prima-facie evidence of that?. The case is not to be solved using *any* argument: imagine a barrister saying "he should not be fined because he is my friend." This argument would not be very persuasive, since the law is not seen as being about granting favours to one's friends. "He should not be fined because it is grossly unfair to do so" is a better legal argument, since law is understood as having something to do with fairness. A fairness-based argument, however, could be less persuasive in what Damaska (1986, discussed below) calls an "activist state," in which the law is seen as being about implementing state policies. The first perspective arbitrarily claims that the correct reading of a rule like Fuller's can only give that rule, as a matter of conceptual truth, complete exclusionary force. Once we accept, following Atiyah and Summers (1987: 17n), that formality admits of degrees, then it is evident that a further reason has to be provided in order to prove that the only way in which legal materials can be understood is as (perfect) exclusionary reasons, i.e. as *rules*.

Consider one possible interpretation of Fuller's rule:

(15) The norm contained in (6) should be applied as a perfect exclusionary reason; the only substantive considerations that are legally relevant for its application are (i) whether a human being is sleeping, and (ii) whether he or she is doing so in a railway station.

The explanation of the formality of law based on the idea of laws being exclusionary reasons claims that (6) is correct as a matter of conceptual truth. Exclusionary reasons exclude all the considerations they do not refer to, hence (6) is correct. But in law (as opposed to other social practices, most noticeably, games) that is not the case: no *conceptual* (as opposed to substantive) argument can show that from the fact that an exception was not explicitly included it follows that it was implicitly excluded. There is no conceptual (as opposed to substantive, as the case might be) warrant for the thesis that the meaning of a rule determines its application.

That this explanation distorts the way in which the law is applied can be shown by a different argument: Atiyah and Summers (1987) claim, as we shall see, that there is an important difference in the degree of formality used in the USA to apply the law when compared to that used in England. In some matters (like *stare decisis*, they claim at 119) the *rules* are basically the same, but their application is significatively different. If the meaning of a rule determines its application as a matter of conceptual truth, though, there would be no room for more or less formal applications of the rules (exclusionary reasons). This would force us to choose one of two ways: either American English and English are different languages (hence the rules mean different things, though the words are the same), or in one country the law is systematically and regularly violated by the organs called to apply it. I think both of these claims would be manifestly false.

To avoid this conclusion, (15) could be understood as a legal rather than conceptual argument. Its force will then depend upon the force of the arguments supporting it. The force and acceptability of these arguments, in turn, will depend upon the canon of legal argument, whose content will be established by the participants' *image of law* (on the canon, *see* Bell, 1986; Honoré, 1974). The concept of an image of law, a label I have borrowed (though with a different meaning) from Bankowski and Mungham (1976), will be further developed below, but for the time being suffice it to say that as a legal argument (15) is likely to be pretty ineffective in most legal systems, at least if we exclude ancient Rome and similar ones (though this is only an empirical claim). If any modern Western legal system contains a rule like (6), (15) is very unlikely to be a good legal argument for its application.

Notice further that if (15) is a *rule* of the same system it cannot solve the problem, because the same question of how formal its application should be could then be applied to it (Detmold, 1989: 453). We have seen that the fact that Pufendorf's Bolognese statute commanded that "the words should be taken exactly and without any interpretation" would not necessarily imply that according to Bolognese law the barber had to be punished.

Now it seems that we are heading straight into a rather uncomfortable sceptical position. No rule can pre-empt the substantive reasons rules are supposed to pre-empt, since no rule can determine the mode (level of formality) of its own application. Hence no formal discourse (better, no discourse with any relevant level of formality) can ever be attained.

But from the fact that a rule cannot determine the mode (*viz.*, the level of formality) of its application, it clearly does not follow that nothing can ever be settled. That merely shows that we cannot look to the *legal material* for an answer, that we have to look instead to the background of the legal practice, to what will be called below an "image of law". This is the reason why the argument so far is not a sceptical argument. There can be constraints on the legal discourse, but those constraints do not come from the content of the legal material: What do you need to know to understand which and why cases can become "abnormal"? Answer: you need to master the canon of legal argument: you need to know the sort of arguments the participants would consider a legal argument, i.e. arguments that deserve their day in court. But no *rule* will tell you *that*.

The idea of "normality" (discussed in Chapter 5) is the link between the evolution of ideas *about* the law and the content of the law itself, between the law that *is* and the law that *ought to* be. That a case is normal is a question that *has* to be answered before any application of the law is possible (needless to say, in the broad majority of cases this question will not arise. But this does not show that it need not be answered. It only shows that because of pragmatic considerations sometimes an answer does not call for external justification). But whether a case is normal is something that is answered not by the laws, but by ideas about the law (an "image of law"), hence the link between the law and ideas about it. This is the reason why Alan Watson is mistaken when he claims that

> If the *rules* of contract law of the two countries [i.e., England and Scotland] are already similar (as they are) it should be no obstacle to their unification or harmonisation that the legal *principles* involved come ultimately from different sources, or that the habits of thought of the commission teams are rather different. It is scholarly law reformers who are deeply troubled by historical factors and habits of thought. Commercial lawyers and business men in Scotland and England do not in general perceive differences in habits of thought, but only—and often with irritation—differences in rules (1974: 96–7).

Insofar as the lawyer or businessman is concerned only with knowing the literal meaning of the black-letter rules of the other country, this must be granted as a matter of course. But they would be lost when faced with private law cases, because they would not know how the law is applied.[3] In fact, it is completely unwarranted to think that "commercial lawyers and businessmen do not perceive differences in habits of thought," and if they do they do so at their own risk. It is a dangerous policy to travel around Europe without trying to perceive "differences in habit of thought" concerning, for instance, the application of traffic laws: any attempt to walk on a zebra crossing in Rome as you would do it in Edinburgh would be considered suicidal (even for commercial lawyers and businessmen).

However, this does not mean that legal questions cannot be settled for participants. Most lawyers and judges (and citizens, for that matter) know

[3] As a matter of fact it could be claimed that they would not, because in the particular case of England and Scotland the "habits of thought" are probably sufficiently similar. This is a controversial point, and many Scots lawyers would disagree (and I would readily admit my complete ignorance on the subject). The main point, however, still stands: if those "habits of thought" are sufficiently different, then knowledge of the content of the rules will not be enough for commercial lawyers and businessmen.

that, though admittedly to different extents. Our question has to be, then: what kind of information do they have? It is not (only) knowledge of the language; neither is it (only) knowledge of the legal material, the *norms* of the system. What else could it be?

In his article "Comparative Jurisprudence: what was it like to try a rat?" William Ewald (1995) deals with a similar problem, from the perspective of comparative law. He is engaged in much the same enterprise as we are now: he wants to understand the animal trials that were somewhat common in Europe during the Middle Ages. He focuses on one particular case, that of the rats of Autun (1522), and on one particular lawyer, Barthelemy Chassenée, counsel for the defendants (the rats).

Ewald argues that none of the traditional explanations of the rationale of the trials of animals really makes sense (he discusses them in 1995: 1905–16). His conclusion is that

> to recapture Chassenée's frame of reference we need to know more than just the legal *rules*; but what else do we need? Certainly also the underlying *principles*, that is, the characteristic underlying pattern of justifications and reasons that he would give for the surface rules. If our task were simply to understand a modern Western legal system we might be able to stop here; but with Chassenée there seem to be at least two further steps we need to take. We need to recover the wider pattern of *beliefs* that underlies the legal principles—his beliefs about pain, animals, the person, responsibility, law—broadly speaking, his metaphysics . . .. We need . . . to find a way into his cosmos, to excavate the pattern of beliefs and sentiments that was characteristic of his age (*ibid.*, 1941).

Until we have understood Chassenée's metaphysics, Ewald argues, we will not be able to understand Chassenée's view of the law—and Chassenée stands here for any typical participant in a legal practice. Granted, we may be able to understand the legal material,

> and if *all* we expect . . . is a rough comprehension of the text of the code, such a knowledge can be had without any special training in history. Indeed, it can be had without any special training of *any* sort, for clearly *this* level of comprehension is available to any literate adult, ancient or modern . . .. If [a law student of the age of Justinian] is to understand the modern terminology and the underlying concepts, he must, I think, however sketchily, try to comprehend their historical development. But the modern law student can take them for granted. They have become part of the atmosphere, a part of the surrounding culture, a part of the *Volksgeist*, and indeed a part of the language itself (Ewald, 1995: 2101–2).

We cannot understand Chassenée's concerns with what we might call "animal law" without understanding what the law looks like to him. That being the case, a theory of law has to have room for this element. Ewald does not discuss the implications for legal theory of his views on comparative law. He only says that a "sophisticated positivist like H L A Hart" would be more inclined to look not at the primary rules but at the "rule of recognition," "and this comparison would lead him into a discussion of many of the issues" Ewald is dealing with (1995: 2081n). But this possibility, if my argument is correct, is not enough (as indeed Ewald seems to think: *cf. ibid.* at 2081n).

Before proceeding to the main argument of this chapter, let me pre-empt an objection to it: the objector could argue that the exclusionary-reasons account only claims that, in order to avoid the conclusion established by a rule, it is not sufficient to prove that reasons to the contrary exist, it must also be established that these reasons are not excluded. This thesis, the objection goes, is fully consistent with the fact that some reasons are not, while other reasons are indeed excluded.

The argument contained in this chapter does not try to refute the exclusionary-reasons accounts by denying that there are substantive reasons that are excluded in legal discourse. I take that to be an obvious and important feature of law, and something that must be explained by any theory that is worth any attention. I will be arguing against an explanation of this feature that focuses upon each and every legal *rule*, claiming that an adequate ontology of rules is enough to understand the formality of law. The alternative account I will argue for here claims, on the contrary, that there is nothing in the concept of a rule that explains the formality of law. At different times different social systems have used rules of different sorts: from rules with a very low, almost non-existing, degree of formality, as in classical Roman law and others, to rules with an infinite degree of formality, as is common in games. There are important differences between the practices in the context of which these rules exist, and these differences are missed if one tries to use the *concept* of a rule to understand them.

But, the objector could insist, there is nothing in the idea of exclusionary reason that denies this possibility. An exclusionary reason is a reason to exclude other reasons, not necessarily *all* conflicting reasons. So an exclusionary reason could be more or less exclusionary, meaning that it could exclude more or less substantive considerations. Now, to answer this claim, we should take care to distinguish what is a matter of kind and what one of degree. Whether or not a substantive consideration is excluded by an exclusionary reason is not something that admits of degree: issues cannot be half-excluded. This is something that can be seen in rules of games, which are our best available example of exclusionary reasons. But in law rules behave, so to speak, in a very different manner. What is excluded, and what included in legal discourse, is not something that is established by the rules to be applied, but by ideas *about* the law. When I say that rules in games are exclusionary reasons I am not saying something important about the rules of football, but about games as social practices. In Fuller's example, the rule (6) does not tell us whether or not the law is that the businessman should be fined. If the rule were indeed an exclusionary reason it would tell us precisely that, since it would tell us whether or not the substantive considerations prompted by the fact of this person being a businessman, etc. are or fail to be excluded. But the rule is silent on that. And furthermore, to know whether or not these considerations are important enough to be relevant we would obviously have to address some of the issues that were supposed to have been pre-empted by the rule, like the relative importance of cleanliness in the station, which alternative uses of the station are to be allowed and so on.

AN IMAGE OF LAW

In this chapter I will label what Ewald calls "Chassenée's metaphysics" an *image of law*. Broadly speaking (I'll speak less broadly below), an image of law is a picture of *what legal discourse is about*. An image of law determines how legal material should be understood and applied, and a study of its content and function becomes, I believe, the sphere in which it is most useful to recognise that "jurisprudence is . . . a joint venture of lawyers, philosophers and sociologists" (MacCormick, 1974: 74).

An image of law is related to an image of the world: legal practices have existed in which people believed, for example, that a contractual obligation was a magical relation between two parties, the law was a set of magical rules that existed independently from their society, and legal discourse was "about" finding and applying them.

At some moment, however, this way of looking at the law changed: people started believing that legal relations were not magical relations, and that there was some regulatory *point* in having legal rules that was not only the magical possibilities the rules created. They started thinking that the explanation for the existence and the justification of the law was linked to its regulatory effects, even though they might still have thought that the law was not a conscious creation of particular human beings (this is a much more recent belief). When this transition had been achieved, normative beliefs about those regulatory effects came to replace those old magical beliefs.

An image of law is usually a complex set of different beliefs that, when put together, form a picture of legal discourse. To make this point clearer, it might be useful to look at one particular example. In eighteenth- and nineteenth-century England what is called the "classical theory of contract" was developed. This theory was not a set of legal materials (norms), though of course it shaped the content of English contract law in a decisive manner. But the content of the rules of English contract law is not the most important issue here. The English "classical" image of law is (for what follows, *see* Collins, 1986; Atiyah, 1995: 7–15). Lawyers and judges in those times believed (i) that contract law was *natural law*, that is, something that was to be found in nature. This means that the law was discovered, not created; now, what they read in that natural law was that contract law was about (ii) commutative rather than distributive justice, which in turn meant that in the application of particular rules of contract law only arguments relating to the justice of the exchange could in principle be heard. Considerations of efficiency, or of distributive justice, were excluded not necessarily because a rule said so, but because that was not the business of the law of contracts. They also had (iii) a strong belief in *laissez-faire* ideology. As a consequence of this belief, considerations of commutative justice could not be heard, this time not because the law of contracts was not about commutative justice (it was), but because the only way in which the justice of a transaction could be assessed was by the parties themselves (*see* Collins, 1986: 138). What commutative justice demanded was to respect agreements freely entered into. Summing it all up,

> By and large this meant that the law of contract was designed to provide for the enforcement of the private arrangements which the contracting parties had agreed upon. In general the law was not concerned with the fairness or justice of the outcome, and paternalistic ideas came to be thought of as old-fashioned. The judges were not even greatly concerned with the possibility that a contract might not be in the public interest. So the function of contract law was merely to assist one of the contracting parties when the other broke the rules of the game and defaulted in the performance of his contractual obligations. The judge was a sort of umpire whose job was to respond to the appeal "How's that?" when something went wrong (Atiyah, 1995: 8).

The belief in a strong ideology of *laissez-faire* (a weaker version will be introduced shortly below) had a related consequence: the interference of the state in the working of the market had to be reduced to a minimum. This called for the separation of law and politics. Therefore a form of reasoning was developed that Morton Horwitz, discussing American law in the same period, calls "categorical thinking" (1992: 27). Arguments that were excluded from the legal realm were categorically different to those that were allowed. Today, for example, we would probably think that unequal bargaining power and duress form a continuum. A classical lawyer could accept an allegation of duress, but not one of unequal bargaining power. If a defence of unequal bargaining power was allowed in, contracts that were agreed between free and equal persons would not be categorically separated from those void by duress: the (substantive) concept of equality of bargaining power would bridge the categorical gap between them, and political arguments would use that bridge to contaminate legal discourse (they were indeed right, as things eventually turned out: today arguments are used before courts that they would have considered obviously political):

> Nothing captures the essential difference between the typical legal minds of nineteenth- and twentieth-century America quite as well as their attitude toward categories. Nineteenth-century legal thought was overwhelmingly dominated by categorical thinking—by clear, distinct, bright-line classifications of legal phenomena. Late-nineteenth-century legal reasoning brought categorical modes of thought to their highest fulfilment. By contrast, in the twentieth century, the dominant conception of the arrangement of legal phenomena has been that of a

> continuum between contradictory policies or doctrines. Contemporary thinkers typically have been engaged in balancing conflicting policies and "drawing lines" somewhere between them. Nineteenth-century categorizing typically sought to demonstrate "differences of kind" among legal classifications; twentieth century balancing tests deal only with "differences of degree" (Horwitz, 1992: 71).

It is today a commonplace to call this nineteenth-century attitude "formalistic" (in the pejorative sense), but this is not because contract law today is not formal at all. Many situations of unequal bargaining power are seen, even today, as giving rise to no legal defence on that account; indeed "bargaining power is nearly always unequal, and, in free markets, it must be unequal" (Atiyah, 1995: 302). Classical lawyers were willing to acknowledge a defence in *some* cases of unequal bargaining power, those in which duress could be proven: given that the law of contracts was seen as being "about" the enforcement of agreements freely entered into, an allegation of duress was obviously something that, if successful, could prevent the enforcement of any contract. Today, in most modern Western legal systems (of course with important variations among them), courts are willing to acknowledge a defence in other cases as well, in cases in which, though there was no duress, one of the parties was not free to agree. Not all the cases in which the freedom of a person to enter into a contract is diminished are important in this sense. What is different is the *kind of arguments* available to defendants if they want to claim inequality of bargaining power as a defence. There is today less widespread confidence in the idea that the parties to a contract are the most appropriate persons to decide what the benefits are worth and that the courts should not interfere with the parties' decisions. There is, therefore, a correspondingly more widespread belief that the fact of an agreement having been freely entered into is not necessarily a reason to exclude other substantive considerations (or: to decide whether or not a contract was "freely entered into" substantive considerations that were excluded before are today allowed in legal discourse). This is what Atiyah (1982b: 118ff) called "the decline of formal reasoning". As a result of this, the same rules of contract law yield, when applied to similar cases, different results, since some features of those cases that would have been considered irrelevant in the nineteenth century would not be so considered today.

An image of law can have different levels of complexity. It can be a very simple idea of the law being part of the basic structure of the world: if Isaac uttered such-and-such words Jacob was blessed, even though he was not the one who was entitled to the blessing, even though he received the blessing only by deceit (Gen. 27: 18–40). As a result the world is different, different in *exactly* the same way in which the world is different after Chernobyl because the relevant safety rules were not followed. Or it can be a complex set of beliefs, comprising moral, political and economic beliefs: it was not *only* the belief in natural law, not *only* a conception of the law of contracts as being about justice in exchanges, and not *only* a strong *laissez-faire* ideology, but an elaborated mixture of them all (and possibly other elements), which explains the dominance of the classical theory of contract in nineteenth-century England and the USA.

Imagine, for example, that this latter belief (in a strong *laissez-faire* ideology) is rejected. That being the case, the fact that an agreement has been freely entered into would no longer be considered as irrefutable evidence of the substantive fairness of the exchange. Therefore, courts will be more willing to make this latter point one subject to controversy, and consequently they will allow arguments about the substantive fairness of the contract as legal arguments. There is no reason why the other elements of the classical theory of contract (that is, the idea that contract law is given by nature, not created, and that of it being only about commutative justice) cannot be retained. This (partial) modification of the image of law will effect a (partial) change in the canon of legal argument: while lawyers and judges will remain equally formalistic as regards their exclusion of distributive justice-based arguments (because they still see contract law as being about justice in exchanges), they will be more prone to "unpick" the contract each time they feel that the parties were not (substantively) equal and free when they struck their bargain. That is, they will be willing to hear arguments that would have been classified as non-legal before, arguments purporting to question the substantive fairness of the contract.

Notice further that the point is not a point about a particular individual's beliefs. It is, rather, about the political and moral beliefs that constitute the normative bedrock of legal discourse when considered as a social practice. This point is important to understand the idea of the justification of legal decisions. Once the law is regarded as a regulatory institution, legal decisions have to be justified. It is no longer possible to answer a challenge by saying "this is simply what we do." The idea of the justification of legal decisions looks at the relevant reference-group (what Perelman and Olbrechts-Tyteca 1968 called the "audience"), and asks the decision-maker to present her decision as grounded in reasons that the members of that group would accept, even if they disagree with its particular content (more on this below at 220f).

The importance of the understanding of this set of beliefs as a condition for the understanding of the law has not, of course, gone unnoticed. In what follows I want to comment on the related issues of Atiyah and Summers idea of a "vision of law", Roscoe Pound's "ideal element in law" and Bruce Ackerman and Mirjan Damaska's discussion of activist and reactive states and their impact on legal practice.

Visions of Law

In their *Form and Substance in Anglo-American Law*, Atiyah and Summers set out to compare English and American law on the basis of the formal/

substantive divide. They found that "substantive reasoning is used far more widely than formal reason in the American legal system when decisions have to be made or other action taken, while in the English legal system the reverse is true" (Atiyah and Summers, 1987: 1), this being their "primary thesis".

If this is the case, then this difference between English and American legal practice calls for an explanation, and Atiyah and Summers put forward a "secondary thesis" as such an explanation: "the differences in methods of reasoning reflects a deep difference in legal style, legal culture and, more generally, the *vision* of law which prevails in the two countries" (*ibid.* at 1). A "vision of law" is defined by them as

> a set of inarticulate and perhaps even unconscious beliefs held by the general public at large and, to some extent, also by politicians, judges, and legal practitioners, as to the nature and functions of law—how and by whom it should be made, interpreted, applied, and enforced. (Atiyah and Summers, 1987: 411).

Atiyah and Summers introduced the idea of a *vision of law* because the explanation for the difference between American and English legal practices cannot be (only) a difference in the legal material. This is because, while there are of course differences in that regard, there are areas, they tell us, in which the rules are "not in the face of it very different in the two countries, but the differences in [their] practical operation are very great" (1987: 119. They are in this particular case referring to the rules on *stare decisis*). Therefore, there must be something, which is not the *content* of these rules, that can account for those differences. That "something" is a vision of law: ST is explanatorily fundamental as regards PT. Needless to say, a vision of law is not something static. It evolves, and it can perfectly well be the case that the content of particular rules or legal institutions might influence that evolution.[4] But it is the *vision*, not the rules, that constitute the final explanation. It is something that belongs to that vision which we should expect to hear if, say, an English judge is challenged by an American colleague to justify her relatively more formal approach to judicial decision-making.

And yet, when, in their concluding remarks (1987, 411–15), Atiyah and Summers develop their idea of a vision of law they simply restate their

[4] This is an important point, and the same goes for the idea of an image of law. The claim here is that, though an image (or vision) of law is explanatorily fundamental as regards the understanding and application of the law and legal institutions, this is not to say that the existence of particular rules or legal institutions cannot affect the way in which the image (vision) evolves. An image of law is, as we shall see, part and parcel of a world-view. As such, the particular ways in which things in the world (including legal rules and institutions) are or have been contribute to the shaping of it. It might even be the case that in cultures like ours, aware as they are and have been of *the law* as a differentiated system (and thus, say, prone to a sort of reflexive self-observation) legal rules and institutions have a pre-eminent role to play in the shaping of the image. It is probably to this phenomenon that Alan Watson is referring when he claims that "legal development is determined by their [i.e. lawyers'] culture; and social, economic, and political factors impinge on legal development only through their consciousness the legal material" (Watson, 1985a: 118). Two issues should be clearly distinguished: one is that of the role, if any, of the image

findings, offering a rather Sganarellian explanation.[5] We are told that a formal (as opposed to a substantive) vision of law is one in which the identification of valid law is predominantly source-oriented (as opposed to content-oriented); in which conflicts between valid laws are thought to be resolved by reference to rules of hierarchical priority (as opposed to their being resolved by substantive, policy-oriented considerations); in which "the forms of law" are predominantly conceived of as "hard and fast" rules (as opposed to flexible legal rules granting discretion or incorporating standards inviting substantive reasoning); in which legislators are assumed to enact "precise, clear and comprehensive statutory rules, and it is believed that most law consists of statute law" (as opposed to legislators being expected to adopt broad directives "which confer upon courts power to develop the law in particular cases") and so on. But at the same time, these actually *are* the differences Atiyah and Summers found between the two systems. Their concept of a "vision of law" turns out to be, therefore, not explanatory of those differences, but a synopsis of them. But if (as they acknowledge) "the idea of a vision of law is synoptic in character" (1987: 411), it cannot hope to *explain* the reasons for the features of which it is a synopsis. Hence it turns out that a vision of law amounts to no explanation at all, or at best to a highly superficial one: their concept of a vision of law warns the reader against looking to the legal material alone, but their explanation of the concept is a mere restatement of the differences they found: thus it cannot explain them. If you want to explain *a*, *b* and *c* on the basis of *x*, you don't produce a very informative explanation if you go on and claim that *x* is whatever has *a*, *b* and *c* as a consequence.

To say that English judges are more formal than their American counterparts is to say that the latter are willing to accept, in legal discourse, arguments that the former would not consider "legal". Why this is the case is *the* question a vision of law has to answer. If it is to *explain*, and not merely summarise, the different levels of formality Atiyah and Summers found in England and the United States, it has to show how it contributes to the definition of the canon of legal argument, how it specifies what counts as a *legal* argument. Therefore, a concept of a "vision of law" that is able to play the role that Atiyah and Summers want it to play throughout the book has to be something more than a résumé of the aspects in which the understanding and

of law; a different one is that of how and why does a particular image come to have the content it actually has.

[5] SGANARELLE [*to* Lucinde]. Give me your arm. [*to* Géronte]. I can tell by this pulse that your daughter is dumb.

GÉRONTE. Yes, Monsieur, that is her affliction. You have discovered it at once.

SGANARELLE. Ha!

JACQUELINE. Just see how quickly he's found out her complaint!

SGANARELLE. We great doctors diagnose correctly at once. An ignoramus would have hummed and hawed. He would have said: *it's this* or: *it's that*. But I put my finger on the trouble straight away, and tell you that your daughter is dumb.

GÉRONTE. Yes, but I wantyou to tell me the cause.

SGANARELLE. Nothing easier. The cause of her dumbness is the loss of her power of speech.

(Molière, *Le Médicin malgré lui*, act II. trans. George Graveley, Oxford University Press, 1956).

application of the law can be more or less formal: it has to explain the reasons (rather than the causes) why that is the case. It has to explain *why* in England most standards of identification of valid laws are source-oriented and not content-oriented, *why* in England conflicts between valid laws are thought to be solved by way of the application of rules of hierarchical priority, and so on.

Atiyah and Summers furnished ample evidence for their primary thesis. In particular, they showed that even in those areas where the black-letter law is substantively similar what the law is for actual cases can be significatively different. If this is the case, it follows that understanding the meaning of the black-letter rules cannot be enough to know how they are to be applied, to know what the law is for any particular case. Hence the importance of their secondary thesis. Their particular explanation of a vision of law, however, turned out to be disappointingly empty. The concept of an image of law can be seen as an attempt to develop their insight so that it can fulfil its explanatory function.

Roscoe Pound's "Ideal Element in the Law"

In his Tagore Lectures delivered at the University of Calcutta in 1948, Roscoe Pound started by arguing that "whether there is an ideal element in law depends not a little on what is meant by the term 'law'" (Pound, 1958: 1). He then went on to distinguish three senses which could be given to the word "law": (i) as an aggregate of laws, a "legal order" (*ibid.* at 2); (ii) the "authoritative materials by which controversies are decided and thus the legal order is maintained" (*ibid.*), what he called the "precept element"; and (iii) a predictive sense, the use of which was a "consequence of development of the functional attitude towards the science of law." Quoting Llewellyn, Pound argues that in this sense "what officials do about disputes is . . . the law itself" (1958: 2f).

After dissecting the meaning of law in these three senses, Pound claims that

> in arguing for and discussing an ideal element in law one must look into all these meanings of 'law.' But one must be concerned specially with one aspect of law in the second sense, namely, laws, the body of authoritative norms or models or patterns of decision applied by the judicial organs of a politically organised society in the determination of controversies so as to maintain the legal order" (1958: 3).

He does not explain why the "precept element" enjoys this priority. So what is the "ideal element in law"? Pound answers,

> The term ["ideal"] comes from a Greek word meaning basically something one sees. Applied to action, it is a mental picture of what one is doing or why, to what end or purpose, he is doing it. Postulating a good law maker and a good judge, it is a picture of how the one ought to frame the laws he enacts and how the other ought to decide the cases that come before him. But behind these pictures of what ought to be the enacted or the judicially formulated precept for the case in hand is a basic mental picture of the end or purpose of social control—of what we are seeking to

> bring about by adjustment of relations and ordering of conduct by social pressure on the individual and so immediately of what we are seeking to achieve through adjustment of relations and ordering of conduct by systematic application of the force of politically organized society (1958: 5).

These ideals need not be consciously adhered to: they "may be held and made the background of their decisions by judges unconsciously or . . . half consciously, being taken for granted as a matter of course without conscious reference to them" (*ibid.* For the ideal aspect of law, *see* also MacCormick, 1997: 10ff).

I think we can see more clearly the importance of Pound's ideal element if we first focus, not upon his Tagore Lectures, but upon a piece written by him some four decades before.

Pound's "Freedom of Contract" (1908), opens with a quotation from Justice Harlan in *Adair* v. *United States* (208 U.S. 161, 174f):

> The right of a person to sell his labor upon such terms as he deems proper is, in its essence, the same as the right of the purchaser of the labor to prescribe the conditions upon which he will accept such labor from the person offering to sell it. So the right of the employee to quit the service of the employer, for whatever reason, is the same as the right of the employer, for whatever reasons, to dispense with the service of such employee . . .. In all such particulars the employer and the employee have equality of right, and any legislation that disturbs that equality is an arbitrary interference with the liberty of contract, which no government can legally justify in a free land.

Pound was puzzled by the fact that this passage expressed something which was the culmination of a line of decisions going back some twenty-five years, and was accepted without question by most American judges and lawyers at the turn of the century. And yet, it was something that to "everyone acquainted at first hand with actual industrial conditions" would obviously be "utterly hollow" and "surcharged with fallacy" (Pound, 1908: 454, quoting approvingly Taylor's *Science of Jurisprudence*). How could something so obviously false be "a doctrine . . . announced with equal vigour and held with equal tenacity by courts of Pennsylvania and of Arkansas, of New York and of California, of Illinois and of West Virginia, of Massachusetts and of Missouri"? (Pound, 1908: 455). The "ideal element in law" is (I believe) Pound's answer to this question.

Let me translate the problem Pound is dealing with here to the language used in this chapter. *Adair*'s doctrine, as expressed in the quoted paragraph above, does not have any relevance as a legal *rule*: it does not belong to the *ratio* of the case, and it is not deduced from valid law. It is, rather, something that will control the ways in which the bulk of the rules concerning contracts will be applied. If, as we have seen, rules are to be applied to *normal* cases, the doctrine fulfils the role of explaining when and why a case is normal (strictly, all it does is to exclude some reasons as grounds for "abnormality," but in a way, this is part of a definition of what makes a normal case normal): no case will be considered "abnormal" because of economic inequality between the parties. The all-important legal category is that of "equality of right" (notice the categorical difference between economic equality and equality of right). We can easily imagine Pound and Harlan discussing a particular case, both of them recognising that contracts should be enforced when they have been freely entered into (call this a legal rule). Harlan would claim that the substantive considerations pre-empted by the rule are all but those showing whether or not the parties enjoyed "equality of right" at the moment of agreeing; Pound would point out that equality of right is only one of the substantive considerations not pre-empted by the rule, (some measure of) equality of bargaining power being another. The discussion is about how *formal* the rule is, how much inequality it can exclude. It is not a discussion that can be settled by a further (legal) rule, but by considerations about what contract law is about and the substantive reasons that it allows: is the law of contract about justice in exchange, about maximising utility, etc? What makes an exchange unfair? How are we to understand utility? and so on.

Adair's doctrine reflects (part of) a canon of legal argument: it explains the sort of arguments that can be used as a defence against the enforcement of contract. And how such an "utterly hollow" canon of legal argument could be accepted without question by so many lawyers and judges was the first point Pound was concerned with in the 1908 piece. The second (and to my mind more important for Pound in 1908) was to criticise the idea of freedom of contract as presented in *Adair*'s doctrine, to offer an alternative image of contract law, one more in tune with the needs and the ethical beliefs of the time.

By 1949, Pound's emphasis had changed. He offered in his Tagore Lectures a more comprehensive explanation of the role of the ideal element in law and also of different ideals and their evolution in legal history. His main thesis, and the reason why this piece is interesting for us, was that

> a body of philosophical, political, and ethical ideas as to the end of law—as to the purpose of social control and of the legal order as a form thereof—and hence as to what legal precepts ought to be in view of this end, is an element of the first importance in the work of judges, jurists, and lawmakers (Pound, 1958: 108).

Pound then goes on to sketch four stages of legal development: (i) primitive law; (ii) strict law; (iii) equity and natural law; and (iv) maturity of law (1958, 109). In each of these "stages" the law is conceived in different ways, and the difference in the idea of law implies different attitudes as to the application of the legal material.

I do not think it is useful to get into the details of Pound's theory of legal evolution, among other reasons because I am unsure about the utility (or even the possibility) of finding "stages" in legal development that have been followed by all "mature" legal systems (assuming that the "maturity" of a legal system is something that can be determined using a criterion other than by reference to one's chosen stages of legal evolution). Having said that, I would like to take one of Pound's stages in order to discuss, not his general claims about the path of legal evolution, but his more particular and interesting ones about the relation between the "ideal" and the "precept" element in law.

In the second stage of legal development, what Pound calls the stage of "strict law", "the legal order is definitely differentiated from other modes of social control." The state has monopolised the settlement of serious conflicts between people, and the idea of law is shaped by two causes: "(i) Fear of arbitrary exercise of the assistance of the state, the rooted repugnance of men to subjection of their will to the arbitrary will of others, and (ii) survival of ideas of form and literal application form the earlier period" (Pound, 1958: 114). From this, Pound extracts the following features of the process of application of the law:

> (i) Formalism—the law refuses to look beyond or behind the form; (ii) rigidity and immutability; (iii) extreme insistence that every one looks out for himself; (iv) refusal to take account of the moral aspects of situations or transactions—to use Ames's phrase, the strict law is not immoral but unmoral; (v) rights and duties are restricted to a narrow category of legal persons—all human beings or natural persons are not legal persons and legal capacity is restricted arbitrarily (Pound, 1958: 114).

There are two objections that can be made to Pound's claim here. The first is particular to the moment of "strict law". It clearly fails to follow from the fact that the legal order is differentiated from other mechanisms of social control, not even when the fear of arbitrariness and the survival of literal ideas is accepted, that the law has to refuse "to look behind the form" (or has to be rigid and immutable, or has to be "unmoral", etc.). Pound's last characteristic of the strict law period makes this point all the more evident: how can it be that the fear of arbitrariness is the "cause" of "arbitrary restrictions" in the legal capacity of natural persons?.[6]

The second and more general criticism is related to this point. Pound assumed that, covering the whole period of legal evolution from primitive law to "socialisation of law" (a fifth stage to be reached after legal maturity) there is something that remains unmodified: an instrumental conception of the law, according to which the law is to be explained by the contribution it makes to the well-being of the relevant society, however this is conceived (in other words, a "regulatory" conception of the law). Pound defined the concept of an ideal of law as a "basic mental picture of the end or purpose of social control . . ., of what we are *seeking to achieve* through adjustment of relations and ordering of conduct by systematic application of the force of politically organized society" (1958: 5, emphasis added). Here, however, Pound was

[6] Notice that "arbitrary restrictions" *could* very well be just restrictions the rationale of which eluded Pound, like the arbitrary formalism of Roman law we encountered in Chapter 6.

smuggling in part of his own ideal of the law: he was working at the wrong level of abstraction. I have argued (in Chapter 1) that the rigid formalism of ancient Roman law (which was not uncommon for its time) can be understood on the basis of (ancient) Romans *not* having an instrumental conception of the law, not *seeking to achieve* anything through law. Whether the law is something that is justified as an instrument for something else or in its own terms is an important part of an image of law. Pound seems to have thought that the law was, so to speak, intrinsically instrumental, hence the only ways in which legal ideals could differ were the ends to be attained with it, the specification of the goals for which the law was an instrument. I do not believe this is useful, and Pound's scheme of the evolution of ideas about the law is thus seriously flawed.

Law in an Activist State

I would now like to consider Bruce Ackerman's *Reconstructing American Law* (1984) and Mirjan Damaska's *The Faces of Justice and State Authority* (1986). The main theme of the first work is the transformation suffered by American legal discourse in the twentieth century. This transformation, according to Ackerman, was the consequence of a change in the political beliefs of the American people. To explain the nature of that change, Ackerman uses two ideal types dubbed by him the "reactive" and the "activist" state (1984: 25).

A *reactive* state is one in which

> legal argument is restricted by something I shall call the *reactive constraint*: no legal argument will be acceptable if it requires the lawyer to question the legitimacy of the military, economic, and social arrangements generated by the invisible hand (*ibid.*).

The reactive constraint was never a *rule* of American law. It was rather a consequence of a set of moral and political beliefs about society, justice and the law; though the content of the law will probably reflect (or feed back, see above, 208 n. 4) this political belief in the invisible hand, the latter has a far more important consequence: it specifies the arguments that can be accepted as legal arguments in the context of legal adjudication, it defines a canon of legal argument. Only arguments that satisfy the constraint are legal (as opposed to, say, political) arguments.

According to Ackerman, the reactive constraint's first consequence for legal discourse will be that the latter will be understood as dealing only "with the appraisal of particular actions against the background of ongoing practices" (1984: 26). The legitimacy of the practice itself cannot be contested before a court of law, because legal discourse is defined by its being a kind of discourse in which that cannot be an issue. The application of the law is about determining and correcting deviations: "each lawyer tries to provide a persuasive account of the ongoing practice that makes the opponent's conduct appear deviant, his own client's behaviour innocent or justifiable or, at the very least, excusable" (*ibid.*). As such, there is a natural end to any conceivable legal case:

> There is only so much that can be said about particular actions before the conversation gets repetitive. The only thing left to do is for the jury to engage in a densely textured judgement upon the defendant's conduct—either it was deviant or it wasn't. If it was the defendant should set things right. If not, not. Next case (1984: 28).

Consider a contract-law case in a community thoroughly socialised into the practice of keeping promises. The efficiency or fairness of the practice itself will not be an issue, and the court will hear each reactive lawyer "attempting to provide an interpretation of institutionalized expectations that makes his client's actions seem appropriate, his antagonist's deviant" (Ackerman, 1984: 26). Once the argument has been heard, the court will pass judgment, and the case will be closed definitively.

The situation changes quite significatively once the political beliefs of which the reactive constraint is an expression are modified:

> assume that, for one reason or another, the dominant opinion amongst the citizenry no longer holds that the country's military, economic, and social problems can take care of themselves without self-conscious tending. Assume, further, that the citizenry insists that law and lawyers have a central role to play in activist governance, and consider how these simple points will transform the profession's conversational repertoire. (Ackerman, 1984: 28)

At the most obvious level, it must be clear that the defining feature of the legal discourse will cease to be that it assumes the validity and legitimacy of social practices generated by the invisible hand. Now the law is seen as being *about* the correction of existing practices, and that will have a profound effect on the canon of legal argument. Arguments that were excluded from consideration in legal discourse because they were, say, *political* not legal, will be deemed to be reasonable pieces of legal argumentation. The whole point of the argumentation will no longer be the discrete one of assessing a particular action against an unquestioned social practice, but sometimes at least the practice itself will be questioned. Arguments designed to question the practice, therefore, will deserve consideration (though of course they might be defeated in many cases by more "traditional" arguments): the canon of legal argument, the whole universe of *what is excluded* and *what is included* in legal discourse changes (Ackerman, 1984: 28), so that arguments that were summarily rejected before (because they were not *legal* arguments, because they did not satisfy the constraint) might very well be good legal arguments now.

The way in which the *facts* are to be described will also change. Under the reactive constraint, the facts were relevant as a description of an individual and concrete action to be measured against the standard given by unquestioned practices, but once the practices themselves can be a subject of legal argument this focus on the concrete and individual action will soon became inappropriate:

> It would be incredibly time-consuming, for example, to describe the practice of driving an automobile by reporting that Roe drove from *A* to *B*, Doe drove from *C* to *D*, and so on. It would also miss the point of activist concern, which is to assess the extent to which the practice, considered as a whole, requires self-conscious legal regulation to operate in an acceptable fashion. Given this concern, individualized descriptions seem nothing more than a series of anecdotes (Ackerman, 1984: 29).

In a way, this is only to be expected. Given that facts can receive numerous different true descriptions, those that highlight the aspects that are significant from the point of view of the image of law will be preferred: "it is interesting to note that generally when people are asked the 'facts' of *Donoghue* v. *Stevenson* they almost always repeat some version of the neighbour principle. The lady with the marriage problem and a snail in her ginger beer and ice cream has disappeared" (Bankowski, 1997: 18). And from this follows that features of a particular case that were irrelevant before, so irrelevant that they were not even mentioned before the court might well end up being decisive for the granting of, for example, an (implicit) exception.

Likewise, the implementation of the policy might be a much more important consideration than the resolution of a particular dispute, and it will provide a yardstick against which the acceptability of arguments could be measured. It can easily be thought, for example, that if the judicial process is an instance of a much broader process of policy implementation it is the *policy* what cannot be challenged before a court, and that any argument to that effect will be considered to be non-legal. But while this can be true, it will nonetheless also be the case that

> While activist law cannot be modified by the preferences of those whose conduct it purports to regulate, it is malleable and flexible in a different sense, changing in turn with each failure or success in carrying the government toward its ideals. Whether it takes the form of objective regulation or model of conduct, it cannot be permitted to be so firmly fixed as to stand as an obstacle to the realization of state programs. (Damaska, 1986: 82)

If the law is no longer seen as being "about" the evaluation of individual behaviour against the background of an unquestioned social practice as reflected in society's legal material (rules, etc.), the main goal of the judicial process also changes: in a reactive state the natural end and goal of the judicial process is the settlement of private disputes according to the prevailing practices as reflected by the legal material. In an activist state, on the other hand, "the activist state's conception of law as an instrument for the realization of its policy makes the legal process independent of dispute resolution." Furthermore,

> requiring a controversy as a general prerequisite for the institution of the legal process clearly makes no sense to an activist government. Disputes do not miraculously arise whenever a social event suggests the need to enforce the law and thus to realize a policy goal in the concrete circumstances of the case. (Damaska, 1986: 84)

In a similar vein, Nigel Simmonds has contrasted a state in which law is "thought of as embodying the popular will in the sense of collective decisions about which goals to pursue" with one in which law is "seen as embodying the popular will in the sense of collective decisions about right and wrong conduct, rather than decisions about the choice and implementation of policy goals". How will these different images of law affect the interpretation and application of legal rules? Probably in the former judges will lack legitimacy to discuss which goals are to be pursued, but will be entitled to adapt the application of the rules so as to foster the goals the rules are supposed to advance. In the latter,

> policy-based interpretation of the law would seem inappropriate, since the law is not regarded as an instrument of policy. But, at the same time, the emphasis on popular will as the source of legitimacy might restrict the freedom of judges and jurists in interpreting and systematically developing the law. Perhaps a formalistic and literal approach would be the result, or perhaps legal interpretation would be handed over to lay decision (Simmonds, 1984: 48–9).

The important issue to keep in mind here is not one of a necessary connection between a particular image of law and a particular style of adjudication. It is, rather, to notice how the canon of legal argument, the criterion that tells legal from non-legal argument, is sensitive to these ideas of "what law is about" in Simmonds' way. Notice that, though the moral and political beliefs that characterise the activist state will eventually affect the *content* of the legal materials, they will also and more pervasively affect the ways in which the old (and, of course, the new) materials are understood and applied. What counts as an "inappropriate" application of a legal norm to a particular case will be different, hence the cases in which certainty outweighs appropriateness and vice-versa will be different.

Both Damaska and Ackerman made broader claims in their characterisation of the reactive as opposed to the activist state. Ackerman, for example (1984, 13ff), offered an historical interpretation of Legal Realism as a "culturally conservative movement" (it was the reactive lawyer's reaction to the birth of the activist state), and undertook to reconstruct an activist ("constructivist") legal discourse (1984, 40ff), a programme that has not been uncontroversial (*see*, for example, Peller, 1985). None of this, however interesting in its own right, is directly relevant to my discussion. The only point I am interested in is Damaska's way of showing how Ackerman and legal discourse is shaped by political beliefs. The canon of legal argument is something that is defined, or at the very least decisively shaped, by moral and political beliefs about what the law is and what it is about. And what the law is for actual cases cannot be known without mastering that canon.

IMAGES OF LAW

The question before us now is, can we allow for the authority of law once it has been shown that the legal material cannot be applied without using the substantive considerations the law was supposed to pre-empt?

The problem was created by one particular way in which an important feature of the law is interpreted and theoretically explained. Legal discourse is *formal* discourse, that is, a kind of normative discourse where participants are justified in not considering substantive questions that are, or might be, relevant for an all-things-considered decision. This feature of the law gives rise to the problem we now face when it is explained on the basis of the exclusionary force of the legal material (rules). This only shows that this is not a correct way of explaining the formality of law.

An enquiry into the nature and function of images of law is another attempt to explain the formality of law, one that is not committed to thinking of rules as exclusionary reasons. It allows, instead, for degrees of formality. These degrees of formality are determined not by the conceptual status of the legal material (rules, principles and so on), but by the constraints that act upon legal discourse as a result of the existence of a canon of legal argument whose content is given by an image of law.

We are now in a position to refine the definition of an image of law given at the beginning of this section (above at 212), and I want to do so on the basis of the already quoted explanation of Pound's "ideal element" in law as "a body of philosophical, political, and ethical ideas as to the end of law—as to the purpose of social control and of the legal order as a form thereof—and hence as to what legal precepts ought to be in view of this end" (Pound,1958: 108, quoted above).

We have seen that this definition of the "ideal element in law" has to be purged of Pound's own ideal. To begin with, Pound's qualification of the relevant ideas as "philosophical, political or ethical" reflects contingent beliefs about the law. For nineteenth-century English or American lawyers or judges, for example, their beliefs about the law were indeed seen as ethical and political, as clearly reflected in Justice Harlan's opinion in *Adair*, or (to use an English case) in Jessell MR's opinion in *Printing and Numerical Registering Co.* v. *Sampson* (1875 LR 19 Eq at 462):

> if there is one thing which more than another public policy requires it is that men of full age and competent understanding shall have the utmost liberty of contracting, and that their contracts when entered into freely and voluntarily shall be held sacred and shall be enforced by the Courts of Justice. Therefore you have this paramount public policy to consider —that you are not lightly to interfere with freedom of contract.

From this, however, it does not follow that an image of law can only be a set of political or ethical beliefs. There was nothing necessarily ethical or political in the ancient Romans' belief that legal relations were invisible objects that existed in the world just as trees and apples do. Needless to say, those doctrines had political or moral consequences. It could even be shown that they fulfilled some political function, helping, e.g. to reinforce the dominance of Patricians over Plebeians in the early days of Rome. But this is not to say that the ideas themselves were political, i.e. that they were believed in *because* of political reasons (as we can indeed say of the nineteenth-century *laissez-faire*). Hence, we have to drop (or at least qualify in this sense) the "political or ethical" qualification in Pound's definition.

Do we have to drop the "philosophical" as well? This seems less important, and more a matter of verbal convention. In a broad sense, it is clear that they are philosophical ideas, in the same way in which any belief whatsoever can be said to be philosophical belief (even the belief that I have two hands is a philosophical belief, as G E Moore famously showed). But in this sense the adjective is uninformative.

A similar consideration is in order regarding Pound's parenthetical remark: those beliefs do not have to be about "the purpose of social control and of the legal order as a form thereof". The point here is even clearer: that the legal order is a form of social control is part of the possible content of these beliefs, not what characterises them.

It could be claimed that precisely because the ancient Roman image of law was not a set of political or ethical ideas about the law as a form of social control we should not use the word "law" to refer to ancient Roman law. This would amount to saying that "autonomous" "legal systems" are, precisely because of this, not legal systems at all. I think, on the contrary, that there is a great deal to be learned from the possibility of their existence (and from the realisation of such a possibility in ancient Rome and in ancient biblical law, among others), hence such a stipulation would prove unhelpful.

In addition to these corrections of Pound's definition, it would be useful to introduce a clarification which, unlike the previous ones, is (I believe) merely an interpretation of his claim. The idea of "of what legal precepts ought to be in view of this end" allows us to introduce that of the canon of legal argument. Since Pound was referring to an ideal element *in law*, I think it is only fair to say that this "ought" should not be interpreted as a moral but as a legal "ought"—it would not be clear, at least without further arguments, why ideas about what the legal precepts ought (morally) to be is "an element of the first importance in the work of judges". If this understanding is correct and Pound's "ought" has to be interpreted as a legal "ought," the whole phrase could be read as meaning: "...and hence as to how the legal precepts should be applied to particular cases in view of this end". The application of legal precepts to particular cases can be, as we have seen, more or less formal. They should be applied without considering irrelevant reasons, and taking into account all the relevant ones. An answer to the question "how should legal precepts be applied?" specifies which reasons for (legal) decisions count as relevant reasons and how weighty they have to be to become relevant: in brief, specifies a canon of legal argument.

An image of law, then, is a body of beliefs as to the nature of the law, and hence as to the kind of arguments that should be considered when deciding how legal precepts should be applied to particular cases. It is, as Atiyah and Summers say, "an inarticulate or implicit legal theory" (1987: 5).

Who needs to hold this body of beliefs? Atiyah and Summers claim that it must be "held by the general public at large and, to some extent, also by politicians, judges, and legal practitioners" (1987: 411). I will have something to say on this issue shortly. For the time being, however, suffice it to say that an image of law is a social construct, hence there must be some degree of (at least tacit, though not necessarily self-conscious) agreement between citizens and legal practitioners. An important distance between one and the other group (or indeed any important controversy about images of law) will undermine the legitimacy of the legal system, as Pound complained when criticising the American *laissez-faire* image of law:

> The attitude of many of our courts on the subject of liberty of contract is so certain to be misapprehended, is so out of the range of ordinary understanding, that they cannot fail to engender . . . feelings [of distrust and partiality]. Thus, those decisions do an injury beyond the failure of a few acts. These acts can be replaced as legislatures learn how to comply with the letter of the decisions and to evade the spirit of them. But the lost respect for courts and law cannot be replaced (Pound, 1908: 487. The disruptive effects of images of law being unsettled is also commented upon by Karl Llewellyn, who called images of law "jurisprudential styles": *see* Llewellyn 1960, 40–1).

Is an image of law equivalent to the more common idea of a legal tradition? I hope that by now it is evident why the answer to this question has to be in the negative. The idea of a legal tradition emphasises the continuity of a legal practice. The existence of something called, say, "the English legal tradition" (or "the common law tradition") is the continued existence of a legal practice (or parts thereof) that can be identified as a unity over a number of years (or centuries). Few people would think that contemporary English judges are not members of the same legal tradition as Edward Coke or William Blackstone, though if my argument has been up to now minimally convincing, it would be impossible to say that they share the same image of law. While the concept of a legal tradition refers to the environmental circumstances in which legal discourse is carried over, an image of law refers to a set of beliefs about that discourse. A legal tradition (or a legal culture) is, like a *habitat*, something someone can *belong* to, while an image of law is, like a religious doctrine, something someone can *believe* in (or, like faith, simply *have*). This does not mean, of course, that traditions do not affect images and vice-versa.

An image of law provides an independent criterion to establish what the content of a canon of legal argument is. This in turn helps to escape a risk of circularity present in the use of the idea of a canon as a key idea to the understanding of legal reasoning and law. This risk is exemplified in John Bell's important article "The acceptability of legal arguments" (Bell, 1986). In that piece, Bell argues that legal reasoning can be understood only "when account is taken of the limits imposed by standards of what counts as an acceptable legal argument" (1986, 47). He then goes on to claim that the canon of legal argument is defined by what the relevant audience finds convincing (1986, 60–1: "what that audience accepts as the criteria for rational debate provides the hints to how [a lawyer] can approach his justification"), and he ends up defining the relevant audience as the *legal* audience, i.e. "those skilled and knowledgeable in law" (1986, 50). To see the circularity one must ask: what is it to be "knowledgeable in law"? The answer seems to be to master the canon of legal argument, i.e., to be able to distinguish good legal arguments from bad ones. Any other definition is liable to become formalistic and to miss the point. But if "those skilled and knowledgeable in law" means "those who master the canon of legal argument" the circularity is evident: the canon is whatever the legal audience finds convincing and the legal audience is a group of all those who have mastered the canon: the canon is thus defined by the legal audience and the legal audience is defined by the canon. If the idea of an image of law is introduced in this picture, this circularity is avoided. The content of the canon of legal argument is defined by the image of law—and who needs to believe in it is itself something that to some extent is defined by the image itself. This is not a circular justification. It only shows something that hardly needs to be said, i.e. that the fact of an image of law being dominant in a legal tradition at a given time is a matter of politics, i.e. a question about power.

Could it be not claimed that the argument is circular anyway? For consider, what makes an image of law an image *of law*? The only answer seems to be that the *object* of the image is something that is not defined by the image, but my argument has been that the image defined what the canon is and the canon defined the audience. If we need an independent "object" of the image, what can it be other than what the audience recognise as legal?

I think this conclusion can be avoided. We begin by noticing that our concept of law is part and parcel of our culture. We think of the law as an independent form of discourse, independent in the sense that it is different from (though it might or might not—the question is not important *here*—be connected to) other forms of discourse, like morality or politics. But this is by no means a generalised fact about every conceivable society. In a society in which the law is not seen as something distinct, does it make sense to say that they have an image of law?

In this point I think Raz's is the correct position: "the concept of law is itself a product of a specific culture, a concept which was not available to members of earlier cultures which in fact lived under a legal system" (1996: 4). In order to understand an alien society, we must relate their concepts and practices to our own:

> To understand other societies we must master their concepts, for we will not understand them unless we understand how they perceive them themselves. Their concepts will not be understood by us unless we can relate them to our own concepts, so the understanding of alien cultures requires possession of concepts which apply across the divide between us and them, concepts which can be applied to the practices of other cultures as well as to our own. Only with the help of concepts which apply to our own as well as to alien cultures can we understand the concepts used by alien cultures in their own understanding of their own practices and institutions and not shared by us. The centrality of law in social life makes it natural that the concept of law would be one of these bridge-building concepts, i.e. one which we could apply to societies which themselves do not use it in their own self-understanding (Raz, 1996: 5; *see* also Moore, 1998: 303) .

If we wanted to understand an alien society's image of law, we would have to start by trying to understand their practices from their point of view. Once we understood them, we can try to relate them to *our* concepts, like law. How do they conceive of practices that have features *we* recognise as legal? The conceptions they have need not be *legal* in the sense that they may lack that concept. We saw that there is a sense in which *laissez-faire* was not a legal but a moral or political belief, but it had an important impact on practices we recognise as legal. Thus the image of law need not be an image *of law* for the holders, since they can even lack the very concept of law, but it is a image of something *we* recognise as law. Depending on particular historical traditions, it might be the case that an image of law includes, as part of its content, awareness of the concept of law, but this definitively need not be the case. Thus we avoid the circularity: an image of law, then, is an image of the world, or of that part of the world that we would identify, using our concepts (themselves the product of our world-view) as legal practice.

References

The *Iliad* has been quoted according to Robert Fagles' translation (Viking Penguin, 1990: the first reference is to the original line numbers; the second to the numbers in Fagles' translation); all quotations of the Bible are taken from the *Revised English Bible* (Cambridge University Press and Oxford University Press, 1989), and those from the *Digest* are from the text edited by Theodor Momsen and Paul Krueger and the translation edited by Alan Watson (University of Pennsylvania Press, Philadelphia, 1985). The reference to David Lodge contained in the acknowledgements section is to his *Home Truths* (Harmondsworth: Penguin, 2000). The rules of football have been quoted according to the official text, available at www.FIFA.com.

Aarnio, A (1998): *Reason and Authority.* (Aldershot: Ashgate, Dartmouth).

——, I Niiniluoto and J Uusitalo (eds) (1979): *Methodologie und Erkenntnistheorie: der juristichen Argumentation.* (Berlin: Duncker & Humblot).

Ackerman, B (1984): *Reconstructing American Law.* (Cambridge, MA.: Harvard University Press).

Alchourrón, C (1995): "On Law and Logic", *European Journal of Law, Philosophy and Computer Science* 2.

——and E Bulygin (1971): *Normative Systems.* (New York: Springer Verlag).

——and E Bulygin (1987): *Introducción a la Metodología de las Ciencias Jurídicas y Sociales.* (Buenos Aires: Astrea).

Alexy, R (1989): *A Theory of Legal Argumentation.* (Oxford: Clarendon Press).

——(1994): *El Concepto y la Validez del Derecho.* (Barcelona: Gedisa).

Amselek, P (1988): "The Philosophy of Law and the Theory of Speech Acts", *Ratio Juris* 1: 187–223.

Atiyah, P S (1981): *Promises, Morals and Law.* (Oxford: Clarendon Press).

——(1982a): "Contracts, Promises, and the Law of Obligations", in Atiyah (1986): 10–56.

——(1982b): "The Modern Role of Contract Law", in Atiyah (1986): 1–9.

——(1984): "Form and Substance in Contract Law", in Atiyah (1986): 93–120.

——(1986): *Essays on Contract.* (Oxford: Clarendon Press).

——(1995): *An Introduction to the Law of Contract.* (Oxford: Clarendon Press).

——and R S Summers (1987): *Form and Substance in Anglo-American Law.* (Oxford: Clarendon Press).

Baker, G (1977): "Defeasibility and Meaning", in Hacker and Raz (eds) (1977): 26–57.

Bankowski, Z (1993): "Don't think about it: Legality and Legalism", *Rechtstheorie* 15: 45–54.

——(1996): "Law Love and Computers", *Edinburgh Law Review* 1.

——(1997): "Parable and Analogy: The universal and particular in Common Law", *Acta Jurídica*: 138–63.

——and G Mungham (1976): *Images of Law.* (London: Routledge and Kegan Paul).

——, I White and U Hahn, (eds) (1995): *Informatics and the Foundation of Legal Reasoning.* (Dordrecht: Kluwer Academic Publishers).

Bell, J (1986): "The Acceptability of Legal Arguments", in MacCormick and Birks (eds) (1986): 45–65.
Bengoetxea, J (1993): *The Legal Reasoning of the European Court of Justice.* (Oxford: Clarendon Press).
Benhabib, S and F Dallmayr (eds) (1990): *The Communicative Ethics Controversy.* (Cambridge, Mass.: The MIT Press).
Berman, H (1993): *Faith and Order. The Reconciliation of Law and Religion.* (Atlanta, Georgia: Scholars Press).
Bix, B (1993).
Brewer, S (1996): "Exemplary Reasoning: Semantics, Pragmatics, and the Rational Force of Legal Argument by Analogy", *Harvard Law Review* 109.
Cairns, J W (1994): "Institutitonal Writings in Scotland Reconsidered", in A Kiralfy and H MacQueen (eds) (1994): 76–117.
Cherry, C (1973): "Regulative Rules and Constitutive Rules", *Philosophical Quarterly*: 301–15.
Christodoulidis, E (1999): "The irrationality of merciful judgement: exclusionary reasons and the question of the particular", in *Law & Philosophy* 18: 215–241.
Cohen, G (1996): "The Obstetric Motif in the Marxist Conception of Revolution". Gifford Lectures, Edinburgh.
Cohen, M R and E Nagel (1934): *An Introduction to Logic and Scientific Method.* (London: Routledge and Kegan Paul).
Coleman, J (1996): "Authority and Reason", in George (ed) (1996): 287–319.
Collins, H (1986): *The Law of Contract.* (London: Weidenfeld and Nicolson).
Damaska, M R (1986): *The Faces of Justice and State Authority.* (New Haven: Yale University Press).
Daube, D (1944): "How Esau sold his birthright", *Cambridge Law Journal* 8: 70–5.
——(1956): *Forms of Roman Legislation.* (Oxford: Clarendon Press).
Detmold, M J (1984): *The Unity of Law and Morality.* (London: Routledge and Kegan Paul).
——(1989): "Law as Practical Reason", *Cambridge Law Journal* 48: 436–71.
Dworkin, R (1967): "Is Law a System of Rules?", in Summers (ed) (1968): 25–60.
——(1977): *Taking Rights Seriously.* (Cambridge, MA.: Harvard University Press).
——(1986): *Law's Empire.* (London: Fontana).
——(1991): "On Gaps in the Law", in MacCormick and Amselek (eds) (1991).
Ewald, W (1995): "Comparative Jurisprudence (I): What was it like to try a rat?", *University of Pennsylvania Law Review* 143: 1889–2149.
Finnis, J (1980): *Natural Law and Natural Rights.* (Oxford: Clarendon Press).
Flew, A (ed) (1951): *Logic and Language.* (Oxford: Basil Blackwell).
Foot, P (ed) (1967): *Theories of Ethics.* (Oxford: Clarendon Press).
Friedrich, C J (1956): "The Ideological and Philosophical Background", in Schwartz (ed) (1956): 1–18.
Frier, B (1985): *The Rise of the Roman Jurists.* (Princeton, NJ: Princeton University Press).
Fuller, J (1964): *The Morality of Law.* (New Haven: Yale University Press).
Fuller, L (1958): "Positivism and Fidelity of Law—A Reply to Professor Hart", *Harvard Law Review* 71: 630–72.
Füßer, K (1996): "Farewell to Legal Positivism", in George (ed) (1996): 119–62.
George, R (ed) (1994): *Natural Law Theory.* (Oxford: Clarendon Press).

——(ed) (1996): *The Autonomy of Law*. (Oxford: Clarendon Press).

Giddens, A (1984): *The Constitution of Society*. (Cambridge: Polity Press).

Gottlieb, S (1994): "The Paradox of Balancing Significant Interests", *Hasting Law Journal* 45: 825–66.

Grotius, H (1646): *De Iure Belli ac Pacis Libri Tres*. (Oxford: Clarendon Press).

Günther, K (1993a): "Critical remarks on Robert Alexy's 'Special-case' thesis", *Ratio Juris* 6: 143–56.

——(1993b): *The Sense of Appropriateness*. (Albany: SUNY).

Habermas, J (1983): "Discourse Ethics: Notes on Philosophical Justification", in Benhabib and Dallmayr (eds) (1990): 60–110.

——(1985): "A Philosophico-Political Profile", in Habermas (1996a): 147–85.

——(1993): *Justification and Application*. (Cambridge: Polity Press).

——(1996a): *Autonomy and Solidarity*. (London: Verso).

——(1996b): *Between Facts and Norms*. (Cambridge, Polity Press).

——(1996c): "Life-Forms, Morality and the Task of the Philosopher", in Habermas (1996a): 187–210.

Hacker, P M S and J Raz (eds) (1977): *Law, Morality and Society. Essays in Honour of H.L.A. Hart*. (Oxford: Clarendon Press).

Hägestrom, A (1953): *Inquiries into the Nature of Law and Morals*. (Stockholm: Almqvist & Wiksell).

Hart, H L A (1948): "The Ascription of Responsibility and Rights", in Flew (ed) (1951): 145–66.

——(1953): "Definition and Theory in Jurisprudence", in Hart (1983): 49–87.

——(1958): "Positivism and The Separation Between Law and Morals", in Hart (1983): 49–87.

——(1967): "Problems of the Philosophy of Law", in Hart (1983): 88–120.

——(1968a): "Kelsen's Doctrine of the Unity of Law", in Hart (1983): 309–42.

——(1968b): *Punishment and Responsibility*. (Oxford: Clarendon Press).

——(1982a): "Commands and Authoritative Reasons", in Hart (1982b): 243–68.

——(1982b): *Essays on Bentham. Jurisprudence and Political Theory*. (Oxford: Clarendon Press).

——(1983): *Essays in Jurisprudence and Philosophy*. (Oxford: Clarendon Press).

——(1994): *The Concept of Law*. (Oxford: Clarendon Press).

Hegel, G W F (1971): *The Phenomenology of Mind*. (London: George Allen & Unwin Ltd.).

Honoré, A M (1974): "Legal Reasoning in Rome and Today", *South African Law Journal* 91: 84–94.

——(1977): "Real Laws", in Hacker and Raz (eds) (1977): 99–118.

——(1991): "Book Review of Reinhard Zimmermann's *The Law of Obligations. Roman Foundations of the Civilian Tradition*", *The Law Quaterly Review* 107: 504–7.

Horwitz, M (1992): *The Transformation of American Law, 1870–1960*. (New York: Oxford University Press).

Huizinga, J (1970): *Homo Ludens*. (London: Paladin)

Kant, I (1797): "On a supposed right to lie from philanthropy", in Kant (1996).

——(1996): *Practical Philosophy*, (ed. by A Wood, trans. by M J Gregor, Cambridge: Cambridge University Press).

Kaser, M (1965): *Roman Private Law*. (Durban: Butterworths).

Kaser, M (1967): "The Changing Face of Roman Jurisdiction", *The Irish Jurist.*
Kelsen, H (1934): *Introduction to the Problems of Legal Theory.* (Oxford: Clarendon Press 1992).
——(1967): *The Pure Theory of Law.* (Berkeley and Los Angeles: University of California Press).
Kelley, D R (1984): *Historians and the Law in Postrevolutionary France.* (Princeton, NJ: Princeton University Press).
Kilbourne, R H (1987): *A History of the Louisiana Civil Code: the formative years, 1803–1839.* (Baton Rouge, La.: Publications Center, Paul M. Herbert Law Center, Louisiana State University).
Kiralfy, A and H MacQueen (eds) (1994): *New Perspectives in Scottish Legal History.* (Glasgow: Frank Cass & Co.).
Kneale, W and M Kneale (1962): *The Development of Logic.* (Oxford: Clarendon Press).
Kramer, M (1999): *In Defense of Legal Positivism: law without trimmings.* (Oxford: Clarendon Press).
Kunkel, W (1973): *Roman Legal and Constitutional History.* (Oxford: Clarendon Press).
Leith, P (1988): "Common Usage, Certainty and Computing", in Leith and Ingram (eds) (1988): 85–115.
——and P Ingram (eds) (1988): *The Jurisprudence of Orthodoxy: Queen's University Essays on H. L. A. Hart.* (Belfast: Routledge).
Lewellyn, K (1960): *The Common Law Tradition. Deciding Appeals* (Boston: Little, Brown &Co).
MacCormack, G (1969): "Haegerstroem's Magical Interpretation of Roman Law", *The Irish Jurist*: 153–67.
MacCormick, N (1974): "Law as Institutional Fact", in MacCormick and Weinberger (1986): 49–76.
——(1984): "Coherence in Legal Justification", in Peczenik, Lindahl and v Roermund (eds) (1984): 235–51.
——(1992): "A Deductivist Rejoinder to a Semiotic Critique", *International Journal for the Semiotics of Law* 5: 216–24.
——(1994): *Legal Reasoning and Legal Theory.* (Oxford: Clarendon Press).
——(1995): "Defeasibility in Law and Logic", in Bankowski, White and Hahn (eds) (1995): 99–117.
——(1997): "Institutional Normative Order: a conception of law", *Cornell Law Review* 82: 1051–70.
——(1998): "Norms, Institutions and Institutional Facts", *Law and Philosophy* 17: 301–45.
——and P Amselek (eds) (1989): *Controversies about the Law's Ontology.* (Edinburgh: Edinburgh University Press).
——and P Birks (eds) (1986): *The Legal Mind. Essays for Tony Honoré.* (Oxford: Clarendon Press).
——and O Weinberger (1986): *An Institutional Theory of Law.* (Dordrecht: D. Reidel).
MacIntyre, A (1985): *After Virtue. A Study in Moral Theory.* (London: Duckworth).
Machan, M (1979): "Legal Questions: What are they, and how are they answered?", in Aarnio, Niiniluoto and Uusitalo (eds) (1979): 121–5.

Manfredini, A D (1994): "Codes and Jurists: Historical Reflections", in Rabello (ed) (1994): 15–26.
Marmor, A (1994): *Interpretation and Legal Theory*. (Oxford: Clarendon Press).
——(ed) (1995): *Law and Interpretation*. (Oxford: Clarendon Press).
Miller, L (1956): "Rules and Exceptions", *Ethics* 66: 262–70.
Mitrophanous, E (1998): "Soft Positivism", *Oxford Journal of Legal Studies* 17: 621–41.
Montesquieu (1756): *Spirit of the Laws*. (Aberdeen: Translated from the edition published at Edinburgh in 1750, with the author's latest corrections and illustrations).
Moore, M (1994): "Law as a Functional Kind", in George (ed) (1994): 188–242.
——(1998): "Hart's concluding scientific postcript", *Legal Theory* 4: 301–27.
Morawetz, T (1992): "The Epistemology of Judging: Wittgenstein and Deliberative Practices", in Patterson (ed) (1992): 3–27.
Opie, I and P Opie (1969): *Children's Games in Street and Playground*. (Oxford: Clarendon Press).
Outka, G H and P Ramsey (eds) (1969): *Norm and Context in Christian Ethics*. (London: SMC Press).
Patterson, D M (ed) (1992): *Wittgenstein and Legal Theory*. (Boulder, Col.: Westview Press).
Peczenik, A (1994): *On Law and Reason*. (Dordrecht: Kluwer Academic Publishers).
——, L Lindahl and B van Roermund (eds) (1984): *Theories of Legal Science*. (Dordrecht: Reidel).
——and J Hage (2000): "Law, morals and defeasibility", *Ratio Juris* 13: 305–25.
Peller, G (1985): "The Politics of Reconstruction (Book Review of Ackerman's *Reconstructing American Law*)", *Harvard Law Review* 98: 863–81.
Perelman, C and Olbrechts-Tyteca (1968): *The New Rhetoric*. (Notre Dame, Ind.: Notre Dame University Press).
Perry, S (1995): "Interpretation and Methodology in Legal Theory", in Marmor (ed) (1995): 97–135.
Pitcher, G (1960): "Hart on Action and Responsibility", *Philosophical Review*: 226–35.
Planiol, M (1939): *Traité Élémentaire de Droit Civil*. (Baton Rouge, La.: Louisiana State Law Institute).
Postema, G J (1996): "Law's autonomy and public practical reason", in George (ed) (1996): 79–118.
Pound, R (1908): "Liberty of Contract", *Yale Law Journal* 18: 454–87.
——(1958): *The Ideal Element in Law*. (Calcutta: University of Calcutta Press).
Prieto, L (1992): *Sobre Principios y Normas. Problemas del Razonamiento Jurídico*. (Madrid: Centro de Estudios Constitucionales).
Pufendorf, S (1688): *De Jure Naturae et Gentium Libri Octo*. (Oxford: Clarendon Press).
Rabello, A M (ed) (1994): *European Legal Traditions and Israel*. (Jerusalem: Nevo Publishing Ltd.).
Radford, R A (1945): "The economic organization of a POW camp", *Economica*: 189–201.
Ramsey, P (1969): "The Case of the Curious Exception", in Outka and Ramsey (eds) (1969): 67–135.
Rawls, J (1955): "Two Concepts of Rules", in Rawls (1999): 20–46.

Rawls, J (1999): *Collected Papers* (Cambridge, MA: Harvard University Press).
Raz, J (1979a): *The Authority of Law*. (Oxford: Clarendon Press).
——(1979b): "Reasons, sources and gaps", in Raz (1979a).
——(1980): *The Concept of a Legal System*. (Oxford: Clarendon Press).
——(1985): "Authority, Law and Morality", in Raz (1994): 194–221.
——(1986): *The Morality of Freedom*. (Oxford: Clarendon Press).
——(1992): *Practical Reason and Norms*. (Princeton: Princeton University Press).
——(1993): "On the Autonomy of Legal Reasoning", in Raz (1994): 310–324.
——(1994): *Ethics in the Public Domain*. (Oxford: Clarendon Press).
——(1996): "On the Nature of Law", *Archiv für Rechts- und Sozialphilosophie* 82: 1–25.
——(1998a): "Two views of the nature of the theory of law: a partial comparison", *Legal Theory* 4: 249–82.
——(1998b) "Postema on Law's autonomy and public practical reasons: a critical comment" *Legal theory* 4: 1–20.
Reinach, A (1913): "The apriori foundations of the civil law", *Alethleia* 3 (1983): 1–142.
Ruiz Manero, J (1990): *Jurisdicción y Normas*. (Madrid: Centro de Estudios Constitucionales).
Schauer, F (1991): *Playing by the Rules*. (Oxford: Clarendon Press).
Schulz, F (1936): *Principles of Roman Law*. (Oxford: Clarendon Press).
Schwartz, B, (ed) (1956): *The Code Napoleon and the Common-Law World*. (New York: New York University Press).
Searle, J (1969): *Speech Acts*. (Cambridge: Cambridge University Press).
——(1995): *The Construction of Social Reality*. (London: Allen Lane, The Penguin Press).
Sergot, M J, F Sadri, R A Kowalski, F Kriwacsek, P Hammond and H T Cory (1986): "The British Nationality Act as a Logic Program", *Communications of the ACM* 29: 370–86.
Shiner, R A (1992): "The Acceptance of a Legal System", in Patterson (ed) (1992): 59–84.
Shklar, J (1986): *Legalism*. (Cambridge, Mass.: Harvard University Press).
Simmonds, N (1984): *The Decline of Juridical Reason. Doctrine and Theory in the Legal Order*. (Manchester: Manchester University Press).
Singer, M G (1963): *Generalization in Ethics*. (London: Eyre & Spottiswoode).
Smart, J C C (1956): "Extreme and Restricted Utilitarianism", in Foot (1967): 171–83.
Smith, B (1993): "An Essay on Material Necessity", *Canadian Journal of Philosophy* 18: 301–22.
Stavropoulos, N (1996): *Objectivity in Law*. (Oxford: Clarendon Press).
Stein, P (1966): *Regulae Iuris. From juristic rules to legal maxims*. (Edinburgh: Edinburgh University Press).
——(1980): *Legal Evolution. The History of an Idea*. (Cambridge: Cambridge University Press).
——(1983): "The development of the institutional system", in Stein and de Lewis (eds): 151–63.
——(1992): "Roman Law, Common Law, and Civil Law", *Tulane Law Review* 66: 1591–603.
——(1999): *Roman Law in European History*. (Cambridge: Cambridge University Press).

——and A de Lewis, (eds) (1983): *Studies in Justinian's Institutes in Memory of J A C Thomas*. (London: Sweet and Maxwell).
Summers, R S, (ed) (1968): *Essays in Legal Philosophy*. (Oxford: Basil Blackwell).
Toulmin, S (1958): *The Uses of Argument*. (Cambridge: Cambridge University Press).
Tunc, A (1986): "'It is wise not to take the Civil Codes too Seriously'", in Wallington and Merkin (eds) (1986): 71–85.
Urmson, J O (1953): "The Interpretation of the Moral Philosophy of J. S. Mill", *Philosophical Quaterly* 3: 128–36.
van Caenegem, R C (1987): *Judges, Legislators and Professors*. (Cambridge: Cambridge University Press).
——(1991): *Legal History: a European perspective*. (London: Hambledon).
Waismann, F (1951): "Verifiability", in Flew (ed) (1951): 117–44.
Wallington, P and R Merkin, (eds) (1986): *Essays in Memory of Professor F H Lawson*. (London: Butterworths).
Warnock, G J (1971): *The Object of Morality*. (London: Methuen & Co.).
Watson, A (1968): *The Law of Property in the Later Roman Republic*. (Oxford: Clarendon Press).
——(1970): *The Law of the Ancient Romans*. (Dallas: Southern Methodist University Press).
——(1972): "Ilogicality and Roman Law", in Watson (1991): 251–62.
——(1974): *Legal Transplants. An approach to comparative law*. (Edinburgh: Scottish Academic Press).
——(1981): *The Making of the Civil Law*. (Cambridge, Mass.: Harvard University Press).
——(1985a): *The Evolution of Law*. (Oxford: Basil Blackwell).
——(1985b): *Sources of Law, Legal Change and Ambiguity*. (Edinburgh: T &T Clark).
——(1991): *Legal Origins and Legal Change*. (London: The Hambledon Press).
Weber, M (1967): *Max Weber on Law in Economy and Society*. (New York: Simon and Schuster).
——(1978): *Economy and Society*. (Berkeley: University of California Press).
Wellmer, A (1991): *The Persistence of Modernity*. (Cambridge, Polity Press).
White, P (1979): "Review (of Neil MacCormick's *Legal Reasoning and Legal Theory*)", Michigan Law Review 78: 737–42.
Winch, P (1987): *Trying to Make Sense*. (Oxford: Clarendon Press).
Wittgenstein, L (1958): *Philosophical Investigations*. (Oxford: Basil Blackwell).
——(1966): *Zettel*. (Oxford: Basil Blackwell).
Wolff, H J (1951): *Roman Law. An Historical Introduction*. (Norman: Oklahoma University Press).
Wonnacott, P and R Wonnacott (1990): *Economics*. (New York, NY: John Wiley & Sons).
Yiannopoulos, A N, (ed) (1989): *Louisiana Civil Code*. (St. Paul, Minn.: West).
Zimmermann, R (1990): *Law of Obligations. Roman Foundations of the Civilian Tradition*. (Cape Town: Juta).
——(1995): "Roman and Comparative Law: The European Perspective", *Legal History* 16: 21–33.

Index

www.ingramcontent.com/pod-product-compliance
Ingram Content Group UK Ltd.
Pitfield, Milton Keynes, MK11 3LW, UK
UKHW020832290926
15470UKWH00009B/1861/J

9 781841 132754